Real Heat

Real Heat

Gender and Race in the Urban Fire Service

CAROL CHETKOVICH

RUTGERS UNIVERSITY PRESS
New Brunswick, New Jersey, and London

Library of Congress Cataloging-in-Publication Data

Chetkovich, Carol A.
    Real heat : gender and race in the urban fire service / Carol
Chetkovich
        p. cm.
    Includes bibliographical references and index.
    ISBN 0-8135-2409-1 (cloth : alk. paper). — ISBN 0-8135-2410-5
(pbk. : alk. paper)
    1. Women fire fighters—California—Oakland.   2. Afro-American
fire fighters—California—Oakland.   3. Fire departments—
California—Oakland—Officials and employees.   4. Sex
discrimination against women—California—Oakland.   5. Race
discrimination—California—Oakland.   I. Title.
HD6073.F52U63   1997
331.7'61363378'0979466—dc21   97-1781
                                                              CIP

British Cataloging-in-Publication information available

Manufactured in the United States of America

To Allyson,
May she become all that she can

Contents

A Personal Preface about Fire   *ix*
Acknowledgments   *xiii*

Chapter 1	After the Door Is Open: Finding One's Place in the Community of Firefighters	*1*
Chapter 2	Work, Culture, and Identity in the Urban Fire Service	*17*
Chapter 3	Newcomers at Entry: Reflecting Back, Looking Forward	*39*
Chapter 4	Initiation: Swimming in the Shark's Tank	*61*
Chapter 5	Proving Grounds	*83*
Chapter 6	Learning in Relationship	*109*
Chapter 7	Becoming an Insider	*131*
Chapter 8	Gender and Race in the Urban Fire Service: Policy Implications	*155*
Chapter 9	Questions of Identity, Community, and Social Justice	*179*

Appendix: A Comment on Method   *193*
Notes   *199*
References   *229*
Index   *237*

A Personal Preface about Fire

THE CEMENT STAIRWAY to my house in the Oakland hills was once shaded by a sixty-foot-tall incense cedar. That tree is gone now, like most of the others in the neighborhood. On the same slope a forty-foot oak tree wages a losing battle against the wounds it sustained in the firestorm. Returning home from a walk with my husband one afternoon, I looked up at the oak and started to cry. "It's like the fire just keeps taking and taking," I said.

WE SAT UPSTAIRS in our bedroom overlooking the bay, enjoying coffee and the newspaper. It was late morning, October 20, 1991. The telephone rang and my husband, Glen, answered; I heard him greet my father. "No, we haven't heard anything about it," he said in surprise. A few moments later he hung up and told me that my father had seen a news report on television about a fire in the East Bay hills. We got up and went to the window. Everything looked normal in front, but when we peered around to the hills behind us we could see how black the sky had become.

We dressed hurriedly, and Glen began to hose down the huge deck of our wood-sided house as I walked up Broadway Terrace toward the park, where I knew I could get a better view of the hills from one of the trails. As I walked, emergency vehicles of all sorts drove in apparent confusion up and down the street. I looked into the eyes of a woman standing in front of her house on Broadway Terrace. Wordlessly we communicated a shared sense of dread, though at this point I, like many others, thought the fire wouldn't come here.

At the park I jogged up a trail and looked across the two freeways to the top of the ridge, on which was burning the biggest fire I'd ever seen. A helicopter with a large basket suspended below it flew over Lake Temescal below me, filled the basket with water, flew to the ridge top and dumped its load. The water had no effect. The helicopter repeated its mission several times while I stood there, not believing what I was seeing. In the ten or fifteen minutes I was in the park the fire jumped both freeways and began burning some brush on the opposite side of the lake. I left the park and hurried down the hill toward home.

By now, the residents of Broadway Terrace were rapidly loading belongings into their cars and departing down the hill towards the flatlands. I ran up the stairs to my house and on the way saw Mary and Mark, who lived just two doors up from us at the top of our little hill, heading down their driveway, their car filled with pets and possessions. Mary looked at me and yelled, "Carol, the fire is two houses away! You have to get out now!"

I ran up the remaining stairs to find Glen still hosing down the house. I gave him Mary's message—we still couldn't see the fire from our house, but the smoke and ash were heavy—and we ran inside to pack up a few things. I went first for some of my work—files and computer hard disk—then for family photographs and finally, jewelry. My husband gathered the bird in his cage and very little else. I stood in the calm of the house and tried to figure out what else I should save. I looked helplessly around, thinking "Why take this book and not that one? Why take this vase and not that clock?" The choices were impossible, and I took nothing more. I looked around at the living room and said good-bye.

We ran down the stairs to our cars and started to get in. Then Glen said he was going back up for his briefcase and I asked him to bring my grandmother's silver coffee service, too. I wanted to wait for him, but he told me to leave and said we'd meet at the BART station. I left as the police were driving up and down the street, shouting through bullhorns the message that residents must evacuate the area.

Many people had apparently chosen to rendezvous at the BART station, or perhaps they just couldn't think where else to go. The area was milling with disoriented residents, people seemingly flooding out of their hill homes toward the still-safe flatlands. Terrible stories came with them. "Everything above Golden Gate Avenue is gone." (My home was above Golden Gate.) A middle-aged European woman near me burst into tears, "Oh, my beautiful, beautiful house. I saw it burned to the ground." Friends tried to comfort her. I thought about my own home and tried to let go.

As time passed, I began to worry about Glen's absence and then to panic. I called my parents from a pay phone to see if they'd heard from him. They hadn't. I couldn't imagine what was taking so long. A reporter came up and asked gently if she could speak with me; she wanted to know what I was thinking, how I felt. The first thing that came into my head was the relative unimportance of material possessions as long as your friends and family members were safe. Then as I spoke I realized that although I had assumed Glen was all right, I didn't know for sure, and I told her not to print what I had said.

An hour or more later Glen arrived. He had stayed to continue hosing down the house until the smoke was so thick he couldn't see or breathe, and he heard Mark and Mary's place explode into flames. His eyes were red, and he wore an expression of infinite sadness. We held each other, and he said, "It's not just our house, it's the whole neighborhood. Everything is gone."

We decided to drive to my parents' home and spend the night there, but first we went to the fire department headquarters to see if there was any volunteer work that could be done by civilians. Though we later heard that there were such jobs, we weren't able to find anyone who could make use of us so we left the city. Even the downtown, miles from the hills, was being dusted with ashes.

The next morning Glen returned to Oakland, to his office. I made a list of supplies we would need to get through the next few days—we had no changes of clothing and no toiletries. My sister came to join me, and we set out in search of toothbrushes and blue jeans. We walked into a discount clothing store, and I tried to think what I should buy. I quickly became overwhelmed and told my sister I had to go outside. I went out and sat on the sidewalk with my head in my hands. She came out. I'd always enjoyed my sister's company, and I told her now, "This would be fun if I weren't so fucking depressed." She said, "Let's start with something easier." So we headed for the drugstore.

By the end of the day we had picked up most of the things on my list and a few unnecessary but nice things as well. We stopped for coffee and then went to a pay phone in the mall parking lot to let my mother know we'd be a little later than expected. My sister spoke to her first, then handed the phone to me with a questioning look. "She wants to talk to you." I got on the phone, and my mother told me that someone from Glen's office had called: Glen and another man went into the fire area; the other man's house was gone, but ours was still standing. I burst into sobs of disbelief. My sister thought that my mother must have given me bad news, and she hugged me. I couldn't let myself feel relief because I knew if later I learned that the message was wrong, the sense of loss would be unbearable.

My sister and I returned immediately to my parents' home and joined them in an anxious wait to hear from Glen directly. Finally he called and said, "Our house is still here." The fire had passed through our yard—two feet from the open wooden deck—but the house was unburned. There is no way to describe what I felt on hearing this, or how I felt when I returned to our destroyed neighborhood and saw my house still standing there, on a blackened hillside marked like a cemetery with fireplaces for headstones, the smell of smoke everywhere. Or how I feel now, four and a half years later, as I write this.

Many people who know that my home is in the fire area have asked if this experience prompted me to study firefighters. The answer, somewhat ironically, is no. I had been thinking about the fire service and even interviewing firefighters in other cities well before October 1991. People who don't know this seem to imagine that the fire inspired me to look more closely at those who fight it for a living—perhaps out of a sense of gratitude that my home was saved, or spared. Like everything else about this work, the dynamic wasn't that simple. Certainly the fire had an impact—on me, on the Oakland Fire Department, and indirectly on the new firefighters I came to know, who entered their training academy some weeks after the fire. But its effect has been one of confusion, contradiction, and uncertainty.

My image of firefighters, still, is the image that they need to hold of themselves in order to do their work: courageous, capable people who are regularly called to battle against disasters not of their own making and who at the end of the day are triumphant. That, of course, was not how it was in the firestorm. Three thousand homes burned, and twenty-five people lost their lives. The Oakland Fire Department came under heavy attack for its handling of both Saturday's brush fire and Sunday's disaster. Instead of being heroes, firefighters were vilified by the press and people who had lost their homes. Bitterness erupted in angry lawn signs and obscene messages scrawled on the streets. Whatever the final resolution of these criticisms—and I leave that concern to others—many firefighters and civilians did their best against impossible odds, working to exhaustion and showing great heroism, and in some cases, succeeding. But when it was all over, the devastation was great and the satisfaction small.

Although I have spoken with a few firefighters about their work that day, most of these conversations have felt distant and artificial. Only on a couple of occasions have I spoken with a firefighter in enough depth to pick up a sense of what this experience meant to them. In both cases they were women, and both seemed profoundly affected. One voiced what I suspect is a general feeling, though not acknowledged by many veterans. She said that before the fire, they had a clear sense of themselves, their work, and their capabilities, but now, "We just aren't sure who we are anymore."

They must regain that sense to be able to do their jobs and I must treat them as though they have, in order to do mine. For the most part, this is the reality of this book. But beneath this reality lies another, and I leave it to you to consider what it signifies.

June 1996
Oakland, California

Acknowledgments

QUITE LITERALLY, of course, this work would not have been possible without the participation of the men and women of the Oakland Fire Department who shared their stories with me. I am indebted to the former chief of the department, P. Lamont Ewell, for opening the doors of the department to me, and to the many other officers and firefighters who graciously admitted me into their firehouses and their work lives. I must also thank those members of the department who overcame their justifiable dread of academic prose to read and comment on the dissertation on which this book was based. The list of those who went out of their way to assist me and to make me feel welcome is too long to include here, but these men and women have my deepest appreciation.

The journey from dissertation to book was for me a difficult one, and I would not have completed it without the guidance of many colleagues. Martha Heller, my editor at Rutgers, saw the project's potential even in its unwieldy early form and helped me tame my masses of material by offering guidance and patiently riding out my fits of frustration. Anonymous reviewers at Rutgers and elsewhere provided important insights into possible directions for the work. Fellow scholars in the 1994–1995 Beatrice M. Bain Research Group at the University of California at Berkeley—especially Lois Helmbold and Shelley Feldman—offered excellent advice on the reshaping of the manuscript. And in the final writing of the book, the members of my short-lived but much appreciated writing group, Maresi Nerad and Colette Patt, gave me excellent advice and encouragement. Lisa Jerry copy edited the final manuscript with skill and sensitivity.

I was exceptionally fortunate in the membership of my dissertation committee. David Kirp, Carol Stack, and Martin Trow were all enormously helpful throughout the project, from early discussions about its possibilities to the final writing. They provided insight and guidance from their very different intellectual perspectives, and, perhaps most important, they were respectful of me and my work and unfailingly enthusiastic even when I was not. For all of this I thank them.

I must also acknowledge those whose personal and professional efforts kept me whole and healthy for the years of this work, and who made me feel not so alone. Through their help, inspiration, comfort, and companionship these people made the work possible. Christine Mayer transcribed many interview tapes with accuracy, reliability, and understanding; she was the only other person to hear the stories as they were told to me. Ann Ferguson, then a graduate student in sociology, listened as I fumbled through the early stages of my analysis and helped me see the meaning of what I had. Odile Atthalin, a gifted Rosen therapist, worked to free my body of the tensions induced by the project. Edith Balbach, a fellow doctoral student in public policy, met me regularly for a glass of wine and a sharing of absurdities; without her company I would almost certainly have lost my sense of humor.

My sister, Kathryn Chetkovich, listened patiently and with great wisdom to hours of monologue about the project and reminded me of what I was about when I lost my way. My parents, Alice and Michael Chetkovich, taught me long ago, in the words of Joseph Campbell, to "follow my bliss"; and they provided me with the means to do so. Above all, my husband, Glen Tepke, has been an unwavering source of love and support beyond anything I could have asked. Perhaps his greatest contribution to this work has been to confirm my belief that it is possible for men to treat women with respect and equality.

The DISSERTATION RESEARCH on which this book was based was supported in part by the National Science Foundation, under Grant No. SBR-9300802. Financial support was also provided by the University of California Provost's Research Fund and the Spencer Foundation. A Spencer Mentor Grant provided me with critical support during the final stages of the dissertation. The NSF and UC grants paid for the transcription of recorded interviews and other expenses of the research, without which the work would have been impossible. Equally important, such support indicated to me that others believed in the project's value. In particular, I appreciate the comments and suggestions of the anonymous NSF reviewers. Any opinions, findings, and conclusions or recommendations expressed in this dissertation are those of the author and do not necessarily reflect the views of the National Science Foundation, the University of California, or the Spencer Foundation.

Real Heat

Chapter 1	After the Door Is Open

Finding One's Place in the Community of Firefighters

Maggie's Story

AT ABOUT SIX WEEKS after their entry into the field, the members of Oakland Fire Department (OFD) Class 1-91 returned to the drill tower in rotating shifts, for the first of a series of additional training sessions.[1] On this, the second day of the training period, the B-shift members gathered in one of the institutional wood-paneled trailers that had served as a classroom during the academy. The room's appearance was no more inviting than it had been during training, but it did *smell* a great deal better: on this occasion, it was not packed with bodies sweating from the exertion of a fireyard training. Instead, the new firefighters were dressed in clean, navy blue uniforms, and they sat—quietly for them—in neat rows of folding chairs behind Formica-topped tables.

In subsequent probationary training sessions, the newcomers received additional instruction and testing in their craft—pulling hoses across the fireyard, raising huge wooden ladders against the tower, pushing on the chests of plastic heart-attack victims, tearing off the roofs of old police cars in order to extricate crash dummies—but today's lessons were of a more social nature. The morning had begun with a few words of encouragement first from the chief and then from the head of the training division; by nine o'clock the group was well into a four-hour session on "Valuing Diversity" organized by the city's Human Resource Development Division.

On this particular shift, the three women all happened to be white, but the fourteen men included whites, blacks, Hispanics,[2] and Asian Americans; as a whole the group reflected the department's ongoing efforts to diversify its work force. These newcomers had made it through a difficult screening process and training academy, but the question remained for each: could he or

she make it in the field—where success was as much a matter of cultural competence as technical skill.

Mary Greene,[3] the session's facilitator, was leading a discussion around
the six themes she had written with colored markers on a flip-chart:

- Need for working more effectively with others who are different
- Assumptions
- Attitudes
- Sabotage
- Stereotypes
- Differences

Casting her eyes around the room, Mary invited the new firefighters to offer
comments about any or all of these topics. As they spoke about their early
experiences in the field, it became clear that the differences that had been
apparent in the academy were magnified after just a few weeks in the field.
Men with traditional backgrounds (those primarily white—sometimes Hispanic—men with personal or familial connections to the fire service) were
arguing that the quality of the "new kids'" experience had a great deal to do
with the recruits' own attitude going in: "You're entering someone else's world,
and you have to be aware of that." "Just do your job, keep your nose clean,
and it'll be fine."

Less traditional probationers were more skeptical. One black man,
Franklin Haywood, was particularly bothered by the veterans' power over the
newcomers' reputations and their seemingly arbitrary exercise of it. He insisted
that a veteran could label a newcomer on the basis of a behavior unrelated to
job performance; if the label stuck, then it would affect the new kid's
reputation.

As the talk turned to how newcomers felt about their interactions with
the veterans, Maggie Steele commented that the men on her crew hardly
seemed to take any notice of her at all. More than anything, she was *puzzled*
by the coldness she'd received: what purpose did it serve? The facilitator then
formulated the question, "Why does the hazing continue?" People began to
respond.

"It's to see how bad you want to be here."

"It's OK as long as it's not demeaning and it makes you feel like you're
becoming part of the team."

Hal Davis, a huge white guy with military firefighting experience, insisted
that "everybody has control. You draw your own boundaries. If somebody
pushes your button, let 'em know, but in a constructive way." Frank Cross,
another experienced white newcomer, explained that it was a kind of test,

that it built character and strength. Someone else added that it was a form of training.

Then Susan Marley interrupted to ask, "What are we talking about?" She pointed out that they'd been using the word "hazing" without defining it; she wasn't sure they were all talking about the same thing. Could people be more specific? Ruth Moore offered an example: being sent to look for something the veterans knew wouldn't be there. Or having lots of extra duties. "But it's OK," she said. Hal brought up the example of Jerry Cole, one of the "characters" at Station 103, who "hazes everyone." Susan responded with a claim that this wasn't *hazing*: the guy is just an inveterate practical joker.

Eventually Maggie spoke up again. "*Being ignored*—not being spoken to— is something I've experienced." Charlie Reyes, a Hispanic man with relatives in the department, claimed it wasn't happening to him. But for people who were experiencing these things, his explanation was, "They're just trying to check you out." Maggie immediately shot back, "*How can they check me out if they don't speak to me?*"

Charlie didn't answer her question. Matthew Taylor, a black man who later had his own problems in the department, said that to be hazed was to be brought into the fold; if you were ignored, then you were being excluded. He added that women were often the subject of derision in firehouses when they were not present. Marshall Lew, one of the few Asian Americans in the class, observed that there was also a certain paranoia about behavior around women; with the sexual harassment concerns, people were simply afraid to say anything. The facilitator commented that there was also an ignorance of how to relate. She asked if life was "different" for the women in the firehouses.

Franklin, who had earlier been complaining of the veterans' disrespectful treatment, agreed emphatically that it was different for the women. "It has to do with familiarity, like with sports." Also, many veterans were set in their ways and uncomfortable with the women. "And it is different when women are there." Hal then asserted that it all depended on the woman; some women were offended by things that didn't bother other women at all. Unflappable women were the ones the guys felt most comfortable with.

Maggie's puzzlement and frustration seemed unabated. For me at least, her question continued to hang unanswered in the air: *How can they check me out if they don't speak to me?*

When I listened to Maggie six months later—a third of the way through her probation—I heard her describe a very different kind of experience and, as she put it, a growing sense of attachment to the job. She had been working downtown at Station 121, an older firehouse with a group of senior veterans. Although she hadn't seen many fires, she was busy enough to be learning and developing a sense of self-confidence. At a five-alarm apartment house fire on Fifth and Market, she'd learned what it was to get "beat to shit" by a five-hour overhaul (tearing apart a burned building to extinguish all hidden fire) and to test the limits of her own capacity. She spoke enthusiastically of her old-timer, all-male crew: they would tease her mercilessly, and she would tease them back, but they could also be serious and helpful when she needed it. One veteran shared her avid interest in windsurfing, and they all seemed to like having her around. Perhaps it wasn't going to be as hard as it had initially seemed to be accepted into the fire department. She was already beginning to feel that she belonged here.

During the six months that followed our interview, Maggie moved around quite a bit, rotating—as most newcomers were required to do—through the stations in different parts of town. She didn't enjoy them all as much as she had Station 121, but neither did she find them intolerable. A few veterans and one or two stations seemed to thrive on the "hard-line bullshit," and a few were openly hostile to women, but in general, as long as you did your job and didn't make any major mistakes, people wouldn't really give you a hard time. She did miss the sense of connection she'd felt at 121, and she believed that many veterans were losing interest in the new kids after seeing so many rotate through. Sometimes the sense of isolation was particularly strong: "Like you come into a double house in the morning and have the officer call everybody 'Buddy' . . . and touch their elbow or somethin' like that, or greet them and . . . [it's] just like I'm not even there, I'm this invisible person, 'cause I couldn't possibly be a buddy, I guess." When something like this would happen, she'd feel as if she were missing out on something, but then she'd tell herself, "Well, I ain't gonna be at this house forever." With a little luck, she'd eventually end up in a place where she could be more a part of the crew, establish stronger rapport, and learn more—as she had at Station 121.

Maggie and I sat in the captain's quarters at Station 122 for our final interview at the end of her eighteen-month probation, some twenty months after our first encounter in the academy. The room was impersonal, bathed in the cold light of fluorescent fixtures, with departmental announcements posted on the walls, desks piled with paperwork, and a neatly made, grey-blanketed bed in the corner. Maggie faced me quietly from a swivel chair a few feet away, tidy in her dark blue uniform but also weary-looking. She sounded strong and collected when we began to talk, but as she offered greater details about her experience and her feelings, her voice took on an edge of frustration, then resignation and sadness. She sighed repeatedly.

I was surprised by the strength of her negative feeling. At the time of our six-month interview, I had mentally placed Maggie in the "plus" column, and although she had seemed less satisfied at twelve months, I still had the sense that she was basically content and adjusting to life in the fire department. Certainly she had seemed capable of finding or making a place for herself. Now I heard her saying that after all this time she was feeling less, not more, connected and that she also wasn't learning much. She complained not of active, overt harassment, but more of a state of starvation—a lack of sustenance, coupled with the pain of being a stigmatized other. Her voice dropped almost to a whisper as she told me how uncomfortable it was for her to sit in a room full of male coworkers, hear the way they spoke about women, and feel the withering hatred that gave rise to such remarks. She was in the deepest sense an outsider, an "invisible person" here, and she had begun to think about leaving the department, maybe leaving the work altogether.

IN THE HISTORY of workplace integration, the story of Maggie and her classmates comes at the end of one chapter and the beginning of another. During the late 1980s and early 1990s, four recruit classes were hired into the Oakland Fire Department under a consent decree that required race and gender diversity; [4] the last and largest of these was Maggie's class. In a decades-long story of conflict over affirmative action issues, the composition of this class represented the resolution of the moment, neither the first nor the last word in the conflict. It was a victory of sorts for those promoting diversity: in keeping with the consent decree, the racial makeup of this class roughly reflected that of the surrounding community (about 62 percent people of color) and boosted the proportion of people of color in the department to 43 percent. But only nine of the fifty-two class members were women, and even after the admission of this group—the largest complement of women ever to enter the department—the work force would be 92 percent male.

The diversity of these recruit classes clearly illustrates how the doors of the fire service are opening to men of color and to all women. In this context, Maggie's entry represents a culmination of efforts to expand opportunities and ensure greater equality. But entry is also only the beginning of another endeavor—the struggle for acceptance faced by nontraditional newcomers seeking places in an occupational community from which people like them have for decades been excluded.

Not everyone succeeds in such an effort. Both minority and female pioneers entering nontraditional work have met with isolation and harassment to some degree, and in some contexts resistance has been quite strong. But there have generally been expectations—by both workers and social scientists alike—that resistance diminishes over time and previously excluded groups eventually achieve acceptance. Is this in fact what happens? How real is the progress of men of color and women? Has the process worked in the same way for all race and sex groups and in all work settings?

Statistical data suggest that although occupational segregation by both race and sex has diminished somewhat over the last two decades, such segregation, particularly by sex, remains pronounced.[5] Traditionally feminine occupations have tended to remain so; women have made inroads into some male-dominated occupations, but a closer look often reveals the progress to be illusory: either the work has been deskilled and devalued, or there has been further stratification within the occupation such that women are concentrated in lower status, lower paid strata.[6] Finally, in certain occupations—most conspicuously, skilled blue-collar work—women's gains have been minimal.

Curiously, overall patterns of segregation remain strong *despite* evidence of considerable mobility at the individual level: many women do enter male jobs, and increasing numbers of men enter female jobs. But they do not stay; in particular, women leave many male-dominated jobs at disproportionately high rates.[7] Why? What accounts for the continuing movement of women out of male-dominated occupations even as other women continue to enter? Is a similar dynamic also found with respect to race? And what kind of policy interventions might be called for if we are to ensure an equitable distribution of work and wages?

Returning to the scene of Maggie and her classmates discussing their entry into the field, we may pose these questions at the level of real men and women in a very particular social context. Will all these people succeed in the fire service? After their eighteen months of probation, will all remain on the job? Among those who remain, which ones will feel truly satisfied with their occupational choice—confident both of their own ability and of their acceptance by coworkers and superiors? How will the process of becoming a firefighter unfold for each of them? What will be the effect of their differing levels of technical competence, previous experience, and social skills? What role might race or gender play?

To the extent that race and gender matter, will the meaning of these social categories differ for different individuals, or will common threads run through the experiences of all members of a given race/sex group? How will the effects of race and sex compare? Will the experience of Susan Marley, a white woman, be more like that of Hal Davis, a white man, or that of Franklin Haywood, a black man? The stories of Maggie and her classmates, related and explored throughout this book, illuminate the important questions of how and by whom membership is achieved, where boundaries are drawn between insider and outsider, how those boundaries are constructed and how they are crossed. But before delving further into the experiences of today's new firefighters, we should briefly consider the history of race and sex integration in the fire service.

Race and Gender in the Greatest Job in the World

In the struggle to realize equal employment opportunity, public safety jobs have been central for a number of reasons.[8] Police and fire departments, with their high level of visibility in the community, are particularly prominent symbols of success or failure in the integration effort. In addition, these jobs themselves offer relatively high rewards—in the form of good pay, benefits, security, status, satisfaction, and excitement—but do not require high levels of formal education. In an economy in which well-paid, secure blue-collar jobs are vanishing,[9] police and fire positions have been in especially high demand.

To illustrate, annual starting salaries for firefighters in major cities fall in the range of $28,000 to $46,000;[10] with overtime pay, compensation can be considerably higher. Firefighters receive relatively generous health, disability, and retirement benefits, and the work schedule is considered an important benefit as well. Urban firefighters generally work a rotating twenty-four-hour shift, which means their workday includes meal and sleep time (sometimes interrupted by calls). Such schedules leave a considerable amount of off-duty time for moonlighting, family life, and recreational activities. In addition, when policies permit firefighters to trade shifts with each other, they can arrange their schedules so that workdays are contiguous, and they can be off duty for extended periods. The twenty-four-hour shift and the intense nature of the work also encourage strong bonds among coworkers, a camaraderie that many firefighters see as another significant advantage of the job.[11]

In terms of the work itself, its effect on those who do it, and their esteem in the community, firefighting is an unusually appealing occupation. Citizens call the fire department when they are in trouble and need help; firefighters are the rescuers in the "white hats," whose arrival is always welcome. Their work is not only constructive but on occasion truly heroic; it is also extremely varied and unpredictable, with the human element guaranteeing that no two calls will be the same. A job well done—whether the revival of a heart-attack victim, the extrication of someone trapped inside a collapsed structure or vehicle, or the saving of a home threatened by fire—can be enormously satisfying and a great source of pride. Firefighters see themselves as members of an "elite," and in the minds of the public their occupation tops all others in terms of honesty and integrity.[12] To many aspirants as well as working firefighters, this is simply "the greatest job in the world."[13]

In such a context, diversity has a particularly strong symbolic value. The presence of men and women of color or white women in any nontraditional role helps to break down confining stereotypes, but the effect is strongest when the role has a special value. In particular, seeing another member of one's social group in a nontraditional role can provide an expanded sense of possibility and pride, even to one uninterested in that work itself. As a woman, I can still recall after twenty years how almost miraculous it seemed when I discovered that the telephone company had sent a woman to install our company lines. Or my pride on hearing that the first rock climber to "free" the nose of El Capitan in Yosemite was a woman.[14] Such sentiments are particularly powerful in connection with an occupation like firefighting, which has such strong associations with courage and heroism.

Patterns of Change

The professional fire service has been predominantly white and entirely male for most of its history. Although black men have worked as firefighters since the early part of the century—in some cases, in segregated departments—their share of these jobs has been far less than their proportion of the labor force. Many departments did not hire their first African Americans until the 1960s, and in the decade after passage of the 1964 Civil Rights Act, characterized as the period of "voluntary desegregation,"[15] the growth in minority representation was extremely slow. The San Francisco Fire Department was typical: the first African American man joined the department in 1955, followed by the second twelve years later; by 1972 there were only five black men in a department of some fifteen hundred. The first female professional firefighter in the nation was not hired until 1974—by the Arlington Fire Department—and San Francisco, the last major urban department to hire women, did not do so until 1987.

Court orders, consent decrees, and voluntary affirmative action programs of the last three decades have eliminated many formal barriers to the inclusion of men of color and women in the fire service. What have been the results of these measures? Is the push for integration working, and for whom? Census data, while not as precise as often desired, give some sense of the changes that have been effected in this work force over time. The 1970 census figures for the "fire protection work force," which included inspection and prevention jobs along with firefighters, indicated that only 1 percent of these positions were held by women, 2 percent by blacks, and 3 percent by persons of Spanish heritage.[16] Twenty years later, white men still dominate the fire service, but there has been some growth in the representation of other groups. According to the 1990 census, 3 percent of firefighters are now women, 9 percent are African American, and 5 percent are of Hispanic origin. Fire inspection and fire prevention occupations are more integrated: 14 percent of the work force is female, 11 percent black, and 5 percent Hispanic. Considering each group's proportion of the labor force, it may be said that racial and ethnic minorities are still underrepresented in the fire service but not as dramatically as are women (of all racial/ethnic categories).[17]

Police work was more integrated than the fire service in 1970, and that trend continues. Minority shares have grown to the point that the proportion of black police officers is now comparable to their proportion of the employed labor force.[18] Female representation has improved as well, with the proportion of women police officers and detectives growing from 3 percent in 1970 to 12 percent in 1990 (note that the later figure is four times the current proportion of women firefighters).

These figures—by race on the one hand and by sex on the other—suggest that in both police and firefighting jobs, racial integration among men has been stronger than sexual integration regardless of race. An even stronger picture of the differing rates of change in racial as opposed to sexual integration can be seen when the intersecting categories of race and sex are examined. For example, the representation of black men in these jobs has increased dramatically, but the representation of black women remains low. While black men represented 9 percent of those in firefighter and police officer/detective positions in 1990, black women held only 1 percent and 2.7 percent of these jobs. Compared to others of their sex, black women were not doing badly (among *women* employed in these categories, black women held 13 percent and 23 percent of the jobs), but compared to black men, the representation of black women was quite low.

In other skilled blue-collar occupations, racial integration has been somewhat less successful, but sexual integration has been truly dismal. Thus, in comparing the experiences of African American women and African American men, we see a paradoxical outcome: when we consider their share of the employed labor force, black men seem to be well represented in many of these jobs, but when we compare them with other *men*, they are actually doing rather poorly—because men as a group hold the lion's share of these jobs. Black women, however, compare reasonably well with other women, but, given the shared gender disadvantage, black women are, in comparison to their share of employed labor, grossly underrepresented. In other words, in skilled blue-collar employment, the disadvantage of race appears to be greatest among men (i.e., black men do not do as well as white men), whereas among women it is either absent or overwhelmed by the effect of gender (i.e., black women do about as well as white women, who do not do very well).

To summarize, then, racial integration has exceeded sexual integration in skilled blue-collar jobs, and the pattern has been particularly pronounced in the public safety jobs of police work and firefighting. Even as these jobs are racially desegregated—some more rapidly than others—they remain largely "men's work." What explains this result? Is it simply a function of time? Will women eventually repeat the progress of black men, and will black men consolidate or continue their gains? If time alone is not the answer, then does the outcome reflect differences in goals or abilities that vary by gender though not by race? Or is there something else about the blue-collar work community, and firefighting culture in particular, that guarantees that these fields will remain a male preserve?

Understanding Participation and Exclusion

A CULTURAL MODEL OF INTEGRATION

These questions motivated my ethnographic work with the members of Class 1-91 of the Oakland Fire Department. Studies of workplace integration usually involve statistical analyses of outcomes and an emphasis on formal structures and procedures. But many important social questions cannot be answered in this way,[19] and it was clear from the outset of my project that informal processes and intersubjective experiences—in a word, culture[20]—were critical to integration. As new kids and veterans quickly showed me, becoming a firefighter involves much more than simply being hired, formally trained, and protected from overt harassment. It also involves learning how to live in the local culture as a native,[21] becoming a full participant in a community of practice, and making the transition from outsider to insider.

Acculturation is a two-way process. On one side, the newcomer arrives with his or her own set of social experiences: family relationships, education, work history, and dimensions of personal identity, such as race, sex, class, and sexual orientation. On the other side, the community enacts a culture reflective of its own history, shared working conditions, and the characteristics of the incumbent work force. In a successful passage from outsider to insider, the newcomer learns the ways of the community, and the community accepts the newcomer as a legitimate member; in the process, a new identity is constructed for the newcomer. The communal identity is unlikely to change radically with the acceptance of any single individual, but over time the absorption of newer generations of workers along with changes in working conditions may result in a new communal identity.[22] In transitional periods, the communal identity may be a contested terrain, with different elements in the community promoting different subcultures.

In other words, a newcomer earns the trust and acceptance of veteran coworkers in part by crafting and presenting a self consistent with either the dominant version of the community's own self-image or, perhaps alternatively, a sympathetic subculture within the community. And in addition, the newcomer must also come to believe in the authenticity of the self he presents to the community: in this case, he must come to see himself as a firefighter. How does all of this happen? What social processes are most critical to the outcome? Most important, do these processes interact with the construction of race or gender to support some and discourage others in their efforts to become firefighters?

SETTING AND METHOD

I first made contact with the staff and recruits of the 1-91 OFD Academy in early March 1992, when they were in their twelfth week of training. [23] Having already conducted a number of exploratory interviews with firefighters in other departments, I had decided that a fruitful approach for a cultural study would be to concentrate on the experiences of people being inducted into the occupation. When I learned that the Oakland Fire Department was conducting an academy, I contacted the department with a request to interview and observe recruits while still in training. The department was interested in the study and granted me access to the academy for observation and interviews with recruits and instructors. In my first few visits to the Training Division I met the academy staff (or "cadre" as it was called) along with some of the recruits and observed hose-and-ladder drills. On my third visit I was formally introduced to the class at roll call, where I described my study and asked for volunteers to participate.

The class included forty-three men and nine women with, as noted, much greater racial diversity among the men: only thirteen of the forty-three men were white, but of the nine women, seven were white (one was African American and the other Latina). Almost three-quarters of the recruits expressed an interest in the study, and I was able to interview most of them before the conclusion of the academy. From among the initial group of interviewees—all of whom agreed to ongoing participation—I selected for follow-up a purposive sample of twenty-six recruits that reflected diversity of age, experience, sex, and race or ethnicity. My sample included seven women, all of those who volunteered to participate and made themselves available for interviews during the training; of the seven, one was black and the others white. Of my nineteen men, seven were white, six black, two Asian American, two Filipino American, and two Hispanic. More detail on the group's variation in terms of age, education, and experience is presented in the appendix; the most striking feature of this variation is the relatively high frequency of firefighting experience and social connections to the department among the white men.

I continued to observe the final month of academy training and joined the recruits—now probationary firefighters—at their graduation. During the next eighteen months, the probationary period for Oakland firefighters, I visited fire stations, attended emergency responses, and reinterviewed the members of my sample group four times: once after approximately one month in the field, then again at six months, twelve months, and the end of probation. My fire station visits gave me an opportunity to meet and talk with veterans, to observe and in a limited way to participate in firehouse life, and to see how recruits interacted with their experienced coworkers and officers. From the fire stations and sometimes from home (where I used a radio scanner to monitor dispatches), I went to a variety of emergency responses, including structure fires, medical calls (primarily false alarms), auto accidents, grass fires, utility calls, and rescues.

I must emphasize here that this was not a study of the Oakland Fire Department, but of firefighters, most of whom happened to work in Oakland. When I was granted access in Oakland I had to choose between a broader project involving more sites and a deeper study relying primarily on one location. Believing that this department is in most ways representative of urban departments in general, and that my exposure to firefighters elsewhere would sensitize me to Oakland's differences, I chose the latter. My observations and conclusions are shaped by the location of the study, but they should not be taken as an analysis of the department, which would require quite a different set of questions, interview subjects, observations, and documents.

My study was also shaped by the advantages and disadvantages of the "sample" of core participants with whom I was able to work. A problem with many gender studies is their failure to include variation on the very dimension of interest (sex or gender); that is, they look exclusively at women's experiences and ignore the question of whether and to what degree men's experiences in the same context differ. Additionally, if there is a comparison, it is often with either white men only or men as an undifferentiated group. The variety of racial and ethnic backgrounds of the men in this class enabled me to consider the effects of race within male sex and to compare the experiences of women to not only those of white men but also those of men of color.

An obvious limitation of my sample, which there was no way to correct within this setting, is the relative absence of women of color. Among the women included here, all but one—an African American woman—were white.[24] The remarks and experiences of the one black female newcomer are very much a part of the story told here, but unfortunately cannot be identified *as* those of a black woman because of the need to protect confidentiality. In other words, the fact that her experiences cannot be reported directly does not mean that they were absent from the analysis. In addition, I supplemented my data with interviews and observations of black and biracial women veterans, and my analysis of their experience also contributed to my conclusions.

RACE AND GENDER AS ANALYTIC CONCERNS

It is difficult to research and write about social constructs such as race and gender without reifying or essentializing them, which I do not wish to do. My research begins from the assumption that in our society the experiences of people of different races and/or sexes vary significantly from one another, *not* because of innate racial or sexual differences but because race and gender are such powerful and omnipresent social constructs. These categories directly constrain our possibilities from the moment of birth, and in so doing they also shape our own behavior, choices, and selves. For example, systematic differences in socialization, opportunity, and power may shape gender-linked patterns of behavior that in turn interact with (and generally reinforce) environmental inequalities.

Other aspects of our experience along with our own agency obviously complicate the picture by producing variation within race/gender groups, overlaps between groups, and contestation of the meaning of categories. This kind of complexity is preserved in the stories I relate here, which illustrate a social process in which women and, to some degree, men of color are systematically disadvantaged—but not in an uncontested, uncontradicted, or invariant way.

This complexity sometimes results in what may appear to be an inconsistent or at least asymmetrical treatment of race and gender: racial identities among the men are sometimes not identified, whereas gender is always clear. The treatment of race is by design: I do not *always* specify race because I believe that to do so reinforces the essentialist position; I do identify race when my analysis suggests that it is meaningful. By contrast, I do not have the ability to avoid specifying gender because any time a name or pronoun is used, the individual's sex is evident, a symptom of the omnirelevance society assigns to gender.

With respect to my own position, it is clear that being female has given me a particular kind of sensitivity to gender issues, and in the conduct of this study enhanced my access to some settings and qualities of experience and excluded me from others. So, too, being white and middle class unavoidably shaped my relationships with respondents and my understanding of race and class concerns in their world. Numerous other elements of my identity and experience, including having lived through the Oakland firestorm, have also shaped my perceptions and interpretations. Like all others, I occupy a particular position in the world, and my work reflects in some complex way the elements of this position—precisely how I cannot easily say. In the end, we cannot know exactly how our understanding would be different if we were other than ourselves, or if that different understanding would be somehow more worthwhile.

Organization of the Book

This book is about the making of firefighters. Each of the next six chapters focuses on a particular dimension of that process, and analyzes the workings of gender and race in that context. As we move through these aspects of firefighter development, we begin to see how certain patterns of social construction and interaction, repeating themselves in different contexts, reinforce each other and determine the outcomes of the process as a whole. Central to this story is the question of identity: Who or what is a firefighter? Who are these newcomers knocking on the door of the fire service? How or where will the community place them when they first enter? What will it take for the newcomers to begin to see themselves—and be seen by the veterans—as firefighters? How does a newcomer learn what he or she must, to assume this role? And will the newcomer's transformation ultimately be validated by a sense of belonging in the community? This series of questions motivates the analyses contained in subsequent chapters of this book.

What is a firefighter? Chapter 2 is a kind of prologue; it places the story of the new firefighters into a particular social and historical setting, without which context we would be unable to interpret and understand their experience. In this chapter we learn what it is to be a firefighter in a traditional urban setting, the relationship between this particular identity and the work and culture of this setting, and the implications of these for the OFD newcomers. Chapter 2 also provides particulars that enable the reader to see both the limits and the possibilites of this case for generalization, that is, ways in which this fire department is and is not like other settings.

Who are these newcomers? Maggie and her classmates first appear in the frame of this study as they enter the fire department's training academy, but for them this moment is only one step along a continuous path from the past into the future. Chapter 3 attempts to locate the newcomers along these individual paths, each of which has a particular direction and momentum that propel the individual's movement into the fire service.[25] It is tempting to attribute these varying life courses to personal differences, but the newcomers' stories reveal the influence of social institutions, including the fire service, that have shaped opportunities and choices. These influences are particularly apparent in the way the recruits see the occupational community they are about to enter and their own place in it.

How or where will the newcomers be placed by the community as they enter the field? In chapter 4 the process of field entry begins to unfold, as newcomers negotiate their way through the traditional social initiation rituals. We begin to see how not only individual style but also race and gender differences interact with the demands and expectations of firefighter culture. At the same time, though, race and gender are not rigid categories; they can have different meanings and implications for individuals in the same subgroup. Tensions, complexities, and paradoxes are apparent throughout as veterans put acceptable newcomers "in their place" and signal unacceptable newcomers that they do not belong. At this early stage in the construction of firefighter identity, gender boundaries begin to appear salient and racial boundaries (particularly among men) subtle, even blurred.

What does it take to see oneself and be seen as a firefighter? The transformation from novice to practitioner requires that the newcomer prove to himself and others his capacity to assume the new role. Chapter 5 explores the various dimensions of this process and reveals that, although race can be relevant, gender is often the more significant social category. Men must prove they can be firefighters; women must prove they can—in some sense—be men. Women must confront not only the negative expectations of a male-dominated community, but in some cases, the caution and self-doubt that often characterize female social conditioning.

What must a newcomer learn to become a firefighter? It might seem that one would first be taught how to fight fires and then prove oneself in the role; if training could be accomplished entirely in the academy, this might be true. But real mastery of the work occurs in the field, in a process similar to and intertwined with the effort to prove oneself. In chapter 6 we see how newcomers develop their skills and professional identity by engaging in practice under the guidance of veterans; the opportunity to learn firefighting (and to become a firefighter) continues to be shaped by one's relationship to the community. Race plays some role in this relationship, but once again, gender differences are more pronounced. The OFD newcomers' experience clearly reveals how different levels of access—to work, community, and identity—produce different outcomes. At the end of their first year in the department, new firefighters have widely varying levels of skill as well as confidence in their own abilities. In addition, we see striking differences in their developing sense of what it means to be a firefighter.

Will the community fully accept the newcomer as a member? Ultimately, a newcomer must be accepted by veteran members of the community to be successful in his or her career. Chapter 7 traces the patterns of social acceptance and rejection in the experiences of the OFD newcomers and assesses the insider-outsider status of different newcomers at the end of probation. With this assessment we can answer the questions presented here: Did all newcomers stay? Who was satisfied? Who did and who did not succeed? The differing importance of race, among the men, and gender is clear in both process and outcomes.

The book's concluding chapters step back from this experiential material to consider the implications of the book's findings for organizational policy and social justice. Chapter 8, analyzing the ways in which social categories are and are not determinative of newcomer success, relates these findings to possible organizational interventions. A broader perspective is offered in chapter 9, where the contrast between racism and sexism in the fire service is taken as a reflection on the deep-seated conflicts in American culture that stand in the way of equality.

Let us turn now to a description of the community into which Maggie and her classmates were inducted.

Chapter 2	Work, Culture, and Identity in the Urban Fire Service

"OAKLAND TO ME is a cotton jacket, brass, iron, and wood department," Ray Montoya explained as I watched him go through his morning check of the rigs at Station 112. He was describing some features that made Oakland a "traditional" fire department—one that relied on tried-and-true, old-fashioned ways and had a culture to match. "We don't have a lot of equipment that's light. We don't have any high tech equipment. . . . You know . . . [it] is wooden ladders and brass fittings and cotton jacket hose. Iron pike poles. Everything is heavy." It was a matter of great pride for someone like Ray to be joining a department in which the traditions of the old "smoke-eaters" were still alive: here there would be a respect for aggressiveness, an unbridled passion for the work of firefighting, and a certain disdain for those safety precautions that might interfere with the task at hand.

Ray knew that not all departments were like this: he'd come from a newer, far quieter, suburban department, and he'd taken a significant cut in pay in order to join what he considered a "real" fire department, where the activity level was high, the firefighting intense, and a guy with ten years on the job would still in some stations be called "the new kid." These interdependent qualities of work, culture, and identity are important because of the ways in which they shape newcomer opportunities and experiences. The story that is about to unfold would be quite different if it had been set in another place (say, Ray's former department), where what it means to be a firefighter may differ from what it means in a place like OFD.

THIS CHAPTER explores the relationship between the work of traditional urban firefighting and the identity and culture constructed by those who do this work. The interaction is mutually reinforcing: the dangerous, highly interdependent nature of the work shapes culture and identity, but these in turn influence how the work continues to be done and what is valued in it.[1] In the case of older urban departments like Oakland, the bulk and weight of the traditional equipment called for exceptionally strong workers willing to push the limits of their physical capacities. With such a work force in place, the work, tools, and community have continued to be defined in terms compatible with its character. In traditional fire departments, physical size, strength, and prowess are highly valued; courage, toughness, and aggressiveness have become the hallmarks of a good firefighter. The community, through testing of newcomers and conditioning of veterans, seeks out and rewards such qualities.

I use the experiences of the OFD newcomers for purposes of illustration here, but they are not the focus of my analysis until chapter 3. With this background portrait of the community they entered, though, we can begin to imagine how differences of gender and race might play out. And in doing so, we can also begin to understand how the story might have differed had it been set somewhere else.

The Oakland Fire Department

Like other urban departments, OFD originated in the rough-hewn volunteer brigades of the mid-nineteenth century; it was formally organized in March 1869.[2] Today it serves a densely populated area with a variety of exposures, including older residential areas, downtown high-rise developments, industrial and storage facilities, under- and above-ground railways, and a busy port. The population of 383,000 is racially mixed—no single group represents a majority—and the city's neighborhoods range from upper-middle-class districts to pockets of poverty and violence. Although the department has been reduced considerably in size as a result of continuing fiscal constraints on the city, it remains an urban-sized department, with 466 uniformed personnel (on-duty staffing of 123), a total staff of 501, and twenty-three stations.[3] Each station contains an engine—the rig that carries water, pumps, and hoses—and its crew or "company." Seven stations (the "double houses") also contain a truck and its crew; this rig carries the heavy ladders and tools needed for such work as forcible entry, ventilation, and extrication.

In terms of activity level, OFD resembles departments in cities of much greater size. In 1993 Oakland recorded a total of 49,157 responses that included 2,111 structure fires. These numbers are comparable to those of the Boston Fire Department (with three times as many firefighters)[4] and much higher than the reported activities of the more similarly sized departments of St. Louis and Minneapolis.[5] Oakland's most active engine companies—numbers 20 and 23—both made over 3,400 responses in 1993, among the busiest engine companies of the country.[6] Oakland's Truck 18, the city's most active truck company, made over 1,400 responses, more than the busiest truck in the city of Detroit.[7]

The Work Force

For most of its existence, the OFD—along with other urban fire departments—was staffed entirely by men and almost entirely by whites: whites were 90 percent or more of the uniformed force until at least the mid-1970s, and the force was all male until the early 1980s.[8] Today the force is 57 percent white, 29 percent African American, 8 percent Hispanic, 5 percent Asian, and 1 percent Native American; 8 percent of the members are women (of whom about 40 percent are women of color).[9] Of promoted firefighting personnel, about 30 percent are people of color and 2 percent are women (black and white). This level of diversity in general and of African American representation in particular is somewhat unusual for fire departments; an illustrative contrast can be made with the nearby San Francisco Fire Department, which is currently 70 percent white, 9 percent African American, 11 percent Hispanic, 10 percent Asian/Filipino, and less than 1 percent Native American; the SFFD is roughly 5 percent female.[10]

Oakland has a long history of minority participation in the city government as a whole and the fire department specifically, but the level of minority group access to jobs and power has often been a subject of conflict. The first black firefighters who entered the department in 1920 were subject to segregated placement, a policy that continued into the 1950s, severely limiting the opportunities. When stations were finally integrated, as one retired black firefighter recalled, the response of the whites was to "make it as miserable as possible" for newly transferred black firefighters, largely by pointedly excluding them from firehouse life.

Opportunities for blacks in the department opened up only gradually; their numbers grew from roughly 5 percent in the 1950s to 7 percent by the early 1970s. At this point, though, their numbers and organization began to improve noticeably, in Oakland as in many other departments; political and legal pressures to open employment opportunities were strong, and the ways of the fire service began to change. The Oakland Black Fire Fighters Association (OBFFA) was organized in 1973 to provide more formal support to black firefighters, to encourage the entry of more blacks into the fire service, and eventually to bring a series of legal challenges against the department on behalf of blacks and certain other traditionally disadvantaged groups.[11]

Oakland's first women firefighters were hired in late 1979 and entered the companies in 1980, at a time when there were estimated to be perhaps only fifty women firefighters in the nation's metropolitan departments.[12] Throughout 1980 a total of four women—one at a time—entered a department in which many incumbents were opposed to their presence and minimal steps had been taken to address such questions as physical privacy in the firehouses.[13] Many veterans believed that women were not capable of performing the job, and in addition they regretted the loss of the all-male social environment and the softening of the traditional culture;[14] in some cases they went out of their way to threaten, ostracize, and intimidate the women.[15] Other men were either supportive or neutral: those veterans who were simply fair-minded were unwilling to treat the women as second-class citizens; some black firefighters were sympathetic because of the parallels they saw between their own struggles and those of the women; still other men believed the entry of women to be inevitable and therefore not worth obstructing, however unappealing it might be.

The hiring of black men accelerated during the 1980s, but the process of sexual integration has been very slow, beginning with the hiring of one or two women at a time, then increasing slightly in the second half of the decade after hiring became subject to a consent decree. The decree was the result of a 1985 lawsuit (*Nero, et al. v. City of Oakland, et al.*) filed by the OBFFA along with a group of applicants—including black, Hispanic, and Filipino men and black women—who had passed the 1984 entrance exam but had not placed high enough on the eligibility list to be hired. The plaintiffs charged that the most recent entry-level selection process had an adverse impact on minorities and women, was not justified by business necessity, and violated an affirmative action clause contained in the city's contract with the agency that administered the test. At the time of the lawsuit, the uniformed force in the department was roughly 24 percent African American, in a city estimated to be 46 percent African American, and the percentages of Asian Americans, Hispanics, and women were also considerably below their estimated proportions in the population.[16]

The 1986 consent decree that settled the case required the city to hire recruit classes reflecting the racial, ethnic, and gender composition of the city's work force and established hiring goals for the classes that followed. In terms of racial and ethnic composition, these classes closely approximated the goals of the *Nero* decree, but the proportion of women ultimately fell far short of the 46 percent goal. As a result, though the number of minority male firefighters has grown significantly (to about 40 percent), women today remain a very small proportion (8 percent) of the department.

To increase the numbers of underrepresented groups, as required by the decree, some hiring was done out of rank order, a process that led to resentments among the members of the affected recruit classes and to an unsuccessful legal challenge by the union along with a small group of white, Hispanic, and Native American applicants.[17] The debate over qualifications, charged with emotion and affecting the relationships among firefighters throughout the department, continues today.

To some extent, however, this divisiveness must be overcome to get the job done. As firefighters put it, fire does not discriminate, and political arguments have no place on the fireground, where companies must work as a team regardless of the members' feelings about one another. We look more closely now at the most prominent features of the work and then consider the culture that has the potential both to unite and to divide those who do it.

The Work

FIREFIGHTING

Though not their most common activity, the fighting of fires—particularly structure (building) fires—is the defining responsibility of the job for those who do it.[18] As traditional firefighters are fond of saying, "We run into burning buildings while other people are running out"—a line reflecting the ethic of aggressive departments, which make an effort to save burning buildings rather than simply protecting the surrounding structures and allowing the fire site to be destroyed (derisively referred to as a "surround-and-drown" approach). An aggressive approach requires an interior attack, in which firefighters actually enter the building, often forcibly, to face enormous heat, smoke, darkness, and flames in order to search for possible victims and to locate the seat of the fire and put it out. Such an approach is facilitated by the simultaneous work of other firefighters (the truck crew) who climb onto the roof of the burning structure to cut holes large enough to release the heat and smoke generated by the fire. Except when a structure has become so engulfed in fire that an "interior attack" is impossible, this is the style of firefighting employed in traditional urban departments.

Most veterans are proud of OFD's aggressive approach to firefighting, and traditionalists complain loudly when held back from an interior attack by a commanding officer who feels that a particular fire should be fought from outside. Many of these men recall the times when safety gear such as face masks or safety gloves were nonexistent or rarely used, and they worry that an increasing concern for safety procedures weakens the department's style. One veteran claimed that regulatory agencies like the Occupational Safety and Health Administration (OSHA) were trying to make the job so safe that eventually you wouldn't be able to leave the station. "It's ridiculous," he said, "it's not supposed to be a safe job."

Verbal descriptions of firefighting pale beside the real thing, but the following passage gives some of the flavor of this work. This is a probationary firefighter talking about one of his toughest house fires:

> It was a front-door still, it was about midnight, I was layin' in bed, and someone came to the door, and I was kinda groggy and I didn't even hear the doorbell go off, but one of the firefighters came yellin' in the dorm, "There's a fire! Down the street!" And sure enough, it was about two blocks down. . . . I've never seen that much fire in a house. . . . Every room was on fire in that place. So I put on my mask and went in, so I was alone for the first few minutes . . . and it was just really intense. . . . I knocked it from the doorway, went in, but wherever I would hit, would just kinda like whip the fire back around the other side, and I'd go to the right, it would whip it to my left. . . . Matter of fact, when the officer came in, he pulled me out, I felt this grab and he yanked me out and started yellin'. . . . So then the officer was with me when we went in, and once I started (hittin') everything, everything just became black, dark, and it was just the most intense heat . . . one line wasn't gonna do anything, 'cause there was too much fire everywhere . . . then Bill . . . came in, so there was three of us on the line, and all of a sudden he yelled and ran back out, came back in with another line. And that's how we were finally able to put it out, was that we had two lines, and we were kinda hittin' it kinda circular. . . . And when we came out of that fire, we were just exhausted, tired, and for a house fire, it was the most intense, stressful, I'm-wondering-if-I'm-gonna-get-out-of-here-type fire and . . . there was a point in there where . . . I know everybody was thinkin' there comes that line where you're thinkin'—I wanna run the hell outta here, this is crazy, we're all gonna die, and this is nuts. . . . But it was like, just suck it up, you got a job to do, let's do it. And I'm always concerned—somewhere in my head I'm always worried that there's somebody in there somewhere . . . and it just gives you that extra edge just to stay in there. And the other thing is you don't wanna back out, 'cause you got the other guys there, everybody's gotta stay in his unit. . . . But when we came out of that fire, there was just three of us . . . we knocked it out together, and it was just like an incredible team effort, and . . . there was this glow and it was like you were just instant comrades. . . . Everybody knew, I think, that everybody really wanted to run the heck outta there, and we all stayed in.[19]

This firsthand description conveys some qualities of the work of structure firefighting. Physical conditions are both threatening and extremely uncomfortable: those entering a building are often confronted with such intense heat and heavy smoke that it is impossible for them to walk upright or to make out their surroundings. They wear face masks and oxygen tanks to allow them to breathe, but the tanks are heavy, the time limited, and the breathing process awkward. The location is almost always completely unfamiliar, filled with obstacles and unknown hazards. While the engine crew works on the ground with water to put the fire out, a truck crew ventilates the building, opening a sufficiently large hole in the roof to allow heat, smoke, and gasses to escape so that the ground crew can do its work. Roof work is not only dangerous, but generally requires a high level of strength, skill, and coordination. If there are possible victims, either crew may become involved in search and rescue (or body recovery), which means working one's way through this foreign environment in darkness and heat, unsure what you may find, taking care not to become trapped or disoriented.

Meeting such challenges requires certain kinds of personal and social qualities. Obviously essential is the physical capacity to do the work, which includes the strength and coordination needed to lift and operate heavy equipment and to move the bodies of other people, as well as the stamina to continue strenuous activity for hours at a time with limited rest. But the work is not only physical; firefighters must be able to "think on their feet," rapidly assess the problem at hand, plan a course of action, and then quickly react when conditions change. Throughout an emergency, a firefighter must maintain a constant and heightened awareness, never losing sight of the broader picture while attending to a specific task. All this requires emotional control— the ability to remain calm enough to think clearly, even in the face of danger and chaos.

Strength, skill, and composure qualify a firefighter to do the job and provide a degree of protection against the dangers of the work. But they are insufficient to ensure success or even survival because firefighting is a team effort. The physical process is one of multiple overlapping or simultaneous tasks that cannot be accomplished by a single person, and the emotional work also requires a team: the knowledge that one is part of a group provides the motivation and reassurance needed to do the job.[20]

Even in routine situations, firefighters need to trust that their coworkers will be adequate to their respective tasks and will not endanger others through thoughtless or panicky behavior. In extreme situations where a firefighter's life is immediately threatened he or she may need to call upon others for extraordinary acts of courage and ability.

MEDICAL CALLS

Like those serving in other municipal fire departments, Oakland firefighters have seen a diversification of their responsibilities and in particular, an increasing emphasis on emergency medical services (EMS). In many areas, the expected response time of the nearest fire crew is shorter than the response time of an ambulance/paramedic unit, and although the fire crew cannot provide advanced life-support services, they can offer basic life support until an ambulance arrives on the scene. Because minutes are important in treating certain conditions, municipal fire departments are increasingly involved in the provision of emergency medical services and new firefighters are generally trained as emergency medical technicians (EMTs).

During the last two decades, EMS calls have risen dramatically both in number and as a proportion of total incidents. Over this period, OFD's total incidents more than doubled—to almost 50,000 in 1993—largely attributable to the growth in EMS calls, which now represent 75 percent of OFD's runs. By contrast, fires have risen slightly in number but constitute a smaller proportion of all responses. Along with the changing nature of emergency responses has come a shift in the type of false alarms: whereas false alarms from street boxes were once a major problem for the department, today the vast majority of "false alarms" are medical calls.

The growing preponderance of EMS calls in many fire departments is not a popular trend with traditional firefighters, who hired on to fight fires and not to be "doctors," and the medical "nonsense calls" are particularly irritating. However, the change is more one of frequency and degree than kind: firefighters have always been called upon to deal with badly injured people, and they still take seriously the demands of such situations. Firefighters are regularly called to the scenes of car accidents, violent assaults, and natural medical emergencies such as heart attacks. Though quite different from structure firefighting, these incidents can pose their own significant challenges, not the least of which is coping with the element of surprise.

In their second month on the job, Rob Marquette and Marcy Genaro were working together at Station 122 when a call came in for a "woman down"; the code suggested an unconscious female victim, nothing more. When they arrived on the scene, an apartment building hallway, they were confronted with the sight of a man stabbing a woman and trying to talk through a self-inflicted wound in his own throat. Following protocol (firefighters do not enter a violent scene until "secured" by the police), the officer immediately turned and told the firefighters to leave. As they did, the police arrived, ran into the building, and began shooting, killing the assailant. The firefighters reentered and began to perform CPR on the woman, but it was hopeless because of her multiple stab wounds. Inside the apartment, the officer discovered an infant who had also been stabbed. The two probationary firefighters began CPR on the baby and got its pulse back, but it also had been too severely injured to survive.

An incident as violent as this one is an extreme example, but it does illustrate the kind of emotional trauma and personal sense of danger that may confront firefighters at the scene of a violent assault. Firefighting is dangerous and sometimes traumatic, but this is their calling, a task for which they are conditioned and prepared. But it is not the job of firefighters to deal directly with violent criminals, and their sense of vulnerability—both physical and emotional—may be heightened in such episodes.

Meeting the challenges of serious medical calls requires the same kind of quick intellectual and physical reflexes and constant awareness called for in firefighting. Additionally, these incidents call for the ability to distance oneself from the emotions of the moment and an ongoing way to cope with posttraumatic stress. As in the work of firefighting, such requirements are met in part by the personal qualities of individual firefighters and also by the social identity created by the crew as a whole. Each individual must remain composed and mentally focused, but they reinforce each other in this effort; in particular, senior veterans and officers can radiate a calm that sets the tone for other crew members. The sense of an invincible team is maintained after the event as well, in the way the group processes its experience.

CONSTANT READINESS, UNSCHEDULED WORK TIME, AND FALSE ALARMS

Not all the firefighter's workday is spent responding to calls, nor do all calls require meaningful activity. Engine companies run more frequently than truck companies because they take the lion's share of the EMS calls, but even a busy engine company spends a considerable portion of its time in nonemergency activities. The three most active engines in Oakland average perhaps nine calls in a twenty-four-hour shift; the median activity level would be six calls per shift. For truck companies, the numbers would be a high of four calls and a median of three.[21]

A single call to a structure fire or some other complicated incident might keep the crew busy for a period of hours, but a relatively small proportion of calls involve this kind of time. Many calls—with three-quarters of the emergency responses in Oakland for medical services, and a substantial proportion false alarms—involve situations in which no emergency exists.[22] Once I began visiting fire stations, it wasn't long before I had collected a large number of false alarm stories; more than once I heard a firefighter tell of arriving at a caller's home for a stomach or back ache, asking the patient how long he'd been in pain, and hearing an answer along the lines of "five years." In addition, there are not infrequent cases in which an ambulance arrives so rapidly and the call is sufficiently uncomplicated that the engine crew simply has no role. Such runs generally occupy no more than a few minutes, with the company sometimes even canceled before its arrival at the scene.

In other words, firefighters spend a high proportion of their shift time in activities other than actual emergency responses. Some of this time is taken up with the types of calls just described, and some involves nonemergency work activities such as fire inspections in the surrounding community, practice drills or other forms of training, physical conditioning, paperwork (for officers), and housekeeping and maintenance chores—including equipment and station maintenance as well as shopping and cooking. Some time of course is also allocated to meals and sleeping. Finally, with chores accomplished and in the absence of calls, firefighters may engage in personal projects or relaxation activities.

This "downtime" itself constitutes an important feature of the job; firefighters must find ways to entertain, amuse, and occupy themselves in those sometimes extended periods between responses or other work activities. This is not always as easy as it might seem. As a San Francisco firefighter commented, "I talked to a guy once that worked in [a slow department]. And they never do *anything*, according to him. . . . They sat around and they didn't do nothing, and they worked to perfection the ability to get on each other's nerves. And it was *horrible* going to work there. . . . I mean, most people would say 'Hey, you don't do nothing, you got a good job.' . . . Actually, the slower the work, the harder it is to get along with people." This feature of the job creates a need for people with appealing personalities, good senses of humor, an ability to entertain themselves and others, and social skills appropriate to the setting. The value of such qualities is enhanced by another important working condition—the twenty-four-hour shift.

THE TWENTY-FOUR-HOUR SHIFT

As is common in urban departments, Oakland firefighters work a twenty-four-hour shift. The schedule involves a rotation of three shifts—A, B, and C—in which personnel on the A shift report to the firehouse at 8 a.m. and remain on duty until the next morning at 8 a.m., at which time they are relieved by the B shift, which works for twenty-four hours and then is relieved by the C shift, which in turn is relieved by the A shift. Most firefighters consider the schedule a significant benefit of the job: two of every three days are free for family, other work, or personal activities.

The cultural significance of the twenty-four-hour shift cannot be overstated: this schedule means that firefighters literally live together. The fire station becomes a combination work-and-home environment, and coworkers constitute a second family, in some cases rivaling or even replacing a firefighter's nonwork relationships. The station itself is outfitted as a home as well as work setting: in addition to the apparatus room and watch room, there are officer's quarters (office-bedroom with private bathroom), a dormitory/ sleeping area for the regular firefighters, a communal bathroom with showers and toilets, a large kitchen, and a lounge or TV room. In most stations meals are eaten at a large table in the kitchen. Outdoor areas, generally furnished with barbecue equipment, may also include a sitting area such as a patio or deck; a private parking area is usually found alongside or behind the station.

Firefighters share personal living space and take meals together while on duty. Some basic equipment and furniture is provided, but the crew must contribute personal funds for food and many other household purchases, including such things as kitchen utensils, special cooking equipment, VCRs, personal telephones, and television sets. If life in the firehouse is to be tolerable, crew members must be trustworthy with respect to both personal possessions and ability, able to interact sociably, and willing, capable participants in household chores such as cleaning, shopping, and cooking. In other words, a good firefighter is someone who can perform not only on the fireground or at a medical emergency, but also as a good roommate or family member.

Firefighters are very conscious of the importance of this aspect of the job; if asked for a list of job qualifications, they often highlight "the ability to get along with others." More than one instructor in the Oakland academy reminded the recruits that "we're training you to be roommates," and "you will spend more time with coworkers than with your family." Academy instructors in Oakland frequently told stories and offered advice on firehouse life, and one or two formal question-and-answer sessions were devoted to this subject. Instructors advised recruits on such details of firehouse etiquette as when to arrive, how to answer the station phones, what to expect to pay for food and house funds, how to get involved in meal preparation, and the like.

Working a twenty-four-hour shift not only puts firefighters into close, extended contact with each other, but it also isolates them from the regular work-home-leisure cycle of most other people, including members of their own families. They may come to rely on each other for social contact and as a respite from their home lives when these are unsatisfying.

Culture and Identity

This constellation of working conditions has evoked from the occupational community a set of specialized strategies for its survival and success. As in any such community, firefighters have their own ways of both coping with the technical, social, and emotional demands of the job and ensuring reliability and solidarity in coworkers.[23] Through the enactment of these cultural forms, an occupational identity—that in some ways reflects both work and work force— is continually reconstructed.[24]

THE SOCIAL INITIATION PROCESS

From the recruitment stage through their initiation into the field, newcomers are subject to a series of messages about what it means to be a firefighter and tests of their own capacity to assume this identity. Firefighting jobs are in great demand, and the formal process of written, physical, and oral examinations imparts to aspiring candidates a strong sense of the uniqueness, importance, and desirability of the job. At Oakland's 1989 written examination nearly two thousand applicants showed up, out of which only about one hundred would be hired. Several of the 1-91 recruits in this study recalled looking across the auditorium at the sea of faces without dreaming they had a chance to make it.

In the academy, trainees are regularly reminded of the uniqueness of this opportunity, the benefits of the job, the competitiveness of the selection process, the dedication required of workers, and the challenges they will face. "Plenty of seats in the audience" was a favored phrase of the OFD training cadre, repeated to remind recruits that getting to be on stage for graduation (i.e., passing the academy) was something that would set one apart from the crowd (the audience). Instructors would push the recruits through long, difficult sessions, then during a break sit down and tell them, "It's the best job in the world. I never had a day I didn't feel like coming to work."

The formal agenda of the academy included training in the many technical aspects of the job, but an additional and equally important function was the social and psychological preparation of the recruits. As one explained, "It's kinda like a fraternity, very much. I've never wanted to be a part of a fraternity, [but] I think . . . I'm part of one now. I feel like I'm going through those— I don't know what the week's called—called 'hell weeks' or whatever, that they go through. I feel like I'm doing that now . . . in order to become a firefighter."

In short, the message was that firefighting is a special calling, a role that involves competitive selection and rigorous preparation. As they move through this process, recruits begin to identify with other firefighters and set themselves apart from ordinary people. Pride in their membership in this "elite team" helps carry them through the rigors of the academy and continues to support them through the difficult times on the job. The commitment they begin to develop to their "brothers and sisters" in the fire service is also a critical element in their ability to do the work.

NEW KIDS SHOULD BE SEEN (DOING EVERYTHING) AND NOT HEARD. At the same time as the recruits of Class 1-91 were being charged with a sense of the desirability and importance of this career, they were also reminded that they themselves were rank beginners—"new kids"—who needed to defer to their veteran crew members and officers for guidance and instruction. Academy instructors offered explicit instructions on how newcomers should behave in the fire station. Recruits were advised to show a great deal of deference to the rest of the crew, to go out of their way to do work for others (always looking for ways to help before being asked), and to be reserved about their own needs or desires. The bottom line was simply: "Show up for work, do your job, and keep your mouth shut."

While unpleasant for the newcomers, this posture is consistent with the realities of the job. For example, the deference shown to veterans reflects the central importance of on-the-job training. No matter how long or sophisticated, fire academies are limited in the extent to which they can simulate the work; the drill tower is a "sterile" environment relative to the field. Most hose-and-ladder drills involve no actual fire, and those that do take place under very controlled conditions. EMT work is practiced with dummies in a classroom setting that is nothing like the real world, a difference that came home to me as I watched a probationary firefighter perform a secondary assessment on an "injured victim." She knelt on the floor by the dummy's head, quickly and coolly going through the motions while tossing off comments like, "Next I check for cerebral fluid coming out of the ears."

In other words, almost all formal training takes place in thoroughly familiar and predictable physical surroundings without emotional content. Missing are the variability, unpredictability, confusion, danger, and emotional challenge of the work itself. Real skill must be developed through exposure and training in the field, under the guidance, tutelage, and sometimes protection of experienced firefighters and officers.

Relative silence and deferential behavior reflect the newcomers' lack of expertise and offer something in exchange for the veterans' assistance. In a session at the academy the recruits were told over and over again how they should plan to do *everything* in the firehouse; following a specific reference to meal preparation, one instructor explained, "You need the veterans to teach you, so if you can help them slice and dice, they'll be more willing. It's really a trade, they're not just taking advantage of you. You want them to show you how to pop out that window, so do something for them."

It was explained that new kids are expected to show up early for work (roll call is at 8 a.m.; they might arrive by 7 or even earlier). Because they wouldn't yet have station keys and they shouldn't ring the doorbell for fear of waking the crew, they were advised that the best strategy is to wait in your car and watch for evidence of someone stirring inside the station or the arrival of another crew member for your shift, whichever came first. You might also pick up a newspaper for the crew on your way to the station, and make the first pot of coffee if it had not been done before your arrival. Once the coffee was made, the new kid should serve everyone else first. In the early days particularly, the new kid should behave like a polite visitor in someone else's home.

Specific assignments are given by the officer at roll call; housework usually follows roll call, and the new kids are expected to do their share and more. As a new kid, you participate in all regularly scheduled duties and emergency responses and in addition work through a list of drills. If left with any free time, you should spend it studying, reviewing equipment at the station, or asking work-related questions of the officers and other crew members. At meal times, new kids are unlikely to be asked to cook at first, but they are expected to help and should jump in to provide assistance before being asked. They are also expected to do much of the dishwashing.

New kids signal their interest in the job by asking questions—for example, about different tools on the truck or how the engine operates or how a certain call should be handled. In response to questions, veterans may spend hours talking, telling war stories, and sharing "nuggets" of information (the tricks of the trade). It is considered extremely bad form for a probationary firefighter to act as though he or she already knows any of this material, and even those with prior experience or knowledge often refrain from displaying it, except when explicitly called upon to do so.

A newcomer's firehouse behavior is also believed to indicate whether he has the qualities of a good firefighter, including aggressiveness and a willingness to work hard. Among the many negative labels that can be assigned to a new firefighter one of the worst is that of "lump"—someone who's lazy and not willing to pull his share (or in the case of a new kid, more than his share). New firefighters are expected to be the first to begin work and the last to quit. Noticing that something needs doing and then doing it without being told often earns a compliment from another crew member ("nice going" or "way to go"). Taking a break—sitting down with a cup of coffee or the newspaper—should be delayed until the crew or officer suggests it; as instructors often cautioned, "You want *them* to tell you to relax." Isolating yourself from cooking or any other firehouse chore is like saying "please screw with me."

One prominent example of this ethic is the norm pertaining to telephone answering. All fire stations have two or more telephones, including the company line, over which official calls and emergency dispatches are made, and the private house line, used by firefighters for personal calls. New kids are expected to show their "aggression" by racing for the telephone whenever it rings. This is often awkward: the new kid may be some distance from the phone, and another firefighter may be right next to it. It can also be embarrassing when the call is for someone else and the new kid neither knows everyone's name nor how many times to press the kitchen buzzer to signal a veteran that he has a call. In some places, the awkwardness of the tradition is heightened into a sort of hazing ritual, in which a veteran standing next to the phone when it rings waits until the new kid dashes across the room before the veteran picks up the phone. Though the ritual is taken less seriously in some stations than others, a failure to move quickly can tarnish a newcomer's reputation.

As noted, these norms are consistent with the apprenticeship process. Newcomers depend on the good grace of their veteran coworkers, and they learn by listening and watching first; if they spend too much time talking themselves, they miss what they need to hear from others. Additionally, in discouraging outspokenness and other forms of "cocky" behavior on the part of new kids, the community is also cautioning them against an overconfidence that could be deadly on the fireground. Firefighters need a high degree of confidence to do what they must do, but an unrealistic belief in one's own knowledge or skill can lead to disaster. By listening, the new firefighter can both learn and show respect for the skill and knowledge of veterans.

REPUTATION IS EVERYTHING. A veteran firefighter explained to me that when you enter the fire department, they give you a jacket, and you have a year for a label to be put on it. Firefighters wear "turnout coats" that have their names lettered across the back, but he was referring to a different kind of label: the reputation you earn. In other words, during your first year you are closely watched; if you perform poorly, you'll be branded more or less permanently.

Silence in combination with hard work in theory gives the new firefighter a measure of control over his or her reputation: if you don't say much, but you display the appropriate qualities in your work, people judge you by your deeds. Firefighters make early and seemingly merciless judgments about each other, and these judgments pass rapidly through the department and may linger for some time. That judging and labeling should figure so prominently in this culture should not come as a surprise; the work of firefighters is dangerous and highly interdependent. When a firefighter enters a burning building with another firefighter, she is trusting that person's sense, skill, and composure; she hopes that her coworker is reliable in all of these dimensions, but if not, she needs to know it. In an emergency situation, a firefighter or officer may behave differently depending on the skill and reliability of others in the crew. If firsthand knowledge of that skill or ability is limited, the officer or firefighter may rely to some extent on reputation.

PITCHING AND CATCHING. The importance to the group of an individual firefighter's skill and composure also means that firefighters engage in a great deal of testing and conditioning of each other in nonemergency situations.[25]

Verbal harassment and practical joking serve these functions for all firefighters, but may be particularly prominent with probationers, whose exposure to major incidents is limited.

Firefighters ride each other with complaints and criticisms, in a game known as "pitching and catching." Brand-new firefighters are almost entirely on the *catching* end of the game; they are expected to listen to abuse but not to respond in kind. As they become part of the group, they can pitch as well. Pitching styles range from the simple insults ("dumb shit") that are routinely showered on new firefighters to more imaginative and amusing barbs.

Recruits are repeatedly warned that any show of temper or defensiveness on their part invites additional abuse. Those veterans who are particularly fond of this style of interaction make many different attempts to get a rise out of someone; if they are successful, they repeatedly return to the individual's weak point. Learning how to react or not to react is an important and subtle skill; once a new firefighter gets to the point where he or she can respond to an insult—which happens fairly soon—there is the question of what level of response suffices. A criticism deflected with a bantering response may be an effective way of standing up for oneself and feeling in control, but if the response is too defensive, it backfires.

Practical jokes, again ranging from the obvious to the subtle, are characteristic of both firefighter interaction and veteran-hazing of newcomers. A new kid may be asked to start a chain saw while being videotaped "for a training film"; but the saw has been rigged to make it difficult or impossible to start. Or he may fall into bed at the end of a particularly hard day only to have his bunk collapse because all the bolts have been removed from the frame.

Many firefighters believe that one who easily loses his cool when insulted or taunted may have difficulty controlling his emotions on the fireground or at a traumatic medical call. Furthermore, a newcomer who takes offense readily and responds "inappropriately" to teasing or joking is not someone that other firefighters want in their house. As an Oakland recruit anticipating entry into the field explained, "the first thing they look for is can I live with this guy for twenty-four hours? . . . If the guy's an asshole they don't want to work with him." Asked how they would determine that, he said, "They kinda throw you some heat and see what happens. You know, if you get back in somebody's face or if you have a temper—you know, they talk about pitching and catching; if you can't pitch and catch or especially if you can't catch, you're not gonna be on everyone's best list."

COMMON STYLES OF INTERACTION:
TEASING, JOKING, AND STORYTELLING

Though respect for experience and divisions based on seniority remain, the probationary firefighter's initiation process does taper off fairly quickly. By the time newcomers have been in the field for six months, particularly if they have seen much action, they are markedly more relaxed than in their earliest days, and they tend to feel and act a bit more like members of the crew (though they are not, of course, full crew members). The testing of new kids shades into the more general exchange of teasing, gossip, and practical jokes that characterizes firehouse interactions.

Firefighters tease each other continuously and sometimes mercilessly about mistakes in job performance, personal foibles, aspects of appearance, and events in their personal lives (if they are unwise enough to have revealed personal information to others). Humor is also often used in descriptions of calls, sometimes in ways that would seem insensitive or inappropriate to an outsider.[26] One probationary firefighter recounted a call from an older woman who had informed the dispatchers that her husband was "kind of cold." When the crew arrived they found that the man had in fact been dead some time. Speculating as to how it could have taken so long for the woman to decide there was something wrong with her husband, the new kid deadpanned, "I guess they must not have been very close."

Storytelling is a prominent feature of firehouse life, both as part of training drills and at meals or other times when firefighters are gathered together in the house.[27] Stories generally involve fire service experiences—strange, interesting or humorous calls, and mistakes or exceptionally good moves by other firefighters. In addition, gossip about other members of the department (sometimes true, sometimes untrue) is extremely common. Within hours of an occurrence in the field or at a firehouse, news of it spreads to several other stations; if it is particularly noteworthy it eventually makes its way through the entire department.

Newcomers, cautioned both to keep their own lives private and to refrain from engaging in the rumor mill, are reminded that you can "telephone, telegraph, tell-a-fireman." At the same time, they are regularly invited to disregard this advice because veterans will often query them about other firefighters, particularly their classmates. Smart new kids deflect these queries by saying "I really don't know" or "I haven't heard any more than you have." In general, this is the correct response, as one probationary firefighter explained: "That's like the first thing that this guy told me at 114, don't say anything about anybody. It'll come back to haunt you. He said just for instance, if I were to ask you about so-and-so, and you said such-and-such, you can be damn well sure that I would go to them and say exactly what you told me. So just don't even say anything about anyone."

But at the same time, participation in the conversation can also give a sense of belonging to the group, and the temptation to talk may be strong. Some new firefighters also note that while they do not feel a need to offer their own opinions of coworkers, they also feel that not *contradicting* talk (in particular, negative talk about others) is a way to display solidarity and trustworthiness.

The styles of social interaction described here are functional within their context; these styles reflect the working conditions of firefighters and meet important needs of the occupational community. Verbal taunts and practical jokes, which test new firefighters, may be used among veterans to release tension, establish and display group solidarity, entertain, and continually condition themselves to stay alert and simultaneously calm. This conditioning function was made particularly clear to me in an exchange with a veteran officer who described to me a regular joke he had played on a fellow crew member. The officer (then a firefighter) would hide a firecracker in one burner of the gas stove each morning; his coworker would come out to make coffee and face a one-in-four chance of having the firecracker explode while he was doing so. In an occupation in which constant awareness of your surroundings can mean the difference between life and death, regular reminders to look over your shoulder or keep your wits about you have their place.

Joking, pitching and catching, and gossip can also be used to display and confirm group solidarity. Though this function is important in many occupations, it may be particularly critical in one in which the work can be simultaneously dangerous and highly interdependent. Firefighters work as a team, depend on each other's efforts to get the job done, look out for each other, and are sometimes called upon to make extraordinary efforts on a coworker's behalf. Their first commitment is to the crew's safety.[28] In circumstances such as these, there is little or no room for personal animosities, and in fact a high degree of loyalty can be useful. Interpersonal bonds are formed both in the firehouse and in the field, and each reinforces the other. In the firehouse, crew members tease each other "like family members" and feel (much like siblings) that it is fine for crew members to criticize each other, but unacceptable for outsiders to do so. Similarly, the trading of practical jokes can be a way of working out hostilities, of demonstrating affection ("when they play tricks on you, that's how you know you're accepted"), or perhaps both.[29] In a setting where getting past interpersonal conflicts and establishing group loyalty is important, each function is relevant.

Gossip, so prevalent in the fire service, also fulfills multiple purposes. This kind of storytelling entertains, informs, and builds group identity when it dis-

tinguishes the group members from outsiders. Stories told about the performance and personalities of other firefighters suggest who is to be trusted and
who is not, in terms of both job competence and personal honesty and loyalty. Gossip about "others" establishes a "we-they" distinction that gives those
sharing the stories a sense of small-group membership and loyalty. This function can be uncomfortably clear to a newcomer or an observer in a firehouse
who is unable to participate in or even understand dinner table conversations
because of the number of in-jokes and private references with which such conversations are peppered.

Finally, in all the behaviors described here—teasing, practical joking, and
storytelling—an element of humor serves yet another set of group needs. Like
other people whose work exposes them to personal danger and human trag-
edy, firefighters have a ready sense of humor that can be raw, sharp-edged,
physical, and rude. The humor that pervades much of firehouse life provides
entertainment, an emotional release, and a sense of distance from or perspective on the more emotionally demanding aspects of the work.

RITUALS AND RITES OF PASSAGE

All cultures include rites of passage marking transformations in the member's
life or career, as well as rituals in which the common ethos is dramatized in
ceremony.[30] For new firefighters, a critical rite of passage is the first structure
fire and the most coveted role in the ground crew is to be "first in on the
nozzle." This means literally being first through the door, entering the heat,
smoke, and darkness of the building at the front of the hose, backed up by
one or two crew members. Breathing through a mask, the firefighter moves
through the building searching for the fire, trying to get as close as possible
before hitting it with spray from the nozzle. Virtually all new firefighters talk
with excitement about their first time in this position, and the event clearly
has great meaning for them. Lillie Carlton, a young veteran, recalled for me
her first structure fire and how she got the nozzle:

> My first fire was at 103 Engine, and it was on the second floor of an
> apartment building. . . . Oh, it was fucking scary. . . . I had to have the
> nozzle, wasn't about to give it to anybody else, but I was goin' in first
> and I didn't know what I was lookin' for. You know, you need to know
> when you're lookin' for that glow . . . don't start shootin' your water
> 'cause you're just gonna bring up steam . . . and I was totally scared.
> Couldn't breathe (right in) my mask [makes gasping noises], I felt like
> I kept hearing my bell go off, like I was out of air. But all you gotta do
> is just keep crawlin', just keep crawlin' 'til you get to it. And then
> once you put it out, you're so stoked on yourself for puttin' it out. . . . I
> was so high on myself. . . . I was talkin' all sorts of shit when I got

back—big time—"I'm Queen Nozzle. What can I say?" And that was the name I gave myself, "The Queen." Call me Queen. I'm Queen Nozzle. Nozzle Woman.

Sometimes a newcomer is assigned to the nozzle, but there are no guarantees, and a new kid who wants into the action has to be prepared to fight for the opportunity. Lillie was ready: with her air tank and mask already in place, she moved ahead of her partner to grab the nozzle as soon as the officer called for a line; then she turned to her partner and told him to grab the hose loops. "And there was nothing else he could do. I got my tank on before him. So I had the nozzle when I went through the front door." The initiation rites of first-time exposure and action are the times when a new firefighter gets to show his or her stuff, to prove to self and others that he or she can do it, and to take steps toward insider status. As in the firehouse exchanges, the new kid is being tested, for aggressiveness, composure, courage, and ability.

Other types of rituals celebrate or ceremonialize important aspects of life in the fire service. Some rituals are small or informal—dinner in the firehouse is an example of a quotidian event that has the character of ritual[31]—whereas others are formal and orchestrated, such as graduation from the academy, and some promotion or retirement celebrations.[32] True to the everyday ethos of firefighter culture, the enactment of these rituals reinforces both pride in the occupation and group solidarity among its members.

Identity, Solidarity, and Boundaries

It should be readily apparent that if a positive function of a firefighter culture is to create solidarity, a negative function may be the exclusion of those who "do not belong." Although this function may be legitimate in terms of informally screening out truly *inappropriate* candidates, the line between this legitimate purpose and the illegitimate intentional discouragement or exclusion of *unwanted* candidates is fine. Apparently neutral norms can be applied in a way that reflects underlying bias, as when hazing becomes racial or sexual harassment, or when veteran judgments and their reputational effects are more positive for majority males than for men of color or women.

These inequities can occur in any work setting, but a deeper level of exclusion takes place when the occupational identity itself is constructed along the lines of a social category such as race or gender. Neither the working conditions nor the occupational culture of firefighters have been determined in a social vacuum; both are embedded within historical relations of race, class, and gender. In theory, the predominance of white, working-class men in the fire service suggests the possible construction of identity and culture along any of those three lines. In reality, however, the particulars of the culture—especially its resemblance to other male cultures[33] and the way in which it has been experienced by newcomers of different race and sex (as I illustrate in the chapters that follow)—strongly argue that the most important feature is gender.

As we have seen, firefighters have a hierarchical society that subjugates newcomers, tests its members with pointed insults and practical jokes, represses emotional displays, and releases emotional tension through rough humor. Firefighters are expected to be large, strong, athletic, unemotional, cool, good with tools, physically hard-working, brave, aggressive, competitive in the manner of team sports, self-confident, and socially skilled in a loud, group-oriented environment. The genesis of this image could be argued at length, but its implications for gender segregation are clear: women will have a hard time becoming firefighters to the extent that to be a firefighter means to be a *man*. Men of color may find some aspects of firefighter culture distasteful or feel that cultural forms are used as an excuse for racial exclusion, but there is no inherent opposition between firefighter identity and the identity of a man of color. Furthermore, the contingency of firefighter culture specifically on a *male* work force is evident in the experiences of female newcomers who must negotiate a set of expectations and cultural norms that are foreign to most and unfriendly to all women.[34] I do *not* argue here that women are by nature unsuited to the work of male-dominated occupations, but I argue instead that this occupation and its culture have been crafted in a way that reflects and enhances the social construction of gender in the society as a whole, exaggerating the barriers to sexual integration.

The following chapters illustrate a pattern repeated in each key feature of firefighter socialization—from the social forces that shape individual choices prior to entry to the final patterns of acceptance and exclusion by the firefighting community. Among men, race clearly matters: the paths of some men are less sure than the paths of others, and experiences of racial suspicions and exclusions do emerge. But gender matters in a different, deeper, and more consistent way.

Chapter 3

Reflecting Back, Looking Forward

*My dad retired out of Oakland, with . . . thirty-three
years on the job. Still to this day he says he's never had
a bad day, comin' in to work. . . . I started takin' fire
department tests in 1984, I think was my first test. I
went to a Firefighter 1 academy at a community college in
'85, I got my EMT in '86. . . . And I took tests up until
probably 1989 or '90, really hard, serious, takin' tests.
Got on a lotta lists, did real good on a lotta lists, just
didn't, you know, wasn't part of the breakdown of the
cultural diversity program. It's kinda tough for a white
male to get on.*

———FRANK CROSS

*I was working out at the Gold's Gym . . . and there's a
lot of firefighters—women firefighters—that go there and
I had never met any women firefighters before that time.
So it was always something that I was interested in, but I
just—it wasn't something that I could do, it just wasn't
something that I thought I could do, 'cause, you know,
women aren't brought up to think that they could be
firefighters. And through talking with these women, I
realized that yeah, I probably could do it. I've been
training for years, so I probably could—as far as strength
goes, and fitness.*

———MARIANNE GRANT

I FIRST MET the OFD newcomers when they were in the middle of the four-
month academy that preceded their eighteen months of probation in the field.
In our initial conversations, we spoke of where they had come from, what it
was that drew them to this work, and how they found their way to the Oakland Fire Department. As the stories of Frank Cross and Marianne Grant suggest, these trajectories differed significantly in some cases, in ways that would
influence the newcomers' future careers and experiences of the fire service.

All newcomers were here because they wanted to be firefighters, and as we shall see, they gave strikingly similar reasons for their occupational choice. But would they all have the same ability to attain this identity? Perhaps more fundamentally, did it *mean* the same thing to everyone? Standing with the newcomers in the academy, we consider what they sought in firefighting, how they came to be here, and what their expectations were about the community and their own place in it. In some cases, the threads of race and sex are prominent, in other cases subtle or insignificant. In the end, what emerges is a spectrum of views on the fire service and its membership that range from the very traditional to the very change-oriented—an array that does in fact reflect differences of race and gender.

The Allure of Firefighting

Virtually all newcomers—male, female, white, black—were attracted to the work for its unique blend of psychic and material benefits. Firefighting offered adventure, challenge, excitement, and unending variety. At the same time, it was a relatively secure position with good pay and benefits along with a schedule that allowed plenty of time for other pursuits. On top of all this, there was the satisfaction of providing service, of being an active participant rather than an onlooker, and in some cases, of being a hero. Eddie Gibbs said it simply: "It's the perfect job for me—plenty of action and time off." Besides its security and decent pay, he noted, "it's a really respectable living"—a combination of excitement and service, something you could be proud of doing. Marianne Grant used similar words, mentioning both the job's excitement, especially the fires, and its respectability: "People usually *like* firefighters. It just seems like a *good* job."

When the newcomers talked about their interest in the job, they sounded very much alike, alluding to the same set of attractions and often using the same phrases. The slight variations in emphasis that sometimes emerged tended to reflect individual histories and experiences more than race or gender differences. For example, someone like Tom Armstrong, who had always enjoyed physical work and sports activities, expected to like the physical work of firefighting, but he also appreciated the schedule: "I also have *other* interests, outside of the fire department. I think it's a job that allows you time to do other things and still have the security of a good job. . . . The reward that you get from the service that you're giving is a great side of it, too." Others, like Laurinda Gibson and John Bowman, had been motivated by family experiences to seek a secure job with good benefits; to find job security *and* "get paid to save lives," as Laurinda put it, was very appealing. John knew from prior firefighting experience that he enjoyed the work and the schedule, but also, he said, "I like variety and I like challenges. And you certainly have that in this occupation."

Jonathan Lawrence echoed these sentiments when he noted that he was drawn by "the excitement . . . you never know what you're gonna be confronted with." Such qualities of the job were also highlighted by people like Rodney Chin and Valerie Dickinson, both of whom had become dissatisfied with their previous work. After thirteen years of a technician's job that "got *really* boring," Rodney Chin was looking forward to both the time off and the variety of firefighting. Valerie Dickinson's work had been well-paid but ultimately unsatisfying in a number of ways, and she also sought both the freedom to pursue other interests and a greater level of physical and mental challenge.

Tommy Bautista had enjoyed his previous work but wanted a greater sense of fulfillment and expected to find this in firefighting: "I wanted to make a mark in life rather than a profit for someone else." Carrie Hopper liked the idea of not feeling helpless around people in need of assistance. "I want to feel like I'm actually bein' a *player* rather than a standby," she said. "There's just no other job like it, that makes you feel like you *were* something to society." Tony Escobar also appreciated "the thought of being able to help people in a situation where they need help, and you're there" but knew from prior work experience that his greatest satisfaction would come in meeting the unpredictable challenges of the job.

On a general level, then, all newcomers described their attraction to the fire service in very similar terms. But on another level, there was a recognition that the job would not feel the same to everyone. In particular, because this job was a more radical departure from prior experience for the women than for the men, the women's enthusiasm was often tinged with a bit more apprehension about how the work would actually feel and how readily they would develop their ability and confidence. Contributing to this apprehension was a distinct concern about veteran reception and judgment. Women noted that in the academy exercises, they sometimes had to find alternative approaches or work harder than their male peers to accomplish the same physical task, and while a woman herself might be comfortable with this fact she knew that her future coworkers might not. Negative comments from the veterans during station visits (required as part of the training) as well as the occasional disapproval of male classmates heightened such concerns.

For their part, the women were extremely diverse in their attitudes toward the physical aspects of the job. For Marla, the combination of hard physical work and mental challenges was a major part of the job's appeal. Though she was a college graduate who wanted a job where she could think, she'd always had an interest in nontraditional work and she most enjoyed physical jobs. On the prospect of working as a firefighter, she said simply, "It's hard, and I *like* that." Toward the end of the training academy when many class-mates were complaining, Marla noted that she'd gotten her wind back after tiring a little and was feeling fine again—in fact enjoying herself. She recalled that when she first arrived at the Tower, she was a bit put off by how much classroom work there was, "but then as soon as we got into the hoses and lad-ders I was sure."

Marianne also had a history of nontraditional, blue-collar jobs, and she was a serious physical trainer. In her new job, she was most looking forward to the firefighting. She expressed a healthy concern about her own level of preparedness, not in terms of the job's physical demands but with respect to her understanding of how the pieces taught in the academy would all come together on the fireground. In training she commented, "It's a little scary be-cause I know enough to be dangerous, but maybe not enough to where I can compensate . . . [but] I think that that'll come with time [and] experience." Like Marianne, Valerie had made a serious avocation of physical training, and she also was looking forward to the fires, particularly "the initial charge—into the building or up on the roof . . . when the variables are changing the most quickly . . . the exhilaration of everybody kind of pulling together and doing their thing."

In contrast to those who specifically named firefighting as an anticipated source of pleasure, Carrie and Laurinda were somewhat more reserved in their anticipation, though neither expressed serious doubts about the work. Carrie found the physical activity of the academy "fairly difficult" but "still fun and a challenge"; she most looked forward to being part of a team trained to assist in emergencies. Laurinda expected initially she'd be most comfortable with the medical calls, but after gaining experience and confidence believed she'd enjoy all aspects of the work.

Jane Macey and Elena Cochrane expressed the most mixed feelings about the physically demanding work of firefighters. Jane felt she could "do it" but was frankly unenthusiastic about some dangers and discomforts inherent in the work:

> My first goal, after I pass probation, is to be an engineer. And *that* is because I don't wanna be in a burning building all the time, and the engineer gets to run the pump . . . [to] some people that would be considered wimpy, well, I don't care. [Chuckles.] Let 'em think what they want, I'm not stupid! I'm not gonna burn my lungs out in three years. Not that they would be stupid for wanting to be a nozzle person the whole time, but I just know there's a lotta risks that go with that, and I don't wanna take those risks for a really long time. . . . I know I'll get time on a truck, but I would not choose to work on a truck. . . .

I don't really wanna climb up on a roof with an SCBA on my back, and an axe on my side, and a saw in my hands, and I hafta climb up this steep roof that I think might be spongy, and I might fall through it, you know. . . . It's just—it's really, really hard work, and then you've opened this roof up, and all this smoke and flames come shooting out at you. I don't know—that's the downside of the career, the danger and discomfort of the moment.

Elena's uncertainty had to do in large measure with her own size and strength. She found the training "kinda hard because . . . I'm small, and that's really a bad thing for me. I'm just beginning to realize. Because the equipment is heavy for me. And my hands are littler. It takes me longer. You know, everything's heavier. And I'm sure it shows, in my performance. That's why the guys probably laugh at me and probably feel what a joke that is, her being a firefighter." She thought she might try to balance this weakness by developing a strength in another area of the work, such as medical calls. When an academy instructor complimented her on her EMS work, she "thought, well that's good, because I might as well star at something, 'cause it sure ain't gonna be ladders."

The women sought the work for reasons similar to those of the men, and they certainly hoped to enjoy it, but they were also in some cases apprehensive of how readily they could do so.

Differing Paths to the Oakland Fire Department

In some sense, the making of a firefighter begins well before the newcomer arrives at the academy, even before the application process, in his or her earlier life experiences. In addition to the myriad social and familial influences on an individual's sense of potential and possibilities, there are specific experiences that can contribute substantially to one's inclination and readiness to enter an occupation such as the fire service. Exposure to firefighter role models can make the choice seem desirable and appropriate; personal training and experience in physical or mechanical work and participation in competitive athletics can enhance preparedness and can ease both skill acquisition and social acceptance. These kinds of background elements vary substantially among newcomers, to a considerable degree along race and gender lines.

Almost all the white and Hispanic men in this study came to the Oakland Fire Department already strongly identified with the occupation—through family members and in several cases their own previous firefighting or paramedic work. Seven of these nine men had relatives or close friends in the fire service, and five had an immediate family member, either a father or a brother, in the Oakland Fire Department. Five of the men had worked elsewhere as firefighters and, in some cases, as emergency medical technicians (EMTs) as well; one had not worked as a firefighter but was an experienced paramedic with police training. All but two had taken fire science classes before entering Oakland's academy.

Although most of these men had spent some time in college, they had worked primarily in skilled blue-collar jobs and found themselves happiest with work that combined mental and physical activity. Ray Montoya had graduated from college and was thinking about graduate school when some friends in a local fire department invited him down to the firehouse; in a short time, he was hooked. "I was looking for something that was different, exciting, because I didn't want to be doin' the same job thirty years down the road and be hating it. I wanted something physical. Something that would . . . [be] helping people. . . . The fire service is a public-aid-type service. It's exciting. It's physical. There's job security in it. The benefits are great." He joined a volunteer group and enrolled in a fire science program at a local community college, where he got his fire science degree and EMT certification. He took tests repeatedly—some out of state—until he was hired.

Paul Brown, reporting a similar experience, indicated that he had intended to follow his father's footsteps into engineering, but after completing two years of university-level training realized he didn't enjoy it. He took up machining, which allowed him to work with his hands, but he still wasn't satisfied. Then he spent time with an extended family member who had been a firefighter for some twenty years, and who "always looked forward to goin' to work. And to me, as a young man, I thought that was great." The man's brother was a captain in another department who managed to get Paul into the part-paid reserves—a difficult thing to do without connections—and that was his start.

Many saw the work as a calling; it was a job they had been seeking for some time and for which they had made sacrifices. For those whose fathers were Oakland firefighters, following in their footsteps was a matter of great pride and a strong motive for pursuing this work. As Andy Lewis said, "As a little kid, I always thought it looked real exciting, and then I followed my dad in his career, and it was always kind of a dream of mine—'cause he worked at 111 Engine . . . to work at 111 Engine, and now I got that chance." Frank also had family in OFD and knew from the outset that Oakland was where he wanted to go. Unable to get into this department after several years of testing, training, and volunteer firefighting, he pursued an alternative career and was well situated when the call from Oakland finally came. "I pondered that, what I was gonna do, and . . . I almost didn't take it. Then I figured I'd kick myself in the ass 'cause it was something I always wanted to do. And my dad bein' retired out of Oakland, well, it just felt good."

Within the African American community, the fire service is a growing presence, and several black men in this study had known people in the fire service, but their familiarity with the work was not of the intimate, long-term sort common among the white and Hispanic men whose immediate family members were firefighters. Marcus Everett began to learn about the occupation, for example, when he met a group of firefighters during an assignment for his previous job. After hearing their stories, he went back to a friend who happened to be an Oakland firefighter. "I said to him, 'Hey, how come you didn't tell me about this long ago?' He said, 'If I would've told you, you wouldn't have believed it.' "

Tom Armstrong had friends who talked up the job. With his strong professional goals in another area, he was uninterested at first but he finally came around: "[it was] just my friends talkin' to me and convincin' me that, 'Hey, you could do anything else you want to do.' It finally sunk in, well maybe this *is* probably the best *job* I could have." Jonathan Lawrence also [had] several friends in local fire departments "and they would always tell me about, 'Hey, man, this is really a great job.' And I'd see the time off that they had, and the benefits package . . . and if you have somethin' that you wanted to pursue and you never had the time for it, this was the right occupation to be in." Eddie Gibbs knew of the job through a relative in another department, and after he joined OFD, he noticed that other relatives began to follow his own lead and were "jumping on the bandwagon—they all want to be firemen because I think people are realizin' the flexibility of the job and—it pays well. And there's also . . . a lot of upward mobility, there's room to be promoted."

Among the African American men, it was unusual for the fire service to be a lifelong interest. In general, these men saw firefighting as "a great job" rather than a personal calling. As Eddie noted, there was a distinction between his feelings and those of the traditional firemen, who "believe this is it. . . . They believe that . . . there is nothing else but this, that you could not want a better job. This is the best job. Which is fine with me, you know, I don't mind if they believe in that. . . . But I can think of a lot of things in my lifetime [that I'd like to do]." Tom expressed a similar kind of reservation:

> You know, sometimes I think about—and I hope I never get this
> way—but there's an *appetite* in this department for fires. And I kinda
> go, Well, am I supposed to think that way? Because the way I see it,
> any time I respond to a structure fire, my life is on the line. So, it's like
> bein' a security guard and you hope somebody tries to steal something.
> I never thought that way and I hope that I never do, I hope that if it
> happens I do the job as best as I can, but—I don't know, there's just
> this appetite that I see that these people have, for fire . . . you know,
> they come in—and even the recruits—they know that there was a
> two-alarm fire last night and where it was and how it was and they

just, they salivate. . . . I mean, I want to get my experience but it doesn't have to come *real* fast [chuckles], you know what I mean? . . . I don't think I'll think that way. . . . I hope that doesn't sound like I don't want to do my job.

Although most of these men had taken one or two fire science or EMT courses before coming to the Oakland academy, they did not have any direct prior exposure to the work,[1] and lacked the specific technical expertise of more experienced classmates. Most of them had worked, however, in blue-collar and/ or physically demanding jobs that prepared them for some of the work of the fire service, and, in addition, they saw themselves as culturally advantaged. All of them were from Oakland, accustomed to a multiracial environment and familiar to some degree with the ways of the inner city in which they would be working.

Among the four Asian American men,[2] one had extended family members in the fire service, but the others came to the work even more serendipitously than did the black men. Stanley Okada was between construction jobs when he happened to meet a firefighter who was unofficially recruiting minority candidates for the department. His decision to follow up on the application "was one of those just-for-the-heck-of-it deals"; not until he was farther along in the process did he realize how much he wanted the job. George Alarcon and Rodney Chin also heard from acquaintances about the job and OFD's openings and said, "Sure, I'll put in," without really thinking twice. Basically, the work seemed to offer better opportunities, more challenge, and greater rewards than what they had been getting. Rodney, for example, had worked as a service technician with the utility company for thirteen years and had become extremely bored; without a college degree he thought his options were limited, but the fire service seemed to open up new possibilities of combined job security and adventure. He felt his life had always been "safe." When the fire service opportunity came up, it was like "Let's get on a roller coaster, I don't care where it takes me anymore. . . . I'm just taking it day by day now, and I'm gonna go as far as I can go."

Only one of these men had any training in firefighting, but they came in with the generally relevant skills of trades work and athletic experience. For example, as a transit construction worker Tommy Bautista had been exposed to both physical work and the occasional emergency response—volunteering at a fire scene, providing services in the aftermath of an earthquake, dealing with injuries on the job. Others had worked in similar settings involving physical activity and mechanical knowledge.

For the women, firefighting was an intriguing possibility that had only recently occurred to them; it was not a familiar, long-term goal. Even if the work was something that had always seemed interesting, as Marianne said, "it wasn't something that *I* could do, 'cause women aren't brought up to think that they could be firefighters." Valerie, seeking a career change, was introduced to the challenges and the potential rewards of firefighting when a close woman friend entered another urban department; the more she learned about the work, "the more it seemed to appeal to a lot of the empty places that I had . . . places that . . . were not being filled by my previous career."

Marla decided to submit an application when her aunt told her OFD was hiring, but she really knew nothing about the job—despite having cousins in the fire service. She developed contacts at OFD, visited firehouses, and found that everyone spoke of the job in very positive terms; the more she heard the more interesting and rewarding it sounded. Elena also heard about OFD's openings through a relative, but she had not really given much thought to the work until her godfather "told me that they were testing. . . . It wasn't like a life-long dream that I wanted to be a firefighter. But once he told me about it, it all just seemed to fit in." Laurinda's father was an Oakland police officer, and her brother's best friend an Oakland firefighter; both of them influenced her decision, and when she decided to work toward a job in the fire service, her brother's friend helped her to prepare.

Although several women had relatives or family friends in the fire service, they had virtually no exposure to the work or familiarity with the lifestyle prior to deciding to pursue it as a career for themselves. Most of the women had something in their backgrounds that might make them slightly more prepared for this work than would be the average woman—including physical jobs, experience working with tools, and physical training—but direct preparation was limited. None of the women had worked as firefighters; only two had taken fire science classes. These two also had EMT training (one had worked as an EMT), and a third woman had EMT training and experience without the fire training. Most common, however, were backgrounds like Carrie's—some exposure to nontraditional work but not necessarily enough to make fire training come easily.

> If you're not exposed to this equipment down here and the fire
> service, some of this stuff can be very confusing. . . . I haven't dealt
> with power tools. . . . I've always wanted to, I've been around a few
> but not enough to really whiz through things here. I've got a little bit
> of an advantage on probably some of the other females in the fact that
> I have swung hammers before and I have, you know, driven large
> vehicles. . . . So that helps. But it's overwhelming. And I would
> suggest to anybody who has the time to do a ride-along program and
> hang around the firehouses [to do it], because when you get here, it'd
> make it a whole lot easier. . . . And especially females—and men also

who haven't been around it—but especially for females, 'cause it's a
lot of physical work and if you're not strong enough to handle some of
the physical work or your mind's not mechanically into it, you're gonna
really have a difficult time. . . . You have to kind of like keep an image.
Kinda like you have to pretend like you know it when you don't.

Though the natural abilities of the women varied, and some took to the
training more readily than others, most could identify with one or more of
Carrie's concerns. The academy was stressful for almost all recruits and "overwhelming" at times for many; lack of a mechanical background or unfamiliarity with techniques for performing physically demanding tasks could magnify
the difficulties of training. Though these women had slightly more exposure
to nontraditional work and training than do women in general, their backgrounds were much less directly related to the work of the fire service than
was true for the men.

As EXPLAINED in chapter 2, not all fire departments are the same, and the Oakland Fire Department offers a very different occupational identity and community than would be found, for example, in a small, suburban department.
We should ask, then, how the newcomers felt about joining this particular
department. What about it—if anything—drew them?

Because the position is in such demand, some candidates would have
taken a firefighter job in almost any department, but most did consider Oakland a particularly desirable location. For probably all newcomers, the
department's most important feature was its high level of activity and variety,
which would not only guarantee interesting work and rapid skill development
but also offer additional prestige. Beyond the matter of action, though, different newcomers had different reasons for preferring this fire department. Among
the men, some clearly admired and identified with the very traditional style
of the department—its age and history, its aggressive style of firefighting, its
respect for old-fashioned equipment and methods, and, even in some cases,
its reluctance to change. This sentiment was most common among the white
and Hispanic men, who tended to have strong family ties to the fire service,
personal firefighting experience, and a confidence that they were perfectly
suited to the job.

A different perspective on OFD was evident among the African American men, who were less likely to have close personal ties to the department
and less likely to be wedded to its traditions. Rather, these men found Oakland appealing because of their ties to the city, their desire to help this particular community, and their wish to serve as role models. They also felt
strongly that their urban backgrounds qualified them culturally, in a way untrue for some of their more technically prepared classmates. Though firefighter

or EMT training and experience were much less common among African American than white men, the black men felt that their familiarity with the inner city and its culturally diverse population would be an important advantage in the job. Tom Armstrong had almost nothing in the way of firefighter training, in contrast to classmates that had degrees in fire science and probably knew "more than a lot of firefighters out there working." But in some ways, he felt that the recruits from Oakland had a better idea of what the work would really be like, "because bein' a firefighter in Oakland and bein' a firefighter in Stockton is a whole other experience. . . . See I think some people just wanted to be a firefighter and it didn't matter where. And the experience here is gonna be something that they probably never thought it would be."

Tom wasn't the only black firefighter to make such a comment; several of them noted that some of their classmates did not seem to realize what the work would be like *in Oakland.* Hugh saw this as a lack of preparation for the job, in an interesting twist on the traditional firefighter's perspective. Whereas a man like Frank Cross would assert the importance of a background in the trades and speak with some disdain of those who lacked this, for Hugh, the opposite was true. He described newcomers from the trades as having been "brought in off the street," a phrase Frank might well have used to describe someone like Hugh, who lacked firefighting experience.

In contrast to these groups of men, the women at entry tended not to have strong feelings about the department or its location. Their ties to the city weren't as well-defined as those of the African American men, and unlike the white and Hispanic men, they were—at least on arrival—relatively unaware of the department's traditionalism and style. As these features became apparent, however, they also in some cases became a source of misgiving. In the minds of at least some women, and a few men as well, the traditions of the department were strongly associated with its hypermasculine style and unfriendliness to women firefighters.

Perspectives on the Fire Service: Traditionalists and Change-agents

Coming from different places and bringing different skills, expectations, and values, the newcomers even at this early point in their careers expressed a variety of perspectives on their chosen field. The complex relationship between these differing perspectives and the social categories of race and gender can be better understood if we characterize the newcomers' attitudes by placing them along a spectrum from traditionalism to change-orientation. This dimension of difference among the newcomers is important, for it emerged in the context of virtually every aspect of the socialization process and describes an important aspect of the newcomer's identity. Furthermore, characterizing newcomers as traditionalists versus change-agents allows us to capture differences relevant to but not perfectly correlated with race and gender.

The relationship between race, gender, and traditionalism can best be represented as a set of overlapping curves along a spectrum. The attitudes of white and Hispanic men would describe an arc from extreme traditionalism to moderate change-orientation, clustering at the traditionalist end. As noted, many of these men had personal and/or familial ties to the fire service and held the "old ways" in high regard. Such men felt that the department's history was proud, and if they believed any change was desirable—in either firefighting techniques or personnel—they thought it should be undertaken gradually and with great care. Not all white and Hispanic male newcomers were extreme traditionalists, and there were certainly enthusiasts among other groups, but no woman, black, or Asian American newcomer expressed the sort of reverence held by some white and Hispanic men.

The distribution curve for the African American and Asian American men would begin at moderate traditionalism and extend to extreme change-orientation, with the high point of the curve slightly toward the change-oriented half of the spectrum. Among these men, a few were very change-oriented (viewing the occupational community with some suspicion and maintaining a detachment from its identity), a few were somewhat traditional (appreciative and proud of the department's aggressive reputation), and the rest held moderate views.

For the women, the high point of the curve would be at extreme-change orientation, but tapering back into the traditional side of the spectrum. Two women were traditionalists in the sense of accepting the less hospitable aspects of the culture; given the historical absence of women from the professional fire service, however, it was impossible for any woman to be a pure traditionalist, for that would deny her own place in the occupation. For a woman, then, traditionalism means *accepting* the culture of the fire service as it is, but cannot mean *identifying* with it. At least three women were decided change-agents, in the sense of expressing great reservations about the culture (at least privately) and consciously working not to support it.

Additional clues to the newcomers' differing ideas of what it meant to be a firefighter could be found in their behavior toward and opinions of classmates, in which traditional versus change-oriented perspectives were quite obvious. Traditionalists among the white and Hispanic men felt strongly that the fire service had been and should remain selective about its membership. Those who had put in years of testing, training, and work at other departments were particularly angry about newcomers who had not displayed these kinds of commitments but nevertheless had been admitted to the class. "I worked hard to get to where I'm at—to work for this department," Frank Cross asserted. "Some people took one test, and they got it. Some people were— not that this matters qualification-wise—but were six hundred on the list. And now they got a job and now the city 'owes them.' "

Men like Frank saw the fire service as a team on which you had to earn your spot, and they sometimes expressed strong feelings about who does and who does not belong in the fire service. They challenged the qualifications of some classmates by claiming that these people lacked the strength, understanding, and proper attitude to be good firefighters and that they might well endanger coworkers. These judgments were not always based on differences in prior experience or race and sex, but there was considerable criticism of affirmative action policies and the "lowering" of standards that had accompanied these policies. Ray Montoya was particularly critical of affirmative action policies that he felt did not screen for the best-qualified people; he believed strongly that effort should be rewarded. It was fine to recruit minorities and women for the fire service, but people should not be handed the job on the basis of race or sex. Though he tried to work with everyone in the class, he had doubts about the mental, physical, or emotional abilities of some recruits.

> Um, these are good people, but there's some that I just shake my head at and say, No, they don't belong in this business. I would like to tell them, if you'd really like to be involved in the fire service, go to prevention. Don't go to suppression. Because you may get yourself hurt, or maybe I might be working with you, and I may get hurt because, because, you know, of a stupid mistake that you might make. . . . I know in this academy who I can trust . . . who I'm gonna rely on because it's a team effort. And I know the other people that I don't trust, I know they mean well, but that's not enough.

Andy also expressed doubts about a number of his classmates and disappointment that because of a "numbers thing" (affirmative action) poor performers weren't dropped from the class. Frank was vehement in his comments about recruits who seemed unprepared for the job:

> There's a lot of people here that don't have a clue, and they're gonna get out there [in the field] and have a rude awakening. . . . Some people think that this is the gravy train, the ride out. Sit in the firehouse and that, but that's not the way it is. It's work. You get out there and work. When things gotta be done, you gotta be *sharp* and on top. You gotta be able to make these split-second decisions that are a matter of life or death. . . . There's some people in the academy that— I don't know. I'm personally *embarrassed* to be comin' out of the same class, considered the same rank, havin' the same experience as these

people. They don't take it seriously. . . . Some of these people, these
people don't even know what fire *is* yet. . . . It's somethin' to always
fear, but you gotta get a handle on it. . . . Some of these people don't
see that—I don't know, they wanna change the system.

Some traditionalists were less outwardly critical of their classmates, but
they clung to the belief that firefighting was special work for people thoroughly
committed to it. Paul Brown was disappointed to hear about people who didn't
really care—to whom it was "just a job"—because it should be something more:
"You're in a position to help people and you have to care about people and
care about your job and in this job there's a lot of pride involved." Howard
Hamilton made a point of saying that he liked to hang out with "people that
bust their butt." It was all right to bitch about it, but you should be willing to
work and work hard. He also believed that many of his classmates were unrealistic about the job; they just took the test and got it, without knowing what
it was really like. Tony Escobar thought most people would do fine, but he
worried that "there's gonna be a group out there that I don't know is gonna
make it. . . . Not that they're not great at somethin' else, but I notice some
people under pressure situations, and this job is pressure. And there's not only
that, but there's some people that I think that . . . aren't gonna be able to
handle the reality of the job."

One or two of the less traditional white men expressed a more easygoing, less reverential attitude toward the job and were less dogmatic in their
assessments of classmates. Steven Brandt commented while in training that
"I'm impressed with the women. . . . At first I looked—when it was starting,
the first day—and kinda said well, gosh, she looks kinda small, she might have
a tough time dragging me out, if there was a problem. But I really, I don't
have any qualms with any of them." Even the most traditional men acknowledged that people could surprise you, and you had to give everyone a chance
to prove himself. Howard observed that "the ones that have lacked whatever
I had coming in [in terms of prior training], there's some of them are gonna
be on the same level with me pretty soon, and so that's not it, either. It's just
a personal thing." He felt some people were simply not suited to the job, but
that quality wasn't something you could necessarily judge by a person's background.

Nontraditional black and Asian American men, generally less identified
with the fire service, expressed less concern about classmate qualifications or
the possibility that some "wouldn't make it." George Alarcon, for example,
felt there was really only "one person that I would say I'm not so sure about.
All the rest I think are gonna be fine." Somewhat more change-oriented men
like Rodney Chin and Stanley Okada were both safety-conscious, and though

they worried about those who might fold under pressure, they were also critical of those who might be *too* "gung-ho" and ignore safety issues in the interest of aggressive firefighting.

While the most traditional (white and Hispanic) recruits gravitated toward others with a strong commitment to the work, the African American men formed relationships around similarities in personal interests, styles, and backgrounds that had little if anything to do with the work. Hugh Thompson, for example, indicated that aside from squad members (with whom all recruits spent considerable time), the classmates to whom he felt closest were those with comparable backgrounds, who had the same "street-smart mentality," and who seemed to be more in touch with what was happening in Oakland. Marcus Everett also mentioned how "having shared some of the same life experiences" made a difference—it "gives us something to build on."

Eddie Gibbs and Leonard Bentley felt personalities drew people together, and—typical of more change-oriented male newcomers—they enjoyed being with those who did not take the training too seriously. Leonard explained that "I think it's more personality similarities [than anything else] because—I talk to guys in here that I really have nothing else in common with, but we like to laugh and joke together. . . . Something that [separates] . . . people in this class are those who take it real serious and then those who don't take it real serious." Leonard also noticed what seemed like an unnecessary level of competitiveness in some of his classmates. He agreed with the idea that "we're all in it together," but then he added that for some people, "it doesn't seem that way." He'd seen a group having problems with a ladder and "this one guy, he let everybody in his group hang—he seen what they were doin' wrong—instead of tellin' em about it." Leonard felt you wouldn't be any farther along as a result of this kind of competitiveness,[3] so why engage in it? "That's one thing that this has shown me, is how people will act under certain situations. I mean, it brings out the worst in some people, and it brings out the best in some people."

Eddie liked to float among different groups, but he also spent time regularly with the "pranksters" who would gather at lunch to relax, read the sports page, talk sports, crack jokes, and take the opportunity to vent. "You got the guys that have been through academies before, the real, real serious, gung ho [types]—sometimes I want to give it a break, you know, I don't want to talk fire every minute of my day." Eddie imagined that some of this fervor came from growing up with firefighters, and in a way he envied those men the advantage such exposure gave them in training. But he didn't believe that these kinds of differences should divide the class for long, concluding that the important thing was that "we're all here now."

The men were all alike in one important respect: both traditionalists and change-agents spoke as if from the inside of the circle. For the traditionalists, fire service membership should be limited to a select group who had earned their way onto the team, and they were among these few. For change-agents, the profession wasn't *so* special, and everyone should be given a chance, including themselves.

But the women, whether traditional or change-oriented, spoke and acted from the margin or even the outside—inevitably, given their provisional status. Though they felt their classmates in the academy to be generally supportive, they were keenly aware of those who were not. For some, the most difficult part of the training was dealing with the hostility of certain classmates to women. In an apparent effort to discourage and demoralize, men sometimes offered their negative opinions in stage-whispers, ostracized women, and dramatized the difficulties of the work. Laurinda, generally something of a traditionalist, reflected painfully on her experience in training during the final weeks of the academy:

> [Some of it] I wasn't expecting. . . . I had a couple guys who just did not care for me at all. I never said a word. I kept my mouth shut all the time. They bossed me around and . . . I wasn't really expecting [it]. I'd been around large groups of men. I worked with all men before, but they weren't demeaning like it was at the beginning [here]. . . . Certain people were just really disrespectful. They'd say whatever comes to their mind. And I had a little problem with that, but working with Susan Dunne [an instructor] . . . she said it's like that at the beginning, and you just get used to it, and then you learn to react back to it. [Laughs.] Which is what I learned to do. . . . I felt a little naive because I came in here thinking everyone was gonna treat everyone like equals, and it wasn't like that. [Laughs.] . . . Like, well first they wouldn't let me load hose. They wouldn't let me throw ladders first, wouldn't let me do any of my evolutions first—"No, I'm going," "No, I'm doing this," "No, I'm doing that," and even if I jumped in, they'd jump up on my tailboard [at the back of the engine] and [take over] . . . during ladder evolutions was the worst because your life's really in jeopardy. You got this 40-foot ladder hangin' over you and they said, "No, we're gonna do it like this." And I said, "No, I need the ladder taken away"—"No, we're doing it like this," and they just wouldn't listen. And . . . then things like, "Oh, women shouldn't be here." . . . It was so negative. . . . It just blows my mind. "Oh, you got the pink slip because you're a woman." . . . It was like a test every day, you know. . . . I can't even think now because I've closed it out.

Laurinda was quick to point out significant variation in male attitudes and behavior. While the women sometimes suffered the impatience and sense of superiority of men with more training or experience, others could be extremely helpful. "Some of the people that have the knowledge and don't bully you with it. . . . Those people are the best."

Unlike the traditional men, women themselves didn't frequently question their classmates' abilities, but they were sensitive to the possibility of their own exclusion from the team even if a failure was someone else's fault. Some women noted that there were men who didn't know what they were doing; yet if something went wrong in a group effort, almost inevitably the woman was blamed. Jane was uncomfortable "working with some of the guys on ladders, 'cause they don't know what they're doing." At the same time, she said, "they'll always blame it on the woman. I mean, that's almost a sure thing, unless you're with some of the really cool guys. . . . If there's a problem, you know, the guy freaks out and thinks it's the woman 'cause she's weaker or you know, 'She just doesn't know what she's doing.' " Jane might be justified in feeling that she had as much right if not more to be a firefighter as did some of the men, but she wasn't in a position to claim this right.

The women generally supported each other and benefited from two female instructors, but their bonds were not uniformly strong. As with the men, differences in interests and personalities were such that the women were not necessarily all drawn to each other, but the differences in their social ties did not reflect the qualities of traditionalism versus change-agency in the way that was true for the men. Instead, their very different views and strategies about how to survive and succeed in a male-dominated environment influenced their associations. For example, both Marla Harrison and Laurinda Gibson could be called "traditional" in their friendships with others who shared a commitment to the work and training activities: Marla was attracted to people who had "the same motivation, desire, effort—people who give 100 percent at all times," and Laurinda was drawn to those who put in long hours and formed outside study groups. But they exhibited very different styles in response to their environment and were not particularly drawn to each other. Marla was in many ways a change-agent: strong-minded, independent, and confident of her ability to find a place for herself in the fire service despite some of her criticisms of its culture. Laurinda was less assured and, in her willingness to accommodate to the community's traditions, a kind of traditionalist.

Elena Cochrane eloquently expressed the tensions felt by a woman struggling to find the right spot for herself. "I respect it's a male-dominated place," she said, but at the same time she didn't want to be "dumped on." She described the kind of behavior she thought was best accepted by the male firefighters: a woman should seem "relaxed," not prudish or strident; she shouldn't have an attitude that says "let's don't talk about that," or "don't treat me like that 'cause I ain't gonna put up with it." She knew the guys wouldn't appreciate that, and she didn't want to "ruin their thing for them." "I can adapt anyway," she insisted. "Nothing really bothers me."

> So I would like to be the kind of person that they can still feel, do anything they want. Even if it isn't real uh, with a lot of manners, you know, because I can handle it. And I just would rather have them not mind me being around, rather than me not hearing it and sticking up for myself, saying, "Well, you can't treat me like that," you know. But I don't want to be dumped on, either, so I don't know, I really don't know what's the right way to be. But I think I would rather just mind my own business, and not you know, make demands on the men, like you can't act a certain way, and you can't say that stuff. Because then they're just not gonna like you bein' around and they're not gonna wanna help you learn. And they're not gonna help you.

Like Laurinda, Elena was a traditionalist in her respect for the community and desire to accommodate to it; but she was a change-agent in the very fact that she sought a place for herself in this world.

Anticipating Entry to the Field

In terms of the work itself, only the experienced newcomers really had a sense of what to expect in the field. But for the social environment of the firehouse, virtually all men were prepared, albeit varying in their enthusiasm for it. Traditional newcomers like Frank Cross and Ray Montoya saw the initiation process as a predictable way of letting new people know they were entering someone else's domain, and they supported the idea that newcomers should earn their way into the fire service. Less traditional white men like John Bowman may not have looked forward to the process, but he anticipated being able to "blend in rather easily." John noted, however, that "there will definitely be a period of adjustment for some people. I do believe that firefighters out there already are adept at making their demands known," he chuckled, "and certainly we're not in a position to negotiate. . . . People will sink or swim. . . . People who have their own agenda are in trouble."

Most of the men, regardless of color, also believed that the *experience* of the veterans was worthy of the deference that newcomers were expected to show. As Tommy Bautista, an Asian American man, explained it, "the older guys have something to teach you—they wouldn't be old in this business if they didn't know something." And John Bowman recalled his previous experience as an EMT, in which a course he'd taken "was great *theory*, but it really didn't prepare me for what I was about to experience. It was the journeyman paramedics . . . who really gave me the nuts and bolts of my education. I think that'll be true here, too." Regardless of how strong the recruits' training was in theory, some veterans in the field could perform better simply because they'd done it for so many years. John respected this fact of firefighter life and said simply, "You know, we *have* to serve our apprenticeship." Even a less traditional newcomer like Tom Armstrong, an African American man, explicitly acknowledged the need to respect the "heavy tradition" of the fire service. "There are certain things you just have to conform to," he said, "and you just do it and you don't hold an attitude about it. . . . You have to respect the fact that these people have *time*."

Like their more traditional white counterparts, the African American men were familiar with masculine culture and knew what to expect in the initiation process. In reflecting back on his experience with a previous work crew, Leonard Bentley commented, "I know how it is when you get a new person, how if they don't do this, they don't do that, they get the instant reputation. . . . And so I kinda know the game of what you do and what you don't do. . . . The first two weeks they'll see what they can do with you—if they see they can't drive you nuts or something, doesn't look like they can mess with you, they'll leave you alone." Echoing Leonard Bentley, Eddie Gibbs added that he expected to "be the butt of many jokes" and that as a newcomer he'd have to do more than his share of scut work. "I know how guys are," he said.

But at the same time, Eddie and the other African American men also expressed a wariness of the community they were about to enter. They explicitly articulated a need for personal respect and an unwillingness to tolerate truly abusive behavior; as Eddie said, "if it's a situation where I'm not liked, I can take my personal space and live with it because I'm not there to be accepted as far as them liking me. But I demand *respect*." For these more change-oriented men, being a firefighter didn't define who they were; they could and did separate this role from their identities as men. And they took great pride in those identities and expected to be respected as men, regardless of their status as firefighters. Jonathan Lawrence summarized their perspective: "Once again, we get back to the respect thing. You may not respect me as a new firefighter, but respect me as an individual, as a person."

The women expressed a different kind of concern. Where most African American men seemed wary of the possible excesses of firefighter culture, the women tended to be more apprehensive and uncertain. Most could not separate their selves from the firefighter role in the positive way that the black men could because for a woman to insist that she was *more* than a firefighter she would have to believe in her right to this role, and few women had this kind of self-confidence in the face of widespread suspicion and a culture hostile to their presence. In contrast to the black men, those women who expressed a concern as to how they'd be regarded were not so much looking for respect *as women*, but rather, for acceptance *as firefighters*, and they weren't at all certain they'd get it. "I don't know if I'm willing to compromise certain things in order to be accepted," worried Marianne Grant. "I'm just not sure how much I'm willing to give up for this job." She saw that "some of the women don't get the respect, and some of 'em do," but that it didn't seem to have anything to do with "competence at their job . . . a lot of it has to do with how they relate to the men."

Most had a sense that they were entering a hostile environment, and all but the most self-confident were unsure about how to respond. Just how were they supposed to act to be accepted? Was it even possible and at what personal cost? Jane felt better knowing that other women had "paved the way," but she also expected the process to be emotionally challenging:

> One of our assignments is going out and visiting every station. And I've gone out there and comments have been made about women firefighters, like that they just don't cut it. . . . And it's really hard to hear because what I've been told is that . . . some of the women should never have made it. But they had to because of affirmative action. So now, we have to overcome not only the fact that we're female, but [the idea] that we're incompetent. We have to go out there and show them that yeah, we *are* qualified to graduate. That it wasn't just handed us—handed to us because it was affirmative action. And so they're gonna be watching every move we make, and everything we do. And granted, I'm not a big boy! You know, I'm not huge and strong. . . . I'm strong but I'm lean . . . so I have to work harder than a lot of the guys. And some of the things I cannot do as well. And that's, that's something that I feel pretty comfortable with, with *myself*, 'cause I can usually get the job done, but what I don't feel comfortable with is that I'm gonna be judged about that.

Carrie also expressed such concerns, but she'd been in male-dominated settings before and had developed a strategy for dealing with the attitude that "it's probably the female's fault" when things didn't go well, or "you can't do it because you're a woman." She had decided that "you can do one of two things with that; you can get mad at that and just be pissed at everybody, and then mess up, or you can just say, 'Well, I got the job . . . I have the badge, you can't take that from me. . . . I do what I have to do and you have to deal with me.' " She knew she wouldn't be able to bring everyone around—you never would, and that wasn't just a problem in nontraditional jobs. "It's just something that you have to deal with; it's a reality."

The most striking exception to the general pattern of apprehension among the women was Marla, who though nervous about being the "new kid," was unconcerned about gender as a barrier to acceptance. Asked if she thought that being a woman would be "an issue" in the process of entry, she replied with certainty, "It's not an issue *for me*." She was confident of her ability to do everything she'd been taught and believed her coworkers would see that. Gender might be a problem for some *men* in the stations, but that didn't mean it had to be a problem for her.

ALL NEWCOMERS, uneasy about entering the field, expected that they'd be endlessly tested and mercilessly scrutinized. But there were differences in the nature and degree of their discomfort, just as there were differences in their ability to see clearly a place for themselves in this occupation. The most traditional male newcomers already had a strong affinity with this community, a sense that while not everyone could be a firefighter, their own claims to the identity would be honored after they paid their dues. Change-oriented men were both warier and more detached. Without embracing firefighter identity in the same way as did the traditionalists, they were mindful of the excesses of the culture, including the disrespect they might confront. They could, however, become firefighters if they worked at it and wanted it enough.

For women the way was less clear. Full identification with the traditional, masculine occupational identity was impossible, but a viable alternative wasn't all that clear. The culture of the fire service had been defined largely by white men; black men had worked in it for decades and were managing to carve out a place for themselves. Women were still foreigners, and the norms both for their own behavior as insiders and for the men's treatment of them as coworkers were ill-defined.

Chapter 4   Initiation

Swimming in the
Shark's Tank

Tom Armstrong and I were talking privately in the lounge next to the kitchen at Station 103 when we were interrupted by a knock on the door. Dean Mulvaney, a young fellow crew member, stuck his head in and announced, "Tom, company line. She said it's pretty important." Tom left me to take the call, and a moment later I heard a loud noise and scream from the other side of the door, followed by loud laughter. By now accustomed to the commotion of firehouses and wary of leaving my tape recorder and notes, I remained seated until Tom returned to explain what had happened. He was chuckling as he said, "So I pick up the phone and I go, this is Firefighter Armstrong, and Dean comes at me with his chain saw and it's, it's goin', right? So I can't tell there's no blade on there and he comes toward me and—ZZZZZ—and he actually *sticks* it on me! And I was like—I screamed! And then there's no blade." He laughed and shook his head. "I guess they got Jeff already. It's crazy. . . . You gotta be ready around here, they do a lot of that. . . . And oh, and Ralph's filmin'. He has his video camera, filmin'." I laughed with him and said, "I would never last!"

Induction into the community of firefighters has traditionally included a fair measure of verbal and physical abuse, including active harassment as well as the silent treatment (pointed disregard of the new person).[1] Name-calling, heckling, practical jokes, and various forms of subjugation are used by the community to test the newcomer's character and composure, to establish his place at the bottom of the social order, and to entertain and bond veteran members of the community. Relatively uncomplaining endurance of these rituals is part of the novice's rite of passage into the community; it is understood that in time, as long as the newcomer behaves appropriately, acceptance will replace subjugation.

Even in relatively homogeneous work forces there are, of course, tensions in the relationship between old-timers and newcomers. The community as a whole maintains itself by taking in novices, but individual members, supplanted in the process, are understandably ambivalent about their successors.[2] Newcomers themselves, while anxious to be accepted, have their own interests and feelings, which at times run counter to those of the senior members. Adjustments and accommodations are made, and conflicts are resolved, in recognition of the stake both groups have in the success of the community. But what happens when workers are also divided by gender and race? Is the process more complicated, more awkward, and in the end less effective? In this chapter, I explore the ways in which these social categories differentiated the initiation experiences of the OFD newcomers. In particular, I consider the universality of the implied promise of eventual membership, the evenhandedness of treatment of newcomers, the consistency of meanings of interactions across race and gender, and the possible race and gender constraints on newcomer response strategies.

Water off a Duck's Back

Tom and his classmates all experienced some degree of ritualistic harassment as part of their initiation into the field. Whether one was the target of a verbal assault or the butt of a practical joke, the appropriate response was to stay cool—to let the harassment flow, like "water off a duck's back." A reaction of anger or defensiveness invites additional harassment and marks one as an individual who easily loses control. Over time, though, the veterans ease up, and the new kids begin to fire back.

Virtually all the men, regardless of race or ethnicity, had a clear idea of what to expect in this regard, and most if not all had prior experience with this process—whether it was joining a fraternity, spending time in the military, participating in team sports, or simply entering a close-knit all-male work group.[3] As Eddie had commented while still in the academy, "I know how guys are. It's like a fraternity, and if they know that something gets your goat, they're gonna do it." And Jonathan Lawrence, another African American man, understood that the veterans would want to know of a newcomer "what this person is made of, what he can do, can he handle it. . . . It's just a test to see whether or not you can adapt." Doing a good job forestalls serious harassment, he believed, and as for the joking, that was second nature to him. "Oh, I'm used to this, I've done this all of my life!" he chuckled. "You're not introducing nothing new to me! And I guess, you know, the firefighters here, they sense that. 'Oh yeah, this guy here, hey, he knows what's goin' on, he can take it!' Because *no one*—I should say *no one* that comes in here can escape some kind of ribbing. . . . You've got to have thick skin to work in the fire department. . . . I'd rather have it that way than, than them not sayin' anything to me period. Truly, I'd rather have it that way. 'Cause you know if they're not sayin' anything to you, they don't care about you."

Traditional newcomers like Paul Brown accepted the ragging as a novice's due, particularly when it was at the hands of an exceptionally experienced and competent crew. As Paul said of the senior crews at 112, "They like to razz you and . . . make sure that you know that you're the new person. . . . That's just their way of lettin' you know that they're experienced, and they've been there for years, and you're comin' into their domain, and don't try and rock the boat. Which is fine." The veterans called him "Bobby Joe Buckwheat," threw his watch in the garbage while he washed dishes, complained about his cooking, introduced themselves by the wrong names, and generally made his life difficult. Paul took it all quietly in stride.

Even when a man didn't necessarily enjoy the game or respect the other players, he understood the game and was prepared to deal with it. Tom Armstrong saw that the veterans would try "to make you 'rise up' as they call it. And if you do . . . you're gonna have a long [miserable] career." He felt the veterans tended primarily to hound people they didn't like, or those who acted like they knew it all, but anyone could be a target. He said he hadn't come in for much slamming, partly because of a strategy of not letting them "know too much." One old-timer who was "known to be able to just rattle your brain" went after almost everyone in the station. "He started on Mulvaney, and Mulvaney kinda lost it, real quick. But then he said something to the other recruit, and that guy went through the ceiling, so that was like his target after that. And he shot at me a couple of times, and he finally told me he couldn't tell where I was coming from, 'cause I wouldn't let him know if he was bothering me or not. You can't let 'em know."

Hugh found the teasing at Station 105 to be so personal and brutal that "I didn't think I was gonna make it." They would "basically tell you that you're not shit, can't fill anybody's shoes, you know, who the hell do you think you are. That type of stuff. Then they'd get into your personal business and you know, tell you they heard you did this, and heard you did that." He simply bit his tongue and eventually the slamming turned to friendly advice. At Station 122 the focus was on practical jokes: they hid his books, clothes, car keys, and money; put weights in his turnout coat, other people's property in his clothes and bags; stuck his books and clothes in the freezer. "I tried to be a good sport 'cause I didn't want to give 'em the satisfaction of blowin' up. . . . [Then] I got transferred outta the station, and when I came back through,

everything was OK. . . . You know, each time you go through a shift or a station, you kinda have to go through a process of bein' accepted or, or at least
tolerated. . . . They test your character, or at least I feel like they're testin' your
character, and as long as you seem to be someone that they can coexist with,
then you do OK." For the most part, new kids who kept quiet and cool—neither revealing information about themselves nor reacting to a coworker's pot-
shots—found that the veterans eventually toned down their assault.

There were exceptions to this general rule of behavior. Sometimes a new
firefighter with a particularly gregarious style would engage in the firehouse
banter by taking on a veteran in a verbal sparring match. Or if the social fit
between newcomer and crew was particularly good, the new kid might participate more as a peer than as the target. In the negotiation of their social
status, then, newcomers could be advantaged by charm, ability, self-confidence,
and personal connections to the department.

Though personal ties would not guarantee acceptance, they often eased
the newcomer's entry. In his second month, Glen Jarvis found himself at a
station where his uncle was well known, and he felt himself very much at ease.
"I just have a lotta fun here, people here are real friendly, and they joke around,
they kid around." As an example, he retold the story of an extensive food
fight in which he had tricked another crew member. During the melee, Glen
had left the room to change his clothes. "And then what I did was I went to
Hal's locker, took off all my clothes and put on *his*, came back out and he
nailed me, thinkin' I'd changed into my own clothes. And he kinda *looked*—
after he nailed me and . . . [I go] 'That's right, Hal, these are your clothes.' "
His crew members called him "the old-time new kid" and complained that
he was too relaxed, but their objections seemed mild.

Of course, participation as an equal could be a risky strategy for a newcomer. Under the right circumstances, it would be accepted, but the newcomer
was opening himself up to more abuse; even if he was prepared to take it, some
old-timers still would not appreciate the presumptuousness of a new kid slamming back too early in his career. As time went on, however, more back talk
was expected and, if clever enough, enjoyed as well.

DRAWING THE LINE

The general rule of keeping quiet could also be violated if the veteran was
judged out of line. A number of men described situations in which they had
refused to go along with a test, told a veteran to "fuck off," or made it clear
that they were prepared to take someone on physically if necessary. Hugh felt
that you were sometimes asked to do unnecessary tasks "just as a measure of
your intelligence"—in other words, the smarter you were, the less likely you'd
blindly obey the veterans. When another firefighter asked him to find some-

thing on the truck at 11:30 in the evening, Hugh told him to go to hell. "I was havin' problems with him and that was like the last straw, that's when I knew he was fucking with me as opposed to trying to help me. . . . And I also heard him talk about how stupid some of the individuals are for goin' for that type of thing."

Though not essential, it helped in these incidents for a firefighter to be self-confident and physically large or capable. Steven Brandt reported a run-in with an "asshole" at Station 112 who was "particularly riding me. . . . He was callin' me a sissy in front of these other guys . . . said it like 'a cat up a tree.' And that's a reference to a pussycat. I mean, you could take it that some-one was callin' you a pussy if they said, 'Oh yeah, when Brandt's on a roof, it's like a cat up a tree.' " At the end of the shift, Steven decided he wasn't willing to put up with it any longer. "I said, 'Hey, we're off duty now, you wanna step outside?' Then he backed off."

Most of the men who described incidents like this conveyed a clear sense of having been pushed too far, and even though they weren't sure how their defiance would be taken, they didn't hesitate in drawing the line when it seemed necessary. These were usually cases in which a veteran had nagged a newcomer repeatedly, it seemed clear that the harassment wasn't going to end, and the newcomer interpreted the episode as an instance of an individual vet-eran behaving inappropriately rather than an expected part of the social en-vironment. Often the veteran would be someone with a reputation for giving new people a hard time. If the newcomer responded defiantly, the crew might be put off, perhaps deciding that the new kid had "a bad attitude," but in most cases, the resistance didn't seem to have any ill effects and could achieve the desired result of discouraging the offensive behavior. And in some cases—when the veteran was widely disliked—a new kid's defiance could actually earn him some respect.

All male firefighters, regardless of race, can be directly insulted and are expected to "take it," but the playing of this kind of game in an interracial setting such as a firehouse is sometimes complicated by racial overtones. While blatantly racial or ethnic insults are generally reserved for private (segregated) conversations, race is sometimes a part of firehouse political arguments about either the society at large or the fire department in particular. Tom described such an episode when asked about the difference race makes in a firefighter's relationship to the outside community they serve:

> I think I have a better understanding . . . and a little more tolerance
> of what's goin' on. I worked at 116 on the B shift, and there was an
> engineer there and—[small chuckle] you know how you just get a
> feelin' about some people? I just have a feeling that he—he's a racist.
> And he listens to . . . Rush [Limbaugh] . . . he's intensely into that

guy! And . . . he was talkin' to me about the welfare system, and
things like that and my point to him was just, "Hey, I'm sure there's a
lotta people that shouldn't get it, but there's a lotta people that would
not survive if they didn't get it, so you can't just eliminate that and
these people have no way to survive." But he said he feels like if he
works hard, he should not have to pay any tax money to help support
[others]. . . . But then at the same time, there're people that pay taxes
to support him. . . . You know, so! They don't *think* . . .

And some people wanna talk to you about stuff like that, you
know . . . and I think sometimes they just think you're gonna just
accept everything they say because you're new. But he's talkin' to me
about how many years he put in to get his job, and then . . . [says]
" 'Cause these minorities from the bottom of the list—" and I was like
"What makes you think that all minorities come from the bottom of
the list? . . . Do you ever think that some of the white guys that had
these jobs when no one else could get 'em came from the bottom?" I
mean, you can say what you want, but whatever's goin' on now, has—
it didn't just start. I mean, for all he knows, if he wasn't white, maybe
he wouldn't have been hired. . . . So then he goes to another classmate of mine and tells him I'm radical. . . . [My feeling is] if you
choose to talk to me about it, then we'll talk about it. But you can't
just talk to me and I can't talk back to you, you know what I mean?

These types of exchange are far more common than are direct comments
on one's own race or ethnicity, but of course they can carry a clear message of
racial prejudice, as here in the implication that minority firefighters are less
capable than whites. Not all racial references are negative, however. On occasion, interracial crews whose members are either very comfortable or self-
confident will trade jokes about racial differences, making mild fun of each
other's customs or of taboo subjects. Direct racial comments and jokes of this
type in interracial groups appear to be most common and most easily accepted
when they're initiated by members of a minority group rather than by whites.
One African American lieutenant is particularly clever in this regard, often
speaking in rhymed couplets and frequently making humorous references to
racial divisiveness. On one occasion when a crew was discussing its dinner
menu and specifically what sort of vegetable to serve with spaghetti, the lieutenant suggested corn. "*Corn?!*" said a Hispanic firefighter. "Who eats corn
with spaghetti?" The lieutenant drew himself up and replied in a serious tone,
"Blacks." A moment of theatrical silence was followed by uproarious laughter.

Hazing or slamming of firefighters across race is not uncommon, but it is
shaped in part by the power dynamics of American society as a whole. Direct
racial insults are generally avoided, though prejudice may be expressed indi-

rectly. New male firefighters of any race are subject to hazing by all others, but interpretations of such interactions may be shaded by racial differences.

THE QUESTION OF RESPECT

The fact that men in all racial and ethnic groups had a sense of how to handle the hazing process did not mean that they all had the same feelings about it or experienced it in the same way. The rationale for submitting to an initiation process is the expectation of eventual acceptance given adequate performance;[4] where there is reason to question such an expectation, there is also reason to question the legitimacy of the process. The many stories of racial exclusion contained in the histories of both the nation as a whole and the urban fire service specifically provide some justification for newcomer skepticism.[5]

Among this group of new firefighters, differences in attitude and experience between racial/ethnic groups sometimes reflected this type of concern in subtle ways. Though white men occasionally criticized the culture's treatment of newcomers, they rarely expressed a worry about not being treated with *respect*; they saw this as something they would earn over time by proving themselves as firefighters. But the African American men did voice this concern, drawing an important distinction between the respect that you had to earn as a firefighter and the respect due you as a person. At the outset, as they were anticipating entry to the companies, they made it clear that although they knew they'd be criticized for their lack of knowledge and experience as firefighters, they were not prepared to be treated disrespectfully as *men*. As Jonathan noted, while it's fine for firefighters to tease one another, "you got to remember you're a man and a woman first. Aside from this job, you know, I'm a man first."

After some time in the companies, three of the African American men pointedly returned to this theme, expressing impatience with the "new kid routine" and a strong preference for crews that were less inclined to haze. These men found aspects of the initiation process degrading and unnecessary, and they resented judgments based on what they considered inappropriate criteria. Eddie described one of his favorite spots by saying, "I had my respect there. It was all about learnin'." The officer was approachable, the crew helpful, and "they weren't throwing that new kid bullshit. . . . It was like, they're very respectful of your manhood. . . . I felt that they were all secure with themselves and . . . we had a good time. . . . They weren't messin' around with you, you know, to try and test you." For Tom, it was OK to be hammered for not knowing your job; however, a personal attack was off-limits, and he'd be more reluctant to take it. "You know, you can't judge the kind of *man* I am by this

job, and some people will try to do that." Like Eddie, he appreciated the atmosphere in stations that were more egalitarian:

> [At 116], like I say, I got a couple of friends there, that I'm pretty close
> with . . . maybe [it's] 'cause they're black, I don't know, but there's a
> different attitude. . . . They're more laid-back over there. It's the same
> thing at 103, though. Same thing at 103, it's just that the difference is
> they're all strangers. . . . But both those stations, they're just, totally
> different. And they, they go about their job the same as everybody
> else, but when they're at the station, it's just a very relaxed (atmo-
> sphere)—they're joking, and everybody's—you know, they don't just
> pick on the new person, everybody gets picked on, everybody gets
> their turn.

Though Hugh recognized the initiation game for what it was and knew
how to respond, he found it distasteful. He didn't really approve of the "tendency to have humor at the expense of somebody else's esteem or feelings—
and I've seen a lot of that, just at the dinner table. I guess that's the part of
the job that I really don't care for." He said it was "like two sets of values":
people knew they should have "human respect" for each other, but at the same
time they'd go along with those who "blatantly violate it or disregard it." To
Hugh, the veterans' "tendency to run people into the ground for their lack of
ability" seemed counterproductive; he felt strongly that people perform better in a more supportive atmosphere.

Eddie objected to the norm of newcomer servility and its importance to
the new kid's reputation. He didn't take well to teasing about his relaxed
firehouse manner and was unhappy being judged for things he saw as irrelevant to job performance. "I have had, well, two lieutenants tell me that they
believe that aggression starts inside the firehouse and that at answering the
telephone they think that I was kind of laid-back. . . . I guess [they expect me
to] knock someone over in order to get to it. . . . I don't like to be grilled every day. I don't like to be spoken to as if I don't know anything. . . . I don't
like being under a microscope . . . [with people] scrutinizing what I'm saying
and scrutinizing what I'm doing and being in control over what they want to
say about me. . . . They go, 'Well, he needs to be more aggressive towards the
phone.' . . . That don't have anything to do with fightin' fires."

A woman classmate who had shared a station assignment with Eddie commented that he was not the only one who did not live up to all of the new
kid norms, but he might have come in for more criticism because "maybe he
makes a *point* of not being a doormat." Eddie's position can be contrasted to
that of Howard, one of the more traditional white men, who saw the firehouse
norms as generally quite fair. If the job was important to you, Howard argued,

you ought to show it. Racing for the phone might be silly, but at worst it was just a game and could be dealt with as such—it wasn't something to get exercised over. "I don't get caught up in that. . . . There are certain hoops that I'm jumpin' through every day, and the way I see those . . . is if you're willing to jump through this little hoop, then . . . you're a worker, you're willing to do something for the job . . . and you're willing to do something to be a part of the group, and you know, some of the hoops for sure are easy to jump through . . . it doesn't cost you much to do it."

He agreed that some "hoops" might be "off base" but you could deal with them by making an act of it. Like racing for the phone. "I don't worry about it. I'll jam for the phone sometimes, and race somebody for the phone, or sometimes I'm just not gonna move." Or he might stay where he was, but vigorously reach for the phone, giving a nod to the tradition. Among his classmates, he said, "there's people that [say], '*Hell*, no, I'm not playing this game. This is a regular job; people in the rest of the world don't have to play these games for other jobs.' But I think they do. Every job has a game."

Somewhere between Eddie's resistance and Howard's acquiescence to the culture, many men simply saw the firehouse tests as little things that weren't worth resisting, particularly when doing so could be costly. These men may have been critical of some aspects of the culture, but they did not openly resist conditions. When confronted with a particularly annoying veteran, they would interpret the behavior as unfortunate but also unusual and shrug it off. John Bowman, a white man, comported himself in accord with newcomer norms and noted that "my reception everywhere has been good, with the exception of 122 where they were extremely indifferent, although I found out later that that's just the way they are." He criticized those who made much of their seniority—"maybe . . . an ego boost, maybe for the entertainment value, and it's not in the best interest of the department." It may have been easier for the veterans at 122 to ignore him than to take an interest in him, but their behavior "certainly didn't do anything . . . to make me a more productive firefighter." John's loyalty went to those who treated him with more respect.

Among the male newcomers, then, there were some in all racial/ethnic groups who found fault with the norms and expectations of the traditional culture. But the most forthright opposition—making a *point* of not being a doormat—was expressed by African American men, who were explicitly bothered by the lack of respect with which newcomers could be treated. The practical effects of this kind of difference in the men's reactions included some variation in satisfaction with the job, station preferences and strength of feeling about different stations, and acceptance by certain crews.

KNOWING HOW TO PLAY THE GAME

African American men in a setting like the Oakland Fire Department may be more sensitive than are their white counterparts to the indignities of social initiation, but in the cultural assimilation process, they and other men of color do have certain advantages not available to women as a group. One of these is the sizable and growing proportion of minority firefighters and officers at all levels of the department: as of this writing, 33 percent of the firefighters, 26 percent of the lieutenants, 14 percent of the captains, 33 percent of the battalion chiefs, and the chief of the department are African American—a total of 29 percent of the uniformed force.[6] By contrast, only 8 percent of the uniformed force are women, including 12 percent of firefighters, 6 percent of lieutenants, and no captains or chiefs. In addition, almost one-third of the women firefighters are from the most recent recruit class. Greater numerical representation changes the environment for minority men in two ways: it allows for a freedom of expression between firefighters (with less suspicion of racial motivation), and it validates the implicit contract between veterans and newcomers that the latter will be accepted into the fold.

A second advantage of African American men is their cultural preparation. In most cases, their life experiences include not only exposure to generic American male culture—in the form of sports teams, male work crews, and the like—but also a good deal of practice with the verbal games of the inner city, an excellent preparation for the "slamming" culture of the fire service. Verbal street contests serve a variety of purposes similar to the purposes of the slamming between firefighters: they test a person's composure in the face of provocation, they entertain, and they provide an outlet for aggressive, competitive behavior.[7]

Eddie Gibbs was proud of his ability to play the game at all levels, using a variety of strategies from laughter and acceptance to heavy hitting. "It's like a shark's tank," he chuckled, "you gotta deal with it—you either swim or you get eaten up." After having problems at a fire, Eddie knew he'd be targeted but said he was ready. "It's easy to diffuse a slam 'cause I won't engage. Right now. But there'll be another time, I won't forget, you know. I mean . . . it's like a game, it's like playin' the dozens . . . the dozens, are you familiar with that term? . . . It's 'Your mother does this, and your mother is that,' and—you grow up playin' that in the inner city." In keeping with the way the game is played on the street, Eddie said, he would seek out an audience and go for the jugular. "I slammed a couple guys in front of people—and the thing is, is that you've gotta do it in front of a bunch of people because the effect is so much greater—you get a group of people laughin' and you don't let up, they can't take it. . . . I'm a heavy, *heavy* hitter."

"The dozens" is played in a variety of settings but is most strongly associated with the urban African American community, where it is predominantly a male activity.[8] In general, it involves trading cleverly phrased, vivid insults—often sexual—aimed at the opponent or his family members (particularly mother or sisters). The challenge is to remain in control, both verbally and emotionally. According to several writers, the game is a way of defining and proving one's masculinity. Specifically, as Herbert Foster explains, "On the streetcorner, verbal ability is rated as highly as is physical strength. Most often, when men gather, a boasting or teasing encounter takes place. . . . Starting a verbal attack is 'mounting' or getting above an opponent. To lose a verbal battle is to become feminized. Strength and masculinity are shown by boasting or 'putting down' an adversary or group of adversaries."[9]

This practice stands in striking contrast to dominant models of female socialization that suppress open conflict and discourage displays of aggression.[10] Women socialized in this way receive little or no training in ritualized forms of conflict such as team sports or verbal street games where the contestants have no real quarrel, so that when conflict does occur among women it reflects genuine disagreement, not ritual.[11] Black women and white women from working-class neighborhoods and families are more likely than white, middle-class women to be exposed to ritual conflict and to display aggressive verbal styles, though even in these groups, gender differences appear and girls tend to display less openly aggressive styles of play and conversation than are seen among boys.[12] A game like the dozens, sometimes played by women but more commonly by men, often serves the goal of asserting one's masculinity—just as the fire service has been in part about being masculine. In an important sense, the advantage of the men in this study is not only to have experienced male culture and training, but to *be* male. It is not insignificant that both in the firehouse and on the urban streetcorner, what is at stake is one's "manhood"—the greatest humiliation is in being *feminized*.[13]

"The Thing Not to Be"

If the initiation process is problematic for some men, it is chaotic or—very differently—nonexistent for women. The traditional abusive procedures are for various reasons not available or considered unworkable with women, and no clear substitute has taken their place. The many veterans who oppose women in the fire service might harass women to discourage them, but they would not "haze" women (in the ritual sense) to initiate them. Those who might be willing to accept women as coworkers are sometimes reluctant to accord them the same treatment they do male newcomers for fear of being

"taken downtown" (disciplined). The result is that women often find themselves in the peculiar position of being ineligible to receive the traditional
forms of initiation and yet subject to a good deal of alienation and hostility.

Veteran firefighter Sylvia Martin explained that when she entered the
department, a number of stations had never had a woman on the crew, and
the men were both unwelcoming and nervous about their behavior. With her
skills and background—including some familiarity with firefighters, exposure
to male work environments, and participation in competitive athletics—she
was unusually well prepared, but it took her some time before her crew began
to see her as anything but a liability both professionally and socially.

> I mean, [at first] they wouldn't even swear. . . . Well, I'll tell you, the
> problem was comin' from the top down. They had a chief come in and
> tell 'em, "Hey. These women are comin' in with notebooks, they're
> gonna be takin' notes, you guys better be on your best behavior," so
> we're comin' in thinkin', "OK, you know, we're gonna do a good job,"
> and these guys are thinkin', you know, they're gonna be in a
> lawsuit. . . . I mean, they had this stuff hammered into 'em before we
> got there. . . . [The brass created] this mass hysteria of lawsuits, and
> these enraged women that are just comin' in and trying to change
> everything. . . . So I was a little resentful of that part of it. But
> [eventually] we started playing volleyball, we started, you know, doin'
> the stuff that they felt like, "Oh, god, a woman can't do this kind of
> thing." And I was right there, you know, "Yeah, I'll play!" So I think
> they really started feeling like, "OK, she wants to be a part of this
> crew, and she wants to pitch in, and she'll be there and helpin' out,"
> and when I finally figured out what they expected of me, it worked
> out pretty good, and I made some real good friends, definitely.
> Individuals. You know, as a group, they still would rather have a jock
> kind of guy that they could beat up. I mean, there's a certain amount
> of hazing that happens with the new kids. And with the women
> coming in, that really was changed, and they resented that because all
> of them had to go through it. And they want all the new guys to go
> through it, and there I was—and I *wanted* to go through it! I didn't
> want any special treatment, or favoritism, or anything like that. "If
> you guys are gonna kick somebody else in the ass, kick *me* in the ass,"
> kind of thing. So I really resented that part of it because instead of
> getting the good and the bad, I got nothing. You know what I mean?
> So I had to figure things out for myself, where they'd be all over some
> male.

For the women newcomers in this study, hazing rituals were often muted,
subtle, or indirect. Practical jokes were relatively infrequent, and verbal harassment was less a form of psychological testing than an expression of hostil-

ity or disapproval. Energetic teasing was most common in places where a woman had found some degree of acceptance, where it served more to express familiarity than to establish rapport.

Elena was personally relieved that she wasn't coming in for the treatment that the men got, but she also recognized that she wasn't getting the respect, either:

> I think my sex has in a lot of ways, um, I feel like I've had it a lot easier than some of the guys [small laugh] because, thank god, most of the guys are gentlemen, and I see 'em doin' things to the guys but they won't do them to me. . . . You know, [they] just play jokes on 'em, and say things to 'em. . . . The guys do it to each other, and I wouldn't want to have to go through it. 'Cause I'm not that witty, you know, I'm just much more of a lady, too. . . . They kinda leave me alone, you know, 'cause there's that—there's always that barrier—they're afraid of going downtown or somethin', I don't know.
>
> And then of course . . . [being a woman has] had its negative, negative things. Like one time I worked my ass off tryin' to get a line off the engine, through the fence, you know, and through all this stuff, and into a house. I kicked the door in . . . took it up through the house, where a guy had a hole in the roof . . . and he was waitin' for the line. . . . And he's like . . . he goes, "*This* is my line?" You know, like [because] *I'm* behind it, and . . . [I'm thinking] "Screw you! This is it!" . . . [So] I've had times when they don't think nothin' of women and they tolerate you, but they certainly aren't gonna give you the respect they'd give regular men. Until you prove yourself, and I don't know if I could ever do that!

Elena's comment on her ambivalence about coworker treatment also revealed how a woman's identity is distorted in this environment. In saying that her coworkers would not give someone like her the respect they'd give "*regular men*" Elena implied that she's an irregular man. In fact, she's not a man at all, but in this context, there is no space to be anything else.

The relative infrequency of direct hazing of women by no means protects them against hostile interactions, and in some ways it serves as yet another signal of their outsider status in this community. Hugh noted that "in my observation, women don't get slammed to their faces, and if they do, generally that means that they have a good rapport with the crew. People who slam the women usually do it out of their presence because they're afraid of some type of administrative retaliation. But when there's a good rapport, generally everyone's interacting like a family." He pointed out that the inconsistent interpersonal treatment of women also made it hard for women to gauge how they were being accepted. There was a difference, he noted, between being socially excluded and simply not being part of a particular clique. Giving

Station 112 as an example, he noted that if he put up with the slamming and the testing and did his job, he could eventually be accepted as a decent firefighter even if he weren't taken in as a friend of the other men in the crew,

> but when *women* come through, it's a whole different matter. . . .
> They're bein' socially excluded. . . . The tendency was [for the
> veterans] to go out of their way not to be social with 'em—they went
> overboard as far as goin' to extremes about not bein' able to trust 'em,
> they went out of their way to be macho and kind of vulgar, you know,
> walk around in towels, things of that nature, or goin' out of their way
> to prove that they're men . . . you know, all of that has an effect on
> the person who it's focused on, and even though it may technically be
> nothing against the rules or whatever, or nothin' that you can sit
> down and draft or anything like that, it's still like a hostile work
> environment.

At Station 112, Elena didn't come in for many practical jokes, and they didn't play "cruel games" on her openly, but they did say and do things that made her feel uncomfortable and unwelcome. Elena recalled that the crew had announced formation of a baseball team with the words "People Needed" on the company chalkboard; then at roll call one morning, one of the firefighters crossed out the word "people" and wrote the word "MEN." They mocked her inexperience and lack of knowledge by posing questions to which the answers were obvious, as though she didn't even know the basics. They complained openly about the hiring of "unqualified people" (particularly women) and argued that it was a waste of the department's money to pay such people to work there. Elena's response was to try to ignore such comments, to take them lightly, and to think of them as new-kid harassment rather than a personal attack. On good days she thought it would all eventually pass and she'd be glad she stayed with the job, but on bad days she wondered if she really wanted to do it.

Virtually all these women heard the abilities of women as a group not simply questioned but denigrated, and the message was clear: you are not welcome here. Some veterans would complain vociferously about the lowering of the department's hiring standards and the futility of employing people with no mechanical background and limited strength. They would elaborate or sometimes even fabricate stories about women's performance difficulties and grumble about how equipment and procedures had had to be modified because "certain people" couldn't handle things the way they used to be.[14] They would withhold positive or encouraging comments, and they would test the women in nonregulation drills designed to showcase their weaknesses (see chapter 5 for details).

Another way of letting women know they weren't wanted without use of overt harassment was the "silent treatment"—a staple of firefighter initiation that was sometimes carried to extremes with women. Laurinda managed to establish a sisterly relationship with most of her crew members at Station 103 and would sometimes trade insults with them (though she wasn't a target of the sort of practical jokes played on her male classmates at the station). She distinguished this good-natured teasing from the truly mean-spirited treatment she received from a young veteran known to be hostile to women, who expressed his disapproval in silence. Laurinda explained, "He hates you no matter—he hates women, period. He won't talk to 'em, he won't look at 'em. If *I* got a phone call, he'd call another new person—Rodney's over there, he'd tell Rodney, 'Phone,' and Rodney would go pick up the phone, and then whoever's on the other line would say, 'Is Laurinda there?' Rodney would have to bring the phone to me."

It may sound like a small matter to be ignored, but in a firehouse with a tight-knit crew for twenty-four hours, this treatment can have a powerful effect. Like other new firefighters, Laurinda understood that "when they joke around with you and stuff you know you're being accepted. But when they don't say anything—silence—oh, it's a killer. It's just *dreadful*." For Valerie, being left alone was puzzling and uncomfortable. "I would prefer to be ragged on and learn something," she said, "than be . . . ignored."

There is also, from the women's perspective, a different quality to their invisibility. Because it is coupled with other forms of hostility directed specifically at women, it does not feel like something that time will overcome. Even after a year in the department and several months in her current station, Valerie frequently felt her presence totally ignored by her other crew members. They talked in a way that suggested that she simply was not there, freely and unapologetically expressing their hostile feelings about women. Whereas other aspects of the culture sometimes bored her or made her uncomfortable, "it's that blatant hatred that is different. That's different. That's the thing that's hard to take. . . . Again, [it's] the way they're interacting with each other, it's how do you insult each other? Well, you call each other a 'pussy.' Or 'Oh, you're such a girl,' or 'You walk like a girl' . . . that's the thing not to be."

In many ways, then, the initiation process does not work for women. While generally excluded from the direct hazing that is the traditional route of social acceptance, women are targets of the indirect harassment associated with being members of an unwelcome group. This is not to say that women's exclusion is complete; some women do manage to gain acceptance in one or more crews, but they generally achieve this in a way that varies from the path taken by male newcomers. Most often the women's participation in firehouse slamming and joking is a result of rapport, not a way of developing it.

THE SEXUALIZATION OF THE WORKPLACE

The silent treatment and open questioning of women's abilities (as a group, not as individuals) are explicit forms of exclusion. Women are *implicitly* excluded from one of the most important bonding elements of the culture: the (hetero)sexualization of the workplace. As in other male-dominated workplaces, sexual materials and comments that objectify women are woven into the fabric of firehouse life. Women cannot participate as equals in this aspect of the culture because they are by definition objects, not subjects, in this discourse. As when a firefighter calls another a "pussy" or "girl," the very idea of the feminine is negative, an insult. For a woman firefighter, the alternative to participation is to ignore what is said and done, but this can be hard to do.

Jane Macey didn't think of herself as a puritanical woman, but she came to find the constant references to sexuality and the presence of pornographic material disturbing, particularly when they seemed to reflect an overt hostility toward women. In an early assignment, she worked with a veteran who "made it clear that he doesn't like women; he thinks they're inferior." Despite repeated warnings, this man kept a collection of pornographic photos posted in his locker, which was sometimes left open. When Jane saw them for the first time, she was shocked. "He's got Polaroid pictures of women in very vulnerable positions. . . . I mean, I've watched porn films and stuff, but when I saw those pictures I was kind of blown away."

Talk could also feel threatening. "We get sexual innuendos a lot— and . . . some of 'em aren't even innuendos. . . . There's nothing subtle about it. One night an officer . . . was talkin' about how he knew a guy who put cigarette butts out on women's tits. And I'm just sitting there, just like I can't believe my ears." Knowing that sexual comments were not necessarily intended to hurt her did not make them easier to take, for they were a constant reminder of the outsider status she held as a woman. Though all newcomers were excluded to some degree, only women were (or could be) alienated in this particular way. "At dinner," she said, "they're talking about some guy that everybody knows, and John Reese goes, 'Oh yeah, you know so-and-so, he's got big hands and a big dick.' . . . And I'm so embarrassed that I don't know how to respond. I feel like comments like that automatically alienate me from the group because I'm not one of the guys and at the same time, I'm offended because I don't want to hear about somebody's dick. . . . I just sat there and . . . looked down at my plate. . . . Those are the times I just want to get up and leave." Increasingly, she found the culture offensive and the environment hostile, but she also believed that "it's not that people are intentionally digging at me because I don't believe that they are, most of the time . . . but I think that it's the ignorance, and the lack of respect, and just the unprofessionalism that runs in this department that's tolerated."

Remarks and photographs that might have been only mildly irritating in another context could feel threatening and deeply offensive in the firehouse, where a woman was often the only one of her sex on the crew, knew her presence was unwelcome and her ability untrusted, and had to depend on her coworkers for her own safety. Veteran Sylvia Martin was quite accepting of most aspects of fire service culture, but she noted the discomfort that she sometimes felt with the men's responses to sexually explicit material. "The photos and everything, that didn't really bother me, but it was kinda the yelling and the screaming—that was a little weird. . . . It's hard not to feel like they're comparing you to [what they're seeing]."

The presence of offensive material and the department's apparent inability to eliminate it made Jane quite uncomfortable, and she was at a loss as to how she should respond. "I don't want to end up alienating people so that my job is really uncomfortable for me, so I'm trying to figure out how to speak up for myself to maintain my self-respect, and setting limits, without drawing negative attention. Because my experience is if you let 'em know what bothers you, they'll do it a lot more." Official policy encouraged victims of sexual harassment to speak up; if she said nothing, her silence could be taken as acceptance of a hostile work environment, and she would have to continue to absorb its pressures. But if she spoke up, she would invite reprisals, and in the worst case, she might so alienate her coworkers that they would not extend themselves for her in a life-threatening situation. "If I'm in a dangerous situation and somebody doesn't go out of their way to help me—be it telling me a certain way to do something or what have you—I could end up getting killed or getting seriously harmed. . . . And you know, I *don't* trust that some guys would come to my rescue as aggressively as they might to someone else's rescue."

Jane tried to deal with her coworkers directly but her informal objections met with limited results; eventually she complained to her officer about both the sexualized environment and the presence, also against departmental regulations, of alcohol in the station. As she expected, her crew members treated her coldly, and she began to experience subtle forms of harassment. On returning from runs she would discover that her car, parked inside the station lot, had been broken into; nothing would be missing, but signs of a break-in would be evident. At dinner one of her coworkers would get up after the meal had begun and start walking around the station, and someone later suggested to her that he might be going through her belongings.

Jane's experiences were typical of the sexualized work environment that all the women faced to some degree. The women reacted differently, according to their personalities and the context. But even the most easygoing women were faced with difficulties, as Carrie explained.

I mean, you know . . . I'm not so strict about what to say and how to say it and that kinda thing, 'cause I tease and I joke just like anybody else and my mouth's probably in the gutter half the time, but [laughing] you know . . . it's teasin' on a level that it's like, let's loosen up here—let's just stop bein' so *tight* about everything. But I think [we should have] more women who are more outgoing and not so uptight about everything these guys say, 'cause these guys are like sittin' on pins and needles sometimes around here wonderin', "If I say this am I gonna get written up?" . . . If you say somethin' then they want to know "Why can you say that and I can't?" or they think you're tryin' to bait 'em into somethin' so you can get 'em, and that kind of thing. . . . What they need to do is . . . learn that yeah, you can say things but you just need to know how far to go. . . . You know, if you're laughin' and jokin' and stuff like that, keep it laughin' and jokin', don't get personal and don't think that . . . something's gonna come out of this—don't think that you can [pauses] come into my bunk and, and do somethin' to me because I've had that happen to me since I've been here and that's, that's, that's upsetting.

She described an occasion when another firefighter started to get into her bed, and when she told him to leave, he did but then returned. She again told him to leave, and he finally did so. Carrie didn't feel that she had done anything to encourage this advance, but the incident made her reluctant to engage in the teasing that was part of her outgoing personal style. At another station she had a firefighter pat her on the rear, and she made it clear to him that this was an inappropriate and unwelcome gesture. She knew what she had to do to control such behavior, but it wasn't always easy; relationships with coworkers were important, and she didn't want to upset or hurt people's feelings or turn them against her.

The way I control it is if I know that the person's like that, I don't tease with them like that. It's like you know, that's out, we're just strictly business now, because you've already invaded my space and . . . I don't have any more respect for you.
    [As for the guy who came into my bunk] . . . I won't trust teasin' with him anymore, but I don't necessarily think that we need to get as radical as . . . us not talkin'. Because when I first got there, he really helped me out on a lot of things, you know, and kinda helped me to assimilate into that house, but that still doesn't mean he can take liberties with me.

She worried that if she spoke up about this incident, she wouldn't be believed because she was both a newcomer and an easygoing, teasing person. As a result, she explained, "I stopped teasin' as much as I used to." But in becoming more withdrawn, Carrie was also giving up an important coping strategy. She had used her joking relationships with other firefighters to gain the social acceptance she needed to get help with her training: "I get a lot more help because they think they can work with me." She was trying to walk a fine line—to be friendly enough that she would gain sympathy and assistance, but not so familiar that her coworkers would assume she was open to their sexual advances.[15]

This type of balancing act was a common requirement for the women in their efforts to negotiate acceptance and pass the psychological tests of their coworkers. All new firefighters were subject to such tests, but for the women, the standard involved not so much emotional composure as tolerance of a male environment. As with their male counterparts, the new women firefighters also had to be likable and appealing as individual people, but they could not be *too* appealing as *women*. In short, they should be friendly but not too friendly, to tolerate some sexualization of the workplace but not so much that they would lose either self-respect or the respect of coworkers, and to be neither too masculine—i.e., unattractive—nor too feminine—and so, unsuited to the job.[16]

In this context it is particularly relevant that a number of the women were openly lesbian. The experiences of these women suggest that being gay was—for the women—advantageous in some respects and disadvantageous in others. On the negative side, the environment is socially conservative and quite homophobic; homosexuality was frequently a topic of humor, and the sexual orientation of individual women was a subject of gossip. One lesbian believed that the only reason the men in her station expressed any interest in her personal life was because they wanted to give her a hard time about being a lesbian. Another woman felt she was being "tested" when crew members expressed conservative views in reaction to a radio talk show covering the issues of gays in the military and the "alleged" sexual harassment of women in the workplace.

On the positive side, however, an openly lesbian woman had the ability to tease and joke with her (largely male) coworkers without either suggesting that she was open to sexual advances or, indeed, having to sort out her own motives in such interactions. In addition, these women are experienced in outsider status and the crafting of nontraditional identities. As a result, they are sometimes, though by no means always, better prepared to adapt to what one woman called the "offensive" traditions of the urban fire department.

TAKING A JOKE: RESPONDING TO SEXUALITY IN THE FIREHOUSE

It is not at all clear how women should act when confronted with pornography, sexual language, and other potentially offensive behaviors, as these moments are subject to conflicting interpretations and expectations. Many men see this "testing" process as a simple matter of equal treatment: this is the way life is in the firehouse, and if you don't like it, then you shouldn't be here. They argue that all new kids come in for some rough treatment and are expected not to complain; women shouldn't be treated any differently, particularly as the environment has softened so much from what it was. Any woman who complains now is going out of her way to take offense.

To the extent that the hazing process is more than an initiation and actually serves some screening function, it may be understood as weeding out or identifying those who *for individual reasons* are unfit. In theory, anyone who performs the job reasonably well and isn't unpleasant to be around can expect eventually to become an insider. But of course the process does not operate the same way for all newcomers. White male newcomers know that in time the harassment will lighten or transform into a game played by equals. Men of color, though sometimes less confident of acceptance than are their white counterparts, can at least see the possibility: there are, after all, men of color inside this community. But no such assurance exists for the women. Given the widespread opposition to women in the fire service, a woman's eventual acceptance is by no means guaranteed, even if she performs well socially and professionally.

The second problem for women is the inherent asymmetry of sexual forms of harassment.[17] The harassment is itself gender-based rather than personal; it refers to sexuality and to some extent takes advantage of both biological and cultural differences between men and women; it is inherently not a game that can be played among equals.[18] When male firefighters argue that "women are just as bad" in the way they talk about men, they ignore the social context of sexual relations and the historical asymmetry of power between men and women, both of which are magnified in the firehouse. As many women firefighters are acutely aware, there is a certain vulnerability in being the only one of your sex in an environment where you know you are not welcome—a threat brought home by occasional acts of physical intimidation against women in the firehouse. In this context as in the larger context of sexual violence and domination, reminders of sexuality, particularly if they emphasize female vulnerability, can be quite threatening. A woman firefighter might be able to put up a photograph of a naked man, but she cannot reproduce the social context that conveys to pornography the power to intimidate.

This is not to say, however, that all sexualization of the workplace necessarily constitutes harassment, that all firehouses are sexualized environments, or that all women react to these situations in the same way. A number of the women in this group explained that their reactions and responses to sexual language or material in the firehouse were highly contextual. They dealt with situations differently depending on their trust and comfort with a particular crew, on their understanding of another firefighter's intent, on the blatancy of the material or language, and on the degree of respect with which they were treated as individuals.

Carrie didn't want to see pictures of naked women all over the walls, and if she found a copy of *Playboy* on a desktop she'd probably put it away; but she wouldn't be "upset" about it, and she wouldn't lodge a complaint. She wouldn't be concerned as long as her coworker treated her well. "If . . . the guy that looks at the magazine . . . treats me like I'm a woman, and treats me like he respects me, then I don't feel that him lookin' in that magazine is disrespectin' me, but now then, if he thinks that I'm weak, and I have only one purpose in life and that kind of thing, then, yeah, that would upset me. . . . It shouldn't bother any woman if the man treats you like you want to be treated. You know, it's when they don't treat you like that—when they treat you like a object or somethin' like that, that's when lookin' at that kind of thing bothers me."

As long as the men's behavior wasn't directed at her, she could ignore it or treat it with humor, as when they'd "almost fall off the engine watching some woman walk up the street." Her response would be to just roll her eyes, expressing her disapproval but in a mild, indulgent way. Valerie used a similar strategy in a crew with which she felt comfortable, a station located in an area with a lot of prostitutes. When she found that the men were "always kinda hangin' out the doors and acting like idiots," she took to calling them "sexist pigs" in a joking tone. They picked up the refrain and began to use the term on each other, which Valerie enjoyed. She participated in the "major amounts of teasing" that went on but also recognized that there were times when she had to draw a line. "You know, we can tease each other about our physical appearance, like if somebody's short and fat or somebody's got spindly little legs or no butt or something like that, I mean that—it's nonsexual, it's *personal*, but it's nonsexual. Every once in a while, somebody's gonna try somethin' to see what they can get away with about teasing in a sexual way, in which case they get shut down immediately."

Valerie's concerns were applicable to all the women: she noted that it was important to have boundaries, but she acknowledged that their placement would vary according to the individual woman drawing the line and the context. Believing that she was relatively tolerant, she added that "a lot of it, too, has to do with what the intent is. And you try to sense whether this is meant in a vindictive way or whether this is just them being stupid." In addition to intent, a woman also had to consider the broader message she was conveying with her tolerance, for fear she might encourage something worse. One of the men remarked on this possibility in his station:

I hear guys say things and it's just, they don't know what to say.
There's women at the table and they don't know whether to say this,
or that, and they'll just end up sayin' something really stupid. And
then, like there's a few women who, they don't care what the men say.
And what is gonna happen is one day they *are* gonna care, and you
can see it comin' a mile away—these guys think, "Oh, we got
somebody here who doesn't care, we can say anything we want, she'll
be cool about it." And one day she's gonna just get fed up and hear
the wrong thing and then she's gonna say something about it and
then, there's gonna be a big mess.

In some respects the women were in a situation similar to that of the male
newcomers trying to define those circumstances in which it *was* necessary and
appropriate to speak up. But there were important differences. The men were
generally larger and stronger—ready and willing to fight if necessary, and more
likely to gain something by this posture.[19] And as noted, the razzing they received tended to be based more on individual qualities and interpersonal differences than on group membership. Furthermore, there were qualities of
hostility and distance in the harassment of women that did not exist with the
men. When Valerie spoke of the "hatred" she could feel sitting in a room with
her crew, she described an experience that had no male equivalent, that was
beyond even the descriptions black men or women gave of interactions with
racist coworkers.

Context does matter in the interpretation of behavior, but context operates on more than one level. In the immediate circumstances of an interaction, it may be a gross misinterpretation for a woman to consider an offhand
comment or gesture to be sexual harassment. But at a social level—regardless
of an individual man's intent or a particular woman's tolerance—a sexualized
work environment bonds men as a group (regardless of race) and excludes
women. In this way, it is very different from the generalized hazing of newcomers. Even if a woman shrugs it off—like water off a duck's back—it won't
stop, and she will never be qualified to participate in the game as an equal.

Chapter 5   Proving Grounds

*I just want to feel some real intense heat and just like go
into a room that's fully engulfed in fire . . . and just see
where my backbone is. Do I squirm out of there, or do I
do what I'm supposed to do? Because you really don't
have any fire at the Tower, and you can play fireman all
you want until you see the real one and you get some
real heat.*

—RODNEY CHIN

*Captain Marshall summed it up in the sense that "Yeah,
we don't trust you." We have to prove ourselves. And I
was talking to Captain Quinn and I told him, you know,
"I agree with what most people feel in this department,
that there are just some people, whether it be male or
female, that just don't belong in this line of work." And,
so . . . they don't trust us. We have to prove ourselves.
And I think that a lot of the gripes that a lot of the people
in my class have coming in are mainly because they're
going in there with an attitude. . . . And I tried to tell
them . . . "Hey, you're going into their world. Just keep
your mouth shut and let your work do the job."*

—RAY MONTOYA

THE TESTING of new kids begins with the social interactions of the firehouse
as described in the previous chapter, but of course new firefighters must also
prove themselves more actively in their work. As Ray Montoya recognized,
before a new kid can be accepted into the fold, he has to demonstrate that
he has both the qualities of a good firefighter and a willingness to "pay his
dues." Given the highly interdependent, sometimes life-threatening nature of
the work, veterans are understandably anxious to know that a newcomer's ability can be trusted and that his composure won't fail under pressure. But they
also want to know that his personal qualities will make him an asset not only
at the scene but also in the firehouse—in particular, that he's a skilled,

motivated worker who knows how to get along with others. The newcomer displays these qualities by performing appropriately—at the scene and in firehouse chores, informal tests, and formal drills. Throughout this chapter, we explore the meaning of a good performance in each context, and consider how the social relations of gender and race influence the newcomers' efforts and ability to prove themselves.

The veterans are not the only ones who need to know the newcomer's capacity. As Rodney Chin's observation illustrates, the novice must also be satisfied that he or she has a place in the fire service, a right to this identity. It's obvious to every newcomer that the job of firefighting calls for something special, but just *how* special must one be? As rigorous as the academy experience is, it cannot provide an answer to this fundamental question; only through field performance does a new firefighter come to know that he or she has the necessary courage, strength, smarts, dedication, and composure to do the job.

The Social Construction of Performance

Both self-confirmation and veteran approval are based on the *interpretation and perception* of performance, which means they are mediated by the newcomer's own view of himself and by his relationship to the community. In the case of self-assessment, for example, a confident newcomer is likely to weight successes more heavily than failures, while a self-doubting novice does the reverse; thus, a similar performance may evoke pride in one newcomer and chagrin in another. In terms of veteran assessment, the perception of performance is shaped by social stereotyping, personal feelings, and active impression management on the part of a newcomer sensitive to the ways of the fire service.

Among the OFD newcomers, we would expect it to be markedly easier for some than for others to prove themselves, and indeed it was. Most obviously, those with prior experience, unusual talent, and/or a high degree of self-confidence were least likely to doubt themselves and could most readily—though by no means automatically—establish their credentials with veteran coworkers as well. Newcomers like Frank Cross, a self-assured white man with firefighting experience as well as family ties to the profession, came in thinking of themselves as firefighters; they knew what the job entailed, and they knew they could do it. They were prepared to show some deference to more experienced veterans, but they did not fundamentally question their own right to be here, and they knew they would be able to prove themselves. For Frank, the critical attention of the veterans was not only justified but worthwhile. "You're always proving yourself," he claimed. "It's something ongoing, until they feel comfortable with you, and then they don't have to worry about it.

They *know* you're gonna be there for them . . . you know they're watching. Which is good, though. . . . You know, I hope it doesn't stop for a long time. 'Cause all it does is continue to better yourself." Such traditional attitudes may have been most common among the white men, but were certainly not limited to this group, as can be seen in the words of Ray Montoya quoted at the opening of this chapter.

Conversely, lack of prior experience and limited self-confidence made for a more difficult probationary experience by increasing both personal discomfort and susceptibility to the supportiveness of the environment. Inexperienced and uncertain newcomers like Tommy Bautista, a Filipino American, and Marcus Everett, an African American, found that anxiety could interfere with smooth performance. In Tommy's early days in the firehouse, his pulse was often elevated, and he found the adrenaline rush at a fire almost overpowering; in his first time on the nozzle, he made the classic new kid mistake of spraying too much water and creating a mess that had to be cleaned up later. He was uncomfortable with his lack of expertise and found the veterans' pop quizzes about firefighting procedures and equipment unnerving, but at the same time he understood that his embarrassment at not knowing could motivate him to learn and remember things. And he respected the process: "It's just that everybody has to put in time to pay their dues, to get respect."

Marcus also understood the veterans' desire to stand back and see what the new kids were made of, but the sense of being under constant scrutiny was even more wearing to him, making him withdrawn and reluctant to try things, for fear of making mistakes. Sensitive to how dramatically the level of pressure could vary from one station to another, he believed his own performance suffered when he encountered an unsupportive environment. When an impatient and unpredictable officer showed his temper, Marcus had to remind himself not to take it personally, and it was a struggle to maintain his self-confidence under these conditions. By contrast, when he found himself in a station where "everybody was treatin' everybody like responsible adults, not like the new kid," he saw himself "open up and, you know, be able to do things . . . without feeling . . . as though I'm the new kid and [have to] do it right the first time."

Unlike Tommy, Marcus came to openly question the fairness of the evaluation process, believing it to be harsher for members of subordinate race or gender groups. Having on occasion observed different patterns of treatment along race and gender lines, he concluded that some of his own negative encounters had been racially motivated. It was "nothing overt," he said, but "I can see a pattern existing." He was used to it, having dealt with the problem all his life, but he found it frustrating and wearying.

Women were the newcomers least likely to have relevant backgrounds and most likely to doubt themselves; as a group they also faced the most thoroughgoing skepticism of their abilities. Though all new recruits heard disparaging talk from the veterans about their class and its training, the challenge to women was particularly direct and sometimes personal. At some point during their initial station visits, the women heard that most if not all others of their sex were unqualified firefighters who were retained simply because of affirmative action policies; as Jane Macey put it, the message was that "we have to overcome not only the fact that we're female, but [the idea] that we're incompetent." Unsure of themselves and aware that many of their coworkers considered them unsuitable for the job, women often felt undermined by the pressure to prove themselves; indeed, at times it simply seemed as if there was no way to do so.

Not surprisingly, these circumstances meant that the women were especially sensitive to variations in station atmosphere. After spending a couple of months "walking on eggshells" at her first assignment, Jane finally began to enjoy going to work once assigned to Station 115, where, she said, "They respected me, already. It wasn't like I had to come in and prove myself at all. . . . It was automatic, 'Here's a firefighter, it doesn't matter her gender, she's one of us.' "

An unusually self-confident and skilled woman might be able to distance herself some from the pressure—as Marla Harrison did, with her refusal to be inordinately intimidated and her belief in her own right to participate—but among the women such a perspective was the exception. Marla's feelings were similar to those of the men, especially the African American and Asian American men, who took a philosophical attitude toward the process. They might not have the enthusiasm of traditional newcomers like Frank or Ray, but neither were they unduly resistant, critical, or anxious. Leonard Bentley, a black man, expressed this perspective when he responded to a classmate's complaint about the constant scrutiny from veterans, saying "Hey, we *all* feel that way. We all have to prove ourselves, 'cause we're new. And that's just the way it is, I mean, you know. Down the line, when they get a new class in here, we'll be lookin' at them like, ah, Jesus, you know, here we go."

These varying perspectives on the need to prove oneself as a firefighter reflect profoundly different senses of self in relation to the community. The newcomers who most easily negotiated the challenges of the entry process were those who believed in both their own potential to assume the role of firefighter *and* the community's willingness and ability to judge their performance fairly. Conversely, those with self-doubts or questions about the community's judgment tended to experience the process of proving themselves as considerably more burdensome, perhaps even impossible. Furthermore, the understanding of the position of self *vis à vis* community reflects a complex interplay of individual qualities with the social categories of race and gender. In theory, a self-doubting white man might have more trouble proving himself as a firefighter than would a confident woman or man of color. But given the historical structure of opportunities in the fire service and elsewhere, white men are more likely to have the experience, training, and knowledge that produce self-confidence. Additionally, to the extent that veteran perceptions are influenced by racial and sexual stereotypes *and* that men of color and women are still underrepresented, white men are also more able to rely on, and have less reason to question, the community's grace.

At the Scene: Takin' Some Heat

The most obvious opportunities to prove oneself come in firefighting situations, and although doing the job at fires is not enough to earn acceptance, it is a critical step in the process. As Tom Armstrong explained, "At fires it's like . . . if you're the guy who goes through the front door and they see well, he's not afraid, he'll go in and he'll do it . . . then they'll kind of trust you."

For most of the men, the idea of doing OK at your first fires didn't mean doing everything perfectly because you were a beginner and bound to make mistakes. The thing was to remain calm and in control, to know enough to follow orders correctly, to avoid very serious mistakes, and to be able to learn from the experience. All these things happened for Tony Escobar in his first structure fire on the night of the Rodney King verdict riots. That evening his crew had been to numerous smaller fires, but when they pulled up at this one, "there was a lot of smoke showing. I knew this one was the real one. . . . At least it was to me. The old-timers are goin', 'Ah, that was nothin', kid. You could *see* in that fire.' " Engine 113 and Truck 114 were there laddering the building, and Tony's officer told him and his classmate to pull the hose off Engine 113 for its crew.

> We pulled it out so I just held the nozzle, and I just stayed there. [A guy showed up with keys to the building.] I just threw my mask on, and they opened the door. A lot of smoke came out, and I just went in. A Piedmont officer [there for mutual aid] . . . came behind me and then Harry Malone [another new kid]. . . . The three of us, we took the line in. And that was kind of interesting, 'cause the nozzle was there on the ground, and I realized that I was kinda hovering over it, you know. . . . And the door opened up, and nobody was doin' anything, so I . . . just grabbed it and went in when I could . . . which was just a thrilling experience because it was like, God, first fire, and I'm first through the door.

Once inside, they encountered a variety of surprises and obstacles, and thinking

back on it, Tony could see where he—along with some others on the scene—
had made plenty of mistakes, including not adequately sizing up the situation
before going in. There was a point when fire began burning behind the attack group, someone yelled "We're trapped," and Tony had to pass the nozzle
to someone in a better position to hit that part of the fire. Shortly after doing
so he became separated from his partners and found himself next to a window. Thinking about the possible need to escape, he kicked a hole in the window but then managed to find his way back to the crew and the nozzle. His
officer later claimed that it wasn't a window but a glass refrigerator door that
he'd kicked open and in addition that Tony had sprayed him at some point
with the hose. Tony laughingly disputed both observations, and in his reflective self-assessment thought he'd really done fine, particularly in staying calm:
"There was just a moment there where I was alone. I was by myself. And here
I was the new kid. The building is on fire. And, you know, I felt comfortable. . . . And I felt very good that I felt comfortable and confident. . . . I didn't
know *how* I would act in a fire. That was the first one I had been in. And I
was very pleased with my thought process and my instincts. . . . There's a lot
of things I have to learn. I wasn't, you know, half as good as I could have
been, just 'cause a lot of things I didn't know. And that is gonna come with
time."

Talking with his officer later, Tony got the impression that the officer preferred that the new kids not go in without him, but that he did not seem to
have a "big problem" with their actions. Neither did Tony himself. "It was
probably a little bit too gung ho on our part. But when I looked around, he
wasn't there, and there was no officer around. The door was open. There was
a fire going. And you gotta go through the front door and find the fire. That's
what we're supposed to do. So I did it. I took the initiative and did it." Looking back on the fire, Tony felt he'd done well in the ways that counted most
and forgave himself for his mistakes. Even kicking out a refrigerator window—
if that's what it was—could be seen as an accomplishment, if you thought about
it, " 'cause you know, those windows are pretty thick."

For a variety of reasons, Tony was well-positioned to establish himself as
a firefighter. A Hispanic man with family ties to the fire service, he was an
experienced EMT who had worked in other kinds of emergency service settings. He was able to handle serious medical calls early on, and he did not
have to wait very long for his first fire experience. But even without a strong
firefighting or EMS background, an athletic, self-confident man could do all
right. George Alarcon, though not huge, was a skilled athlete who had no
doubts about his own physical and mental abilities. Even before his first major fire, he seriously questioned neither his ability to do the work nor the veterans' eventual acceptance of him. "I've always felt that athletically speaking,

I was right up there with just about anybody as far as that goes and I just relate that to the fire scene. If these guys are climbing ladders and pulling hose and stuff, I can keep right up with 'em. . . . I may not know exactly what to do, but I feel like I can be right in there with anybody."

Among less self-confident men the lack of experience was a bit more problematic, and a sense of comfort in the new identity could take somewhat longer to achieve. Marcus, an African American man with no special training or connection to the fire service, had a long and anxious wait for his first serious structure fire. When it finally came, he made some mistakes—such as entering too high and almost being overcome with heat—but he worked past those and found the experience to be "just what I needed," a chance to apply lessons, build self-confidence, and show something to coworkers. He received a pat on the back from his crew at the time, but, whether or not they were truly impressed, it was clear that the event was a significant turning point in Marcus's view of himself.

For the women, whose abilities were widely distrusted and who were subject to self-doubt as well, the timing and frequency of their exposure to action was an even more determinative force in the shaping of their identities as firefighters. Initially terrified, Laurinda Gibson explained that things started to change for the better as soon as she got a little activity behind her. "The turning point it feels like to me was at 108, about my second shift at 108," she noted, "when I started feeling confident about the medical runs and did CPR a few times." Prior to this time, she had been very much on edge. "I mean, I was so stressed out, to the point where I couldn't sleep at night." She kept thinking to herself, "I know these guys don't want me here."

For both Laurinda Gibson and Marla Harrison, early assignments to busy east end stations meant rapid exposure to a variety of incidents, and this in turn made a significant difference in their self-perceptions and comfort in the job. Laurinda appreciated her luck in station assignments because it allowed her to gain experience quickly and spared her the common anxiety of having to wait for that first serious call. With repeated exposure, first on serious medical calls and later in fires, she began to feel much more assured about her own place in the work and more able to weather the occasional abuse she received from exceptionally hostile coworkers or officers. Marla expressed similar sentiments; in thinking back over her first six months, she recalled an early conversation with an officer about her preparedness for the job. The first time she met Captain Simmons he asked, "You gonna be able to handle it? You gonna stand up under the pressure?" At the time Marla wasn't sure, saying simply, "I don't know. I guess we'll have to see." But by the end of six months, her feeling was, "*Yeah!* . . . anything you wanna give me, I'll be able to hold up."

By contrast, Marianne Grant spent much of her early probation in less active houses, where she also found that officers and coworkers could facilitate or inhibit a new firefighter's opportunity to prove herself, by keeping her in or out of the action at fire scenes when they did occur. After working lobby control ("a bullshit word to say that you do nothing") at a high-rise fire, Marianne was coming "to the decision that I'm not going to wait around for people to tell me what to do—I'm just going to do it, and if it's wrong, fuck it." She was frustrated by the behavior of some of the veterans and officers: "They'll let you fuckin' not do anything . . . when it's the good work, and when it's the bullshit work, they'll have you do it." Marianne knew herself to be stronger than a young male firefighter in her station, but while he was entrusted with a variety of tasks, she was either restricted to engine work or kept out of the action if she did ride the truck.[1]

For someone like Marianne, the lack of opportunities to prove oneself—whether the result of being in a slow station or being purposely kept out of the action—meant not only a delay in acceptance by coworkers, but also slower development of self-confidence. She was particularly sensitive to her own insecurity and to how this could in turn affect her interactions with coworkers. Disappointed with her relative lack of exposure to fires in her first six months, she couldn't express a firm belief in her own ability to do what the job required, for the simple reason that, as she put it, "I'm not really sure what the job *does* require." She anxiously anticipated the time when she *would* know because "confidence really does equal power in my opinion, it can change the way people view you. Being aggressive in this job really helps. But it's hard to be aggressive on something that you don't know what you're doing." Marianne was one of the strongest women in the department, but her confidence did not grow until she was able to spend some time in busy east end stations.

Valerie Dickinson's exposure to fire was gradual, but her previous training and work in EMS enabled her to take responsibility on those calls and to derive some satisfaction from them. "It's like anything else," she said of firefighting, "I mean . . . you're stupid for 99 percent of the time because you've never done anything before." But with the EMS runs, it was different. "I'm first in the door, or I jump right on the patient . . . because I have a comfort level with it that makes me more assertive with it. . . . But I know that once I get more comfortable with the fire thing, I'll do exactly the same thing. It's just a matter of getting the experience."

Having EMS experience and skill gave Valerie something to contribute and also a source of self-esteem while she waited to acquire firefighting expertise. But when asked about a sense of learning confidence on calls, she returned to the work of firefighting:

I keep coming back to the same thing, over and over again, as I'm thinking about this, and it's interesting because it—what it does, it seems to me it kinda points up the areas of which I feel the least comfortable about with myself, right? I mean, and for me it's the physical—it's a demonstration where the physical endurance thing is tested. 'Cause you *don't know.* I mean [a drill is] . . . finite, has a beginning and an end, you know when the drill starts and when it stops. But when you're at a fire, you're going and going and going and going and it keeps asking *more* and *more* of you, and do you have it to give? . . . The thing I keep coming back to is that fire that was on Bailey. . . . I was there for *five hours,* and . . . the thing I came away with is OK, I gave it everything I had for five hours . . . fought through the nausea, fought through the exhaustion, just picked it up, tried it some more, that sort of thing . . . having to tear a roof apart with a mask on, all that kind of stuff, and came out the other side, *absolutely* beat to *shit,* but—made it.

Finding out for certain that she had the stamina to do what was needed was an important moment of passage for Valerie. She had established her value as an EMT and was developing a reputation as a hard worker and cooperative team member, but without the physical test of firework she could not fully *know* her capacity.

Like Marianne, Valerie was an exceptionally strong woman with physical and mechanical skills who desperately needed the exposure to prove to herself that she could keep up. These women understood that the ultimate test of one's suitability for the fire service was at the fire scene: if you couldn't hold your own at a fire, particularly in a physical sense, you were unlikely to garner respect from your coworkers, however much they might praise your positive attitude or your efforts around the fire station. Someone who didn't live up to firehouse norms might be tagged with a negative nickname but could be pardoned with the qualification "but he's a good firefighter." By contrast, someone who worked hard but was considered a poor firefighter might be described as a "really nice guy" (or, more commonly, "lady") who "doesn't belong in the fire service."

Among the qualities that veterans look for in newcomers at the fire scene are courage, composure, aggressiveness, and the capacity to do what's asked without making serious mistakes. Most new OFD firefighters managed to acquit themselves reasonably well in terms of courage, composure, and the avoidance of major mistakes in their work. Those with the most experience—generally, the white men—may have had somewhat smoother initial performances, but in general there was little systematic variation by race or sex in terms of these particular aspects of performance.

What did seem to vary, however, was the inclination and ability to show aggressiveness. Though new firefighters were supposed to follow the instructions of their officers or senior crew members, male newcomers frequently reported free-lancing. Several talked of simply taking the nozzle when they were momentarily without officer direction (and then fighting to hang onto it), of grabbing equipment before it was requested, of stepping in to take over work from others. By contrast, the women's descriptions of their early fires tended to emphasize concern for doing the right thing, a desire to clarify instructions before acting, and a disinclination to assert themselves when they were kept out of the action.

Marianne knew that as hard as she might work around the firehouse, she would not earn her coworkers' respect without performing aggressively at fires. But being stationed in a slow area and being by nature reluctant to act when uncertain what to do, she found her opportunities to prove herself were limited. In her first call, a dumpster fire, one firefighter told her she had to hustle for the nozzle, whereas her inclination had been to wait to see if they wanted to pull the more convenient red line or the larger inch-and-a-half line off the engine. "To be aggressive is not difficult for me, but I like to know what I'm doing first," she said. "It's hard for me to prove myself because it's assumed that I'm not aggressive just because . . . I don't jump into things not knowing what I'm doing. . . . It's a little harder, too, if you don't make your own situations. But I'm also not willing to make a situation where I do something stupid—just to try and look good!"

Carrie Hopper described a similar reluctance to act without explicit instruction; in her first car fire she also had waited to see which line would be pulled and felt this was only sensible: "You have to wait for an officer to tell you what to do—you can't just get out and start pulling hose off the rig—you better know what they want." By contrast, when Marcus arrived at his first car fire, he momentarily debated with himself about which line to use but then moved without instruction: "it was enough smoke I didn't know if it was going to go any further, so my first thought was to grab the inch-and-a-half and then the next thing . . . I looked and the red line was right there and so I grabbed the red line and I began to hose it down." When Frank was sent to the roof with a saw, he refused to give it up to another firefighter and insisted on cutting the hole himself; when Elena Cochrane was sent with a hose to the roof of a high-rise, she turned the nozzle over to another firefighter, followed orders, and returned to the ground. Despite the fire department's paramilitary nature and the stated importance of following the chain of command, the men's initiative was either rewarded ("Nice goin' ") or the subject of a mixed message (chastisement with praise), which they generally interpreted as approval. The bottom line was that the veterans wanted to see action, even if it was not perfectly controlled, as long as the job got done and no one got hurt.

But the women tended to be reluctant to engage in this kind of behavior.[2] It seemed foolish to them to act independently when they were not sure what they were doing and would run the risk of doing something both wrong and dangerous. Did this caution signify a lack of commitment to the job? There was no indication that these women were any more reluctant than their male counterparts to take on the rigors of firefighting; indeed, given the obstacles they had to overcome to enter and remain in the fire service, they could not have been a timid group. Moreover, with the passage of time and increasing confidence in their knowledge and skill, their willingness to take the initiative also grew.[3]

What the women's initial hesitations did reflect was probably a mix of social conditioning with an acute awareness of the cost of their mistakes. With respect to social conditioning, mainstream American gender-role socialization has encouraged deferential, self-effacing behavior in girls but—in contrast to the behavior expected of boys—rarely promoted risk-taking or self-assertion.[4] Most women begin to learn at an early age not to put themselves forward, and the lesson is reiterated and elaborated into adulthood.[5] This training is more pronounced for some women than others; some research suggests, for example, that African American women may be less subject to these cultural stereotypes at least initially than are white women,[6] but the pattern is general enough to pose a problem for women trying to enter male-dominated occupational domains.[7] In a culture like the fire service, the caution and self-doubt in which many women are trained are exactly wrong for the environment, where one is expected to behave aggressively even before he knows for certain what needs to be done.

At the same time, though, women have excellent reason to be cautious, given the unfriendly spotlight on their performance. When the fact of their low numbers is combined with the negative expectations of women by many men in the fire service, the pressures on performance are particularly high, and the cost of making a mistake is magnified. Where a male newcomer might shrug or even laugh off a mistake by figuring he'd get it right the next time, many women would justly fear that their coworkers would conclude they were not fit for the job. In the gossip mill of the fire department, stories circulate about all firefighters, and all rumors are subject to distortion as they move from station to station. But people who are disliked or whose abilities are suspect are particularly vulnerable, and the mistakes of tokens are always widely and rapidly known (and sometimes embellished).[8]

The Meaning of Housework

While all new firefighters felt the need to get a few good fires and some seri-ous medical calls under their belts, most of the men were quick to assert that proving oneself was not limited to the fireground, particularly after some ex-posure had begun to demystify the work. Hugh, for example, came to believe that "basically . . . it's not so much how you perform at the incident as it is how you perform around the house. If you have a pretty good work ethic, you tend to get more respect. If you do good with your housework, you help out in the kitchen, you do your drills up to par and that type of thing, you're seen studying, that tends to lend itself to more respect than not doing anything all day and then kickin' ass at a fire. 'Cause basically everybody can put a fire out." In the station, the goal was to prove that you were not a "lump" who was looking for a free ride, but rather someone who was prepared to earn his place in the fire service.

Among the men, the most traditional newcomers not only anticipated but also approved of the firehouse norms. Frank had actually expected that it would be worse for the new kids than it was: "You know, I expected to be doin' all the shit jobs . . . everything, but it's really not [like that]. You do your share and everybody else does theirs." Following a lunch that he had helped to prepare he got up to do the dishes. "I could've just sat there and rolled dice," he said to me later, "you know, the loser would've done 'em. But I just jump in and do 'em. And that's noticed, that gets noticed right there." John Bowman's approach was less spirited but just as judicious:

> I've not only witnessed but had it bluntly put to me the more
> aggressive you are, the more favorably you're going to be evaluated.
> And that involves anything from answering the telephone to getting
> in on the medical calls. So you're expected to do virtually every-thing. . . . I've been in the kitchen at 6:30 in the morning and
> somebody else will come in and see that the coffee's made and say,
> "Oh, way to go!" And you score big points just for doing something as
> simple as that. So if you can keep your eyes open and . . . anticipate
> what needs doing before somebody tells you to do it, you're a step
> ahead.

Jonathan, an African American man with a traditionalist's approach, agreed that willingness to work was an important part of proving your fitness for the job. "If there's a job that I have to do, then I do it, regardless, what-ever it is, from fighting a fire to cleaning the toilets. See those are the things that a lot of us are judged by. Being able to get along. How well do you pitch in and help when it comes to cleaning up after a meal. Things of that nature. Those things make you a team player." He'd arrive early and be going over the rigs before his shift started and not stop working until the officer or crew told him to slow down.

On the other hand, more critical newcomers like Eddie and Hugh viewed the process as demeaning and resented it. It was one thing to pitch in and help, but something else to be expected to do it all. Eddie thought the emphasis on housework was misplaced; he asserted that his lack of interest in doing dishes should not reflect on his capability as a firefighter. While Hugh indicated that he understood the need to prove oneself, he also said, "I'm not really gung ho about the new kid do everything, do this, do that. . . . The old-timers aren't the ones who got me the job. I'll respect them for their experience and what they can teach you, but as far as me owing them something—" He disliked having to bend over backwards: "It's like you have to do a lot of unnecessary stuff to earn some people's respect. Instead of being based on your ability to do the job and your work ethic, with some people you just have to go out of your way to do unnecessary stuff, you know, unreasonable things." To Hugh, the expectation that the new kids would "do everything" implied a belief on the veterans' part that the newcomers *owed* them something.

Overall, though, differences by race or ethnicity were very slight; most men fell somewhere in the middle of this spectrum in terms of their attitudes on housework norms, and there was both within-group variation and across-group overlap. By contrast, gender could be significant—not in terms of attitudes or expectations, but in the value of housework as a proving ground.

Throughout the academy, the women had heard about the informal testing of new firefighters and understood that they would be expected to "do and be everything" in the station and on the fireground, but accomplishing this was sometimes trickier than expected. Once in the companies, they found that when you are assumed to be "the weak link in the chain," the process of "proving yourself" takes on a special meaning. For most of these women, proving themselves ultimately meant showing their *firefighting* capabilities, particularly aggressiveness, physical strength, and mechanical aptitude. Although EMS skills were important and a willingness to work hard in the firehouse was essential, neither of these constituted "proving yourself" in the arena most critical for acceptance or self-confidence.

Following the advice of academy instructors, the women were conscientious about demonstrating their work ethic. Valerie was in "constant motion" from 8:00 a.m. until 8:00 p.m. (or later). On her first day at Station 116, Laurinda never sat down—"I think I even read standing up"—despite the example of another recruit who watched TV. Carrie did more than her share of housework " 'cause I want them to know I'm not afraid of work. I am not afraid to get my hands dirty. . . . And I do more than my share . . . [but] sometimes I wonder if they notice or if they really even do care."

Like the others, Marianne, knowing she was being watched constantly, thought it was just common sense to stay busy all the time. The veterans wouldn't say anything to you if you violated the expected work ethic, but you'd get a reputation. When she changed station assignments, Marianne heard that her new crew had received a "good report" on her from the previous crew. But she was sensitive to the fact that this "good report" was of limited value: "I mean, to say that I'm a 'hard worker,' I mean, that *is* good, but what does that mean? . . . I think there is a difference between hearing that you're a good worker or that you're good at fires." It wasn't that she'd performed poorly at fires, but simply that she hadn't had the opportunity to prove herself in that most critical setting.

In short, women were no more resistant to housework than were their male counterparts, nor was there a general expectation that they would do more of it. But they did seem to get less credit for it: a man might be able to "prove himself" to some degree by doing work around the station, but a woman couldn't. It would be noticed if either didn't jump to do such work, but if both did it well, then the man would be more likely to get positive recognition for it. Ray knew that the veterans respected him for his hard work around the station, but Carrie questioned whether anyone noticed that she did chores for other firefighters. Hugh felt that displaying the right work ethic in the firehouse was as important as performing on the fireground, but Marianne was sensitive to the limited value of a reputation based on being a hard worker. Visiting at Station 101 I heard from the veterans what a wonderful worker Mark Lopez was, but I never heard a similar comment about Elena Cochrane, despite her having taken on extra cleaning duties on a slow day.[9]

This difference in experience reflected different underlying assumptions about men's and women's abilities. Hugh asserted that hard work in the station would shape a newcomer's reputation because, as he put it, "*everybody* could put a fire out." But the general belief was not that everybody could fight fires; in particular, it was widely assumed that most (or even all) women could not do so. Accompanying this belief was the suspicion that women would substitute housework for firefighting if they could get away with it: more than one veteran complained about women who had entered the fire service allegedly because they liked to hang out in the fire station, not because they wanted to fight fires. Men might be suspected of laziness—either in the firehouse or on the scene—but no one suggested the possibility that a man might prefer baking cookies to fighting fires. Consequently, when a man threw himself energetically into firehouse tasks, he indicated his willingness to work; when a woman did so, she indicated her willingness to work *around the firehouse*—a demonstration of much more limited value.

This pattern also reflects the way in which this workplace is gendered.

In many work settings, the local equivalent of "housework"—cleaning, coffee-making, occasional food preparation—is women's work, and it is devalued. But in the fire service, housework is masculine because there *is* no "women's work" in this setting. Even conventionally feminine skills such as cooking are masculinized: firehouse meals emphasize hearty, strong-flavored fare, in which there is little need or room for culinary refinements. To the extent that firehouse tasks are valued, then, they are firefighters' (men's) work. When these chores are not valued, they are simply left undone. In a sense, when men do such work, it is masculine; when women do it, it is invisible.

Showing Special Skills

If something's gotta be done, you don't wait for anybody to do it. You just jump in and do it. . . . You know, after you've been to a house—might take you a few shifts—by now, you know what's gotta be done. After meals you get the dishes. Somebody's gotta do 'em, you're the new kid, you do 'em. If you come back from an incident and you've used some equipment on the truck . . . you make sure they're loaded and ready to go. You don't wait for somebody to tell you that, you just do it. And then they'll jump you, first round. That's what they call 'em, you know, "first-round draft picks."

—FRANK CROSS

Everyone knew the importance of keeping busy throughout the shift—keeping one's eyes open and jumping in to do something before being asked. Being the first to make coffee in the morning or doing more than one's share of housework did not take any special talent, but when it came to "jumping in" on emergency responses or more technical chores around the firehouse, it helped to have some prior knowledge and experience. In the early months of probation many new firefighters waited anxiously for their first fire, but those with more expertise felt that they could begin to prove themselves through the performance of drills or technical tasks, where they could take care of business before being asked, or assume special responsibilities without instruction.

For example, all firefighters were expected to look over the rigs in the morning to make sure they knew where everything was, but if one's knowledge was adequate, he could also verify that all the equipment was in proper working order and fill out the daily check sheet. An especially talented newcomer might make occasional equipment repairs, as Frank Cross did when he worked on the power tools at Station 112. "Our generator was out. . . . They were gonna send it back, and I said, 'Let me see what I can do.' About forty minutes later, I had that thing purring like a kitten. The lieutenant comes out and goes, 'Damn! We're gonna keep you around here.' " Riding the truck at another station, he thought to chock the tires to keep the rig from rolling down a hill it was parked on. "Using your head, especially at an incident, gets noticed. . . . Just like chockin' them tires—nobody told me to do that. I just don't want the damn thing rollin' down and hittin' me [chuckles]. . . . And that was noticed, you know, Captain said, 'Hey, nice goin' on that.' "

Paul Brown's ride-along experience in Oakland prepared him to handle the medicals, and he would initiate the patient evaluation without waiting for instructions. "If you show initiative and show that you want to do it, then they'll pat you on the back . . . rather than having to kick you and you know, 'Do this' or try and show you. They would rather you do it than have to show you directions."

Most newcomers were intimidated by truck work because of the number of tools involved, the scope and variety of the work associated with this rig, and the relatively limited training recruits received on truck work in the academy. But a little experience could make a big difference, as Andy found on his first truck call, an extrication. When the crew sent him back to the rig for equipment he had no trouble supplying what they requested: "First thing they said was, 'Andy, grab hacksaw, bolt cutters, and the jamb spreader.' Well, in the Tower we weren't taught anything about jamb spreaders . . . [but] I've heard of those and I've used them before. . . . I went back, and I grabbed the stuff. . . . A lot of it is winning over the crew's confidence. When I come back with all three of those things, they go, 'Hey, we tried to stump him with the jamb spreaders, and it didn't work—well, we'll get him on the next one.' So they find these obscure things, you know, until they stump you."

Tony hadn't been a firefighter, but he had plenty of emergency medical experience; his crew quickly saw that he could and should take charge of the complicated medical calls. They appreciated his knowledge and complimented him on his EMS work, and this esteem undoubtedly enhanced Tony's ability to perform on the fireground as well. Ray's previous firefighting and EMT experience gave him not only the ability to do more than the average new kid but also the certainty that he could do what was required and that the veterans would see that. He said of his favorite officer, "Quinn has control of me, but it doesn't feel like it. He knows, he has confidence in me that he knows what I can do. He told me, 'I want you on the nozzle, I know you can do it, just do it.' " Ray was doing truck work at fires much earlier than most of his classmates and taking greater responsibilities sooner. At a structure fire where the crew had opened a skylight but the fire still wasn't ventilating, one of the veterans finally found the real hot spot and the captain said, " 'OK, let's cut it open.' " Standing there, Ray saw that "the chain saw was right next to me and I said, 'Heck, I'm grabbing the chain saw.' So I started it up—thank god it started up on the first try [laughs]—and Quinn was tellin' me, 'OK, kid, I want you to cut it here,' and I cut the hole."

One common early drill was for the newcomer to go over a truck with an officer or senior firefighter and review the uses of each piece of equipment that the rig carried. The officer might open up a compartment and quiz the novice on its contents, either by asking for a piece of equipment by name and then waiting to see if the newcomer pulled out the right item or by pulling out an item and asking what it was called. Once the tool was out of its compartment, the officer would continue to ask questions about the tool's possible uses and necessary safety precautions. Because truck-related training in the academy was limited, this drill was an occasion when people with relevant backgrounds could shine and people with no related experience could look particularly weak. The contrast was especially evident when experienced and novice probationers worked together, as when an officer at Station 122 conducted a truck drill with Elena Cochrane and Paul Brown. Although Paul didn't have all the answers, he knew more than Elena, and right or wrong, his responses were almost always more confident than hers, so that even when she gave a correct answer, it sounded like a lucky guess. A firefighter who watched the drill frequently interjected critical remarks, sometimes general but sometimes aimed at Elena, as when he informed her in a mock serious tone that "this is a truck, not an engine," as though she didn't know the difference between the two rigs.

Dodging Bullets and Looking Good

There was of course good reason to expect newcomers to learn the names, locations, and uses of all equipment. At an emergency scene there wouldn't be time for an extended search of the rig; a firefighter ought to be able to go immediately to the right compartment and pull out the requisite tool. In this context, the informal testing of a newcomer's knowledge seems perfectly justifiable, even necessary. John Bowman acknowledged that the quizzing could be personally stressful but insisted that it was "justified, because that sort of competence affects your ability to perform." Referring to a senior firefighter at the very traditional Station 112, he noted that many of his classmates were intimidated by the man but John felt that this veteran was simply interested in assessing people's ability: "He wants to know if you know your job. When . . . I was working at Station 112, and it was my second or third shift there . . . he said, 'OK, Bowman, where's this? Where's that?' And of course he knew all the items to ask for that were impossible to find. . . . [But] I think that's more of an awareness-heightening tactic on his part, and you need to know your rig."

As in other interactions between veterans and newcomers, there was an element of gamesmanship on both sides. Andy explained that the job was really about "dodging bullets": as a new kid you were constantly on the spot, and you had to be ready for whatever might come your way. At certain stations that meant the crews would regularly try to stump you with their questions—sometimes making things up, using unfamiliar names, asking about extremely trivial details. A canny newcomer would expect this and be ready for almost anything, as Frank was when the veterans at 112 Truck asked him about the ring cutter:

> We got it up in the front seat. They wanted to know how many teeth were on it. It's got this little tiny blade about the size of a dime, and there's ninety-six teeth on that thing.
> C: Did you count them?
> You bet I did. I heard somebody else do that once before, they asked what that was, so I was ready for it. . . . Somebody came in a couple times at 112 and said, "Hey, yeah, count the teeth on the ring cutter, 'cause I guarantee they'll ask you that." Sure as shit. I counted them son-of-a-bitches . . . and I was ready for 'em. . . . They said, "Where's the ring cutter, kid?" and I said, "Front seat, officer's side, on the dashboard." And the guy goes, "Wow," you know, like I got him, and he says, "How many teeth's it got?" And I said, "Ninety-six." [Laughs.] And he goes, "Damn!" . . . You gotta be fast. . . . You gotta beat 'em at their own game.

By his own report, Frank apparently thrived on the game, but other newcomers weren't always so delighted. Rodney Chin's initial discomfort at the hands of the "gung ho" young veterans at Station 108 was so great that he dreaded coming to work. Looking back he appreciated how much he had learned, but he sometimes wondered if there might not be a less offensive approach. "They just fire off random questions at you all the time, and when you don't know the answer, they kinda feed off of each other and they give you a really hard time. So the first month, I was dreading it here . . . because I hate being wrong, and I hate not knowing. So now that they can't ask me any more questions I don't know, I find that I'm real glad they did it. I mean, they could have done it a different way, but ultimately, I know more, I've been trained better here than anywhere else I've been."

Rodney felt the new kids should support each other, so when he heard that Laurinda was being sent to 108 he made sure she was prepared, going over all the questions she was likely to be asked. Laurinda thought he was exaggerating, but soon learned otherwise and was extremely grateful. "[Rodney] . . . really came through [for me] because they started grillin' me the minute I walked in. They just thought they were going to pound me into the dirt. And I think I answered [almost] every single question."

All newcomers were at times impatient with the game, especially when the test seemed particularly pointless, or when the tester was someone not held in high regard or who seemed to have unacceptable motives. For example, a traditional newcomer like Andy respected senior crews like those at Station 112, and he never criticized them for their treatment of newcomers; in fact, he would consider it "an honor" to pass their tests. But he was less tolerant of testing at the hands of younger or less able veterans. During overhaul work after a trailer fire, Andy was pulling rubbish down from the top of the trailer when "this gal who I know has just been in like three years . . . she comes up to me and says—'cause I wasn't usin' the pike pole and I kinda was holding it and pulling some stuff down with my arm at this time—and she goes, 'Do you want me to hold that pike pole for you?' And that's that whole thing of like, if I were to give it to her, then she would go, 'Hey, new kid, don't ever give up that—' It's always these little tests, you know. And here's this gal who is tryin' to test, and there I was, I was thinkin' like, 'Who the hell are you to test me?' "

Intent was important to Andy, but he was equally if not more concerned with a veteran's "right" to test him. By contrast, less traditional newcomers were somewhat more concerned with intent than with who was doing the testing, though the two factors were of course related. Leonard Bentley, in most respects an easygoing man, was most impatient with games that seemed to be intended primarily to humiliate. At Station 122, for example, they might quiz a newcomer by asking questions to which a wrong answer would be particularly embarrassing—such as tossing out the name of a street right behind the station and asking the new kid where it was located. They also seemed to take pleasure in pushing the newcomer without letting up. One evening at 10:00 p.m. when Leonard sat down to watch TV (his chores and drills completed), the engineer insisted that he couldn't watch TV because he had to tell him where the rope bag was kept on the engine. When Leonard was able to do so (as a result of a tip from another firefighter), the engineer asked him if he thought he knew everything. Leonard replied, " 'I don't think I know where everything is, but I don't see why we have to do this,' you know. So they kinda left me alone . . . but I think they think that maybe I have a bad attitude or something. But, you know, I'm not a kid."

Other nontraditional newcomers—including some Asian American men—might have been equally disdainful of the firehouse proving ground but treated it more ironically. Particularly after their initial anxiety began to wear off, they knew that they were simply playing a game, and they did so with either amused detachment or lighthearted resignation. In their own minds, they were able to sort out the legitimate expectations from the rituals of humiliation, and among the latter, to sense what they had to do to get by.

George, for example, quickly figured out how to give the right impression even if it wasn't entirely accurate. He and a classmate who were stationed together at a traditional double house would sit at the kitchen table with their books out. Much of the time they'd be talking, but if anyone else came by, their books would be laid out around them, and it would appear as if they were studying. He would work some of the time and relax some of the time, but he managed to be seen at those times when he was applying himself. "The other day," he chuckled, "Janice and I were inside the apparatus room, we had a Halligan tool and we were talking about how to take off a door handle and Joe [the officer] walked by and said, 'What're you guys doing?' and I told him exactly what we were doin' and he took off and I told Janice because I know it's true, I said, 'Joe just loves that. He loves to see us tinkering around. You got some brownie points by being caught doing that.' "

Playing the game this way allowed George to succeed with an otherwise critical officer. "He's tough on new kids that he doesn't think are gonna do well. And you know, half of it—at least in my case—is that it's not that I'm any more competent, but that I know how to look good around the lieutenant." But he added that his performance wasn't just show—as a new kid, you knew the veterans would drill you and you really should know that stuff and be able to give it back to them quickly. The men's responses to the veterans' tests, then, ranged from the traditionalists' enthusiastic effort to beat the veterans at their own game to the more change-oriented men's somewhat grudging compliance. In the middle was a more calculating kind of impression management that nevertheless acknowledged the legitimacy and even value of the process.

Testing for Failure

For some women the informal testing seemed designed to show up their weaknesses and make them think twice about their ability to do the job. Veteran quizzing of newcomers was an opportunity for some new firefighters to display desired mechanical knowledge, but for others it could be a harrowing experience. Jane, for example, was quizzed extensively by a firefighter who had traded onto her shift for the day, "and I didn't have all the answers, and he was really—you could tell he was just down on me. . . . I felt real bad, too, I felt real humiliated." Elena had understood firefighting to be a job one could enter without prior experience, but she found instead that people are "pissed off that they've hired people like that, 'cause they want people that have mechanical abilities and have some knowledge of electrical and stuff." This realization made her feel very "small": "All I can do is wait table. . . . Not that I can't learn. But I don't think I learn as good as some people that have been exposed to it more."

In some circumstances, practical drills could also have a depressing effect on the women. Many of them had difficulties initially in starting some of the more temperamental power tools, a task that all recruits were expected to practice regularly. Under a patient and skillful tutor such practice could be helpful, but when the drill was supervised by a more hostile or unforgiving coworker, the "lesson" could feel like harassment.[10] When Elena had problems starting a saw, the young coworker who was watching her insisted that she continue working with it for nearly two hours, well beyond the point when the exercise was of any value. Her arm was sore for days afterward, and as she angrily recounted the story she described it as a "haunting" and "terrorizing" experience. When Carrie had difficulty starting a saw, her coworker told her it was her lack of strength. "He says, 'Well, it's an upper body thing' and I say, 'I don't think so.' 'Cause I can bench press 200 pounds, and I don't believe that this saw would . . . [take] 200 pounds. I mean that cord isn't gonna have 200 pounds of pressure on it. And so it's not that, it's a technique. . . . And when they say things like that, that is just reinforcing the concept that women cannot do the job."

Because of the general skepticism about female firefighters' capabilities, their testing seemed to be negatively weighted in a way not experienced by the men. If something went wrong for a woman, she was less likely than a man to receive the "benefit of the doubt." Her difficulty was seen as a reflection on her ability—indeed, on the abilities of all the women—rather than a momentary lapse or external problem. Laurinda experienced this type of judgment while working at a fire where she had trouble starting a blower; later, she learned that another firefighter had failed to fill it with gas. Not knowing at the time what the problem was, she became frustrated, embarrassed, and also puzzled because she had not had this difficulty before. Another firefighter tried to start it and also failed. At this point a hostile coworker arrived with another blower, took hers away, and said, "Kick that woman out of here! She couldn't even start a power tool!" When a more supportive coworker defended her, saying it wasn't her fault, the first man replied, "I don't care!" Such incidents could be particularly damaging to a woman's self-confidence, adding to her reluctance to take chances or to act aggressively in the absence of certainty.

The many veterans who believed that women did not belong in the fire service shaped the testing and proving process by not only raising the stakes for women, but also setting sometimes unreachable goals or refusing to credit the women for what they could accomplish. For example, new firefighters were sometimes subjected to nonregulation physical drills, such as raising a particular ladder with a smaller group of people than called for under department regulations. The overt rationale for this procedure was simple: sometimes field conditions required nonregulation approaches; however, the practical (some would argue, intended) effect was to make some firefighters—smaller women in particular—look bad to themselves and their coworkers. Jane confronted this situation when she was participating in ladder-raising exercises at her station. A young veteran—the same firefighter who had drilled Elena on the saw—began by pulling out a number of ladders to be raised. OFD policy is that any ladder over twenty feet is thrown with two or more people, but this firefighter was throwing twenty-two-foot and twenty-four-foot ladders and expecting the probationary firefighters to do the same. Jane threw the twenty-two, but had been having a shoulder problem and didn't want to try the twenty-four (which the male probie did), so she went inside the station to do some other work. The firefighter who had been working with the probationers came in later and asked if she didn't want to throw the twenty-four, a comment that let her know he'd seen her leave without doing it. At subsequent encounters, Jane said, he shunned her and also made it clear to others that she had refused to throw the twenty-four-foot ladder, thereby encouraging other firefighters to ostracize her. Though occasionally an exceptionally strong woman was able to pass the test, with some minimal gain to her reputation, when the average woman was faced with this kind of test, her choices were to try it and risk failure or injury or to walk away and be ridiculed. The fact that she might be capable of the regulation ladder raises or of good engine work was not enough in the eyes of some veterans to "prove" her capacity to do the job.[11]

Some of this testing was probably simple harassment, and some was likely motivated by the veterans' refusal to trust the current formal certification system under which people generally do not fail. Marianne explained both sides of it:

There's a different set of rules for us. 'Cause you know, we start out, we have to prove ourselves anyway. Although I've come to the conclusion that for the most part, it just doesn't matter. It doesn't matter. They don't think that we can do the job. You can't prove yourself. No, there's a certain number of people that maybe you can, but the vast majority of them think that this is a gift and that's it. It doesn't matter what you show them, that's just what they think. And going through—before this year test, probationary test, they just kept talking about, you know—'cause I was nervous, obviously I'm nervous—and they're like, "Well, you *can't* fail." And I'm like, "Well, you can fail." And they're like, "No, *you* can't fail. You don't understand. You're a woman, you can't fail. *Joe* can fail. You can't fail." And that's pretty much the attitude.[12]

Many women veterans were particularly weary of what they saw as a no-win battle for respect; they had come to believe that it simply did not matter what they did; they would never be good enough for some coworkers. A black woman veteran explained it this way: a man comes in with 100 points; if he performs poorly, then they subtract points from his score. A woman comes in with zero points, and she has to try to accumulate points from there, which is almost impossible to do. But the most traditional male veterans insisted that the women's experience simply reflected the reality that "women can't do the job." Part of this conflict centers around the question of exactly what constitutes the job and whether it's necessary that everyone be as physically capable as the strongest man, or if other kinds of abilities are equally useful. The traditionalists argue that the job has to be done one way—though they also make explicit allowance for old-timers who have "paid their dues" and can't pull the same load any longer. The more progressive firefighters assert that a good team should be made up of people with a variety of skills and that brawn isn't the only way or even the best way to fight fire.

But much of the testing process highlighted physical abilities, and although technique was important, its absence could be compensated for by sheer power. Newcomers unfamiliar with the physical tasks might struggle with them, but if they were large and strong, their chances of avoiding embarrassment were better. One afternoon at a phase check, the probationary firefighters were asked to raise and adjust the position of the forty-foot ladder, the second heaviest in the department. Though they knew how to raise the ladder, they were inexperienced in adjusting it (moving it from one position to another along the side of a building). Several groups struggled with the awkward process, eventually succeeding in situating the ladder to the instructor's satisfaction. The last group, however, had a great deal of difficulty and appeared as if they might lose the ladder a number of times. The instructor kept them at the task for an extended period, while veterans and other probationary firefighters watched. Though the ladder group included two women and two men, it was generally assumed by the bystanders that the women's lack of size and strength were to blame for the group's difficulty. In a typical aside, one veteran observed that it was hard to lift and control a ladder like this one when you had two people on the crew "who weigh less than the ladder does."

The reactions and comments of the veterans on this occasion and at other moments of the probationary testing process tended to highlight the failures of women specifically. Men sometimes had difficulties starting saws or controlling ladders; these events were usually seen as isolated incidents, and the newcomers often received coaching on how to improve. The women's difficulties, by contrast, were interpreted as evidence of a more general pattern, and their failures did not always elicit helpful feedback. This kind of differential processing of information by observers is consistent with research on in-group and out-group perception, which indicates that judgments of the out-group (in this case, women) by members of the in-group (men) are more likely to be subject to stereotypes than are judgments about other in-group members.[13] Whereas a great deal of individuation is seen among in-group members, out-group members tend to be aggregated into a small number of stereotypical categories,[14] where they are sometimes evaluated more harshly.[15] Perceptions of out-group members tend to be subject to a different set of cognitive processes than perceptions of in-group members.[16]

These kinds of distinctions operate even in numerically and socially balanced environments, but in a setting like the fire service, the problems of token representation of low-status groups also arise. The fact of being a member of a numerically subordinate group (well under half the total) can significantly affect one's role options, performance, evaluation, and self-perception, and in the case of low-status tokens—for example, women in a sexist culture—the result is almost always adverse.[17] The effects, particularly intense when the token is a "solo" representative, are probably aggravated for those working in culturally "inappropriate" settings.

Of course, all these conditions hold for women in the fire service. Nationwide, women constitute less than 5 percent of the fire service (8 percent in Oakland), and in individual stations they frequently find themselves in solo conditions. They suffer the low status associated with being female in our society and working in a distinctly masculine occupation. These circumstances highlight all aspects of their performance and put a level of pressure on them beyond what their male counterparts experience. By virtue of their unique status they are more noticeable than the men, and they tend to be seen as symbols rather than individuals. The performance of individual women in this group was taken as a reflection on all other women, and vice versa. Furthermore, their mistakes were often attributed to their sex; if a woman failed to start a power tool or misunderstood an instruction, she was often told directly or indirectly that the problem was being female, not something she could work on and change.[18] " 'You gotta think more mechanical,' " Carrie was told. " 'Now that's a woman thinking . . . 'cause you're a woman, you're just not thinkin' mechanical.' "

THROUGHOUT THIS CHAPTER, we have seen that all inexperienced and unselfconfident newcomers experienced greater than average difficulty in establishing themselves as firefighters, both in their own eyes and in the estimation of their veteran coworkers. The overwhelming importance of establishing a good reputation put all newcomers under tremendous pressure to perform well and simultaneously heightened any reluctance they might have to act. To the women, though, the odds were particularly daunting. They shared with African American men the disadvantages of inexperience and membership in a subordinate group, but in a male-dominated environment where physical strength was prized and female ability suspect, the women's opportunities to perform well were more constrained. Finally, even if gender-role socialization had produced women and men of equal self-confidence, women—for whom the price of failure was high and the benefits of success limited—might still be reluctant to put themselves forward. It might well be true that the only way to establish yourself was to take the risk of making mistakes, but if the mistakes were the only things that were noticed, then all you proved was that you couldn't do it.

Chapter 6

Learning in Relationship

[My classmate] Paula got the nozzle taken away from her at the fire, and you know what kind of (voodoo) thing that is around here, and it really made her mad because it was her first fire, and she's not real aggressive and you know, she wanted to try and do good, she's not out to do bad, to do anybody any harm, and another firefighter came and took the nozzle from her, and she was really doing what she thought she was supposed to. . . . And that happens a lot, you know, 'cause there's aggressive guys out there. And Bill [my officer] really took offense to that and talked to the guy afterwards. Which isn't really his place to do because it's a tradition, if you're not aggressive enough, the nozzle gets taken away from you. . . . And Bill even admitted that it was, you know, something that happens when you're not aggressive enough, and there's somethin' that needs to be done, and Paula wasn't doing it, but she didn't, you know, she was willing for somebody to tell her where to go or whatever, she woulda done it, and Bill kinda backed this guy up into the wall and kinda told him, "You know, it wasn't right, man." But then we came back here, and everybody's like, "Well, she wasn't puttin' the fire out."

—LAURINDA GIBSON

Learning by Doing

IN THE PREVIOUS CHAPTER, we saw how newcomers had to put themselves forward to *prove themselves*—to establish their capacity to become firefighters. In this chapter we see how they also must assert themselves to be able to learn their trade and continue the development of their occupational identity. Having begun to show the veterans that they are worthy of being taken seriously, the newcomers must continue to hold their senior coworkers' interest, attention, and support—something Paula was on this occasion unable to do—if they are to master the lessons of firefighting.

Why should a newcomer need this additional instruction? OFD's Class 1-91 went through an exhausting, sixteen-week academy that included seemingly countless hours of hose-and-ladder drills along with classroom and practical training in emergency medical services, wild land firefighting, hazardous materials containment, search and rescue operations, and countless other special topics. Isn't this training adequate preparation for the work? The answer is no; even with such extensive formal instruction, only in the field can newcomers actually learn to be firefighters. As Steven Brandt put it, "They can train you all they want, but they can't light a Victorian on fire. . . . You don't really know what to expect 'til you go to one." The current trend toward more elaborate formal training reflects both the widening scope of firefighter duties and the increasing state requirements for certifications of firefighters. But all this is really only preparation for field training, which remains the "real thing." Important contingencies of the work—including its emotional realities—simply cannot be reproduced in the academy, and even those lessons that can be conveyed in an artificial setting tend not to "sink in" until their relevance is revealed at an emergency scene. Fires and other emergencies are unpredictable; so many different things can happen on the scene that no formal training can anticipate them all, and there is no sense in trying. There comes a point where the newcomer simply must learn by doing, a fact recognized implicitly or explicitly in all apprenticeships.[1]

What does it mean to learn by doing? As Laurinda's story about Paula vividly illustrates, the experiential learning process is *social*; what and how one learns are determined by the relationship between newcomer and community. Each party has expectations of the other, and when these are met, training proceeds smoothly; but when one side or the other fails to meet expectations, the newcomer's development, at least along traditional lines, is significantly inhibited. In the anecdote above, Paula didn't meet the veterans' expectations of a newcomer (to be aggressive in handling the nozzle, including fighting to hang onto it); simultaneously, her coworkers didn't meet her expectations (that they would show her what to do). Though she may have learned something about how traditional firefighters behave, she did not learn how to work the nozzle.

Apprenticeship involves learning not only how to *do*, but also how to *be*; it is the development of both skill and identity through the practice of each, and access to practice is central to successful apprenticeship.[2] In this episode, Paula's access was inhibited on two levels: she was excluded from participation in the task and simultaneously shown that she wasn't a firefighter; the community didn't accept her enactment of the identity. In such a moment, the community signals that its training may be less concerned with cultivating qualitites than with testing for them. That is, in this work culture, the process of *learning the work* often looks very much like the process of *proving oneself*, a model of apprenticeship that may be common in male-dominated workplaces but is not the only way to learn a trade. In a different work culture, Paula's coworker might have coached her in proper technique; instead, he took the nozzle away, and in so doing he also took away an opportunity for her to learn.

This episode is particularly important for the questions it raises. The veteran was behaving in accord with the norms of traditional firefighter culture, and in so doing, he was also interfering with the professional development of a female newcomer. Was he motivated in part by sexual prejudice? If not, he presumably would have taken the nozzle from a male newcomer under the same circumstances. Would that newcomer, then, have fought to keep it? Would the story have played out differently if the two firefighters had been men, but of different races? Certainly there is room, under "cover" of apparently neutral practices like this one, to act out one's bigotry. Of greater import here, though, is the possibility that the practices themselves are not neutral, that in their effects, they do favor some groups over others. In this chapter we look closely at the field training process, at how it works, and for whom.

The Firefighter Apprentice

HE WHO HESITATES IS LOST

The norms of traditional field training dictate that whatever form the lesson takes—whether trial and error, direct instruction, or simply example—the initiative rests with the newcomer. The process of learning to be a firefighter is itself a test, not of knowledge or skill but of attitude: as in other occupations where on-the-job training is crucial, assertiveness is looked for and rewarded.[3] OFD newcomers quickly saw that it was an unusual veteran who would actively teach; more often, the veteran would sit back and watch you, without offering either assistance or instruction until the novice had tried something solo or had asked for help in a way that demonstrated interest and awareness.

On the scene this meant that if your role happened to be central—such as being on the nozzle or ventilating a roof during a fire—and your performance wasn't up to par, you might well have the task taken away from you. Alternatively, if the role were less important, you would be permitted to work at it incorrectly for an extended time before help was offered. In either case, active coaching would be unusual. Similarly, with respect to probationary drills and exercises in the station, newcomers were supposed to make things happen.

An apt newcomer would be prepared for this environment, and ideally he or she would find the dominant mode of training not only familiar but also entirely appropriate. Frank's attitude, exemplary in this regard, was typical of the most traditional of the white and Hispanic men: "And the way I see it, it's my responsibility to ask to do the drills, and if they say no or whatever, then that's on them. But it's not their deal to come see what I have to do. Some of 'em will. But others will sit back and see what you do with your day. I haven't had any problems, though, gettin' people to help me. You just have to show 'em that you're interested and that you wanna learn something and . . . the next thing you know, you get more than you ever expected. . . . You show 'em that you're ambitious and you want to learn, they'll be more than happy to [help]—but you gotta show 'em that. They're not gonna come up and say, 'Hey, I'm gonna teach you this.' "

Not all male newcomers were so uncritical of the veterans' stand-back-and-watch-you approach, but most were at least familiar with the basic process and able to get from it what they needed. For the women, though, the veterans' posture was generally unfamiliar, and they sometimes found it puzzling or annoying. The women also had to wonder at times if the lack of coaching reflected a lack of support or interest in them as firefighters. When one reviews Paula's case from the beginning of this chapter, it is important to remember that the tradition of fighting over the nozzle does not mean that it is always taken away from a new kid who isn't performing. The aggressive response to Paula's hesitation could happen either out of "tradition" *or* because someone wanted to discourage her through such action.

Marianne had just such questions about an overhaul incident in which she'd been told to "take out the floor" of a burned building. Uncomfortable with axe work—as were many newcomers—she had a hard time with the job, and her coworkers let her exhaust herself before someone finally told her how to do it. She was angry that the veterans withheld instructions, though when I told her that a white male lieutenant had shared a similar story with me, she realized the unhelpful behavior hadn't necessarily been targeted at her because of her sex. In a setting where the women are constantly reminded of their shortcomings and alien status, it becomes difficult for them to tell when they're being treated like everyone else, particularly when that treatment reflects an unfamiliar style.

DON'T LET THE VETS GET YOU DOWN

Playing the role of apprentice, like proving oneself, required the ability to put oneself forward, make mistakes, and take harsh criticism in stride. Though everyone wants to avoid major mistakes in order to build a good reputation, no career is error free. The willingness and ability to risk making mistakes and to learn from them without being discouraged distinguishes successful from less successful students.

This wasn't so hard for OFD newcomers who were self-confident, forgiving of themselves, philosophical about mistakes and criticism, and able to stand up to veteran abuse.[4] Frank said every call could be a learning experience if you put yourself forward, applied what you knew, made mistakes, and took your lumps. He said he didn't mind if someone pulled him aside and suggested a different way: "That's great, 'cause that's how I'm gonna learn." Most of the time, he maintained, the comments were constructive. "You know, it's not like they said, 'You dumb fool! What the hell's the matter with you, you stupid—!' You know, they won't do that. They'll say, 'Hey, this is the way we should've done that,' you know, 'get yourself hurt that way, or wipe yourself out.' " But if someone *did* go too far, you just had to let them know. When Frank had an officer scream at him, he shrugged it off or even screamed back, as he did once when the hose got stuck while he was attacking a house fire. "And usually an officer'll grab the hose and help you . . . move it, you know, advance it. And I'm yankin' the son of—and he's yelling at me, 'Get in there! Protect the—!' You know, 'We're gonna lose her,' or something. I can't remember what the hell he's doin'. But he's *yellin'*, and I just turned around—'Can't get the fuckin' hose!' You know, he's barkin' up my ass." Frank laughed as he recounted the incident. "Anyways, you know, it was no big deal after. He goes, 'Way to go, standin' up for yourself!' "

What's notable in Frank's stories is his comfort with himself and the environment: most of the time things work fine, and when they don't, you do what you need to do and don't worry about it afterward. Tony expressed a similar philosophy and summarized the attitudes of most men when he said he'd advise a newcomer to be "hard on yourself and gentle at the same time." For him, being watched and critiqued was helpful; he not only respected his crews, but he also assumed "a position where I don't let a lot of things bother me. . . . And a lot of times I don't care what people think, as long as I know the goal I'm tryin' to reach."

Andy elaborated by repeating a relative's advice: " 'There's gonna be good days and there's gonna be bad days.' . . . You're gonna have days where you're gonna leave and you're gonna go, 'God, there isn't one thing I did yesterday that was worth a shit.' . . . And then you'll have days where you just go, 'God, this is just the greatest job.' " Andy added that you had to remember not to take personally the things people said either to you or about you. "I always think that if somebody's sayin' somethin' shitty about me, hey, maybe they got somethin' wrong with them, that they're tryin' to work out. Maybe they feel like they need to do this. Whatever. . . . It's personalities."

These white and Hispanic men were familiar with the environment and confident of their own abilities. Hugh Thompson, a black man, was more of a novice and less comfortable, but he also emphasized the importance of not getting hung up on your mistakes and the criticisms of crew members. "Some people are a lot more cruel than others, and . . . I've made some mistakes where people were out to hang me . . . but the next shift, they may talk about it or whatever, but then you just kinda realize, you know, life goes on, so. I think some people have a problem gettin' hung up on it, you know, and they really think that people are judgin' 'em forever based on that, and they don't really concentrate on progressin' past it."

Men as diverse as Frank, Andy, Tony, and Hugh all had enough self-esteem to withstand the seemingly inevitable battering that came with field training. For less secure newcomers—women, especially—the trials of apprenticeship took a much greater toll. Marianne spoke vehemently about both the need to take chances and her own extreme discomfort in doing so when the environment felt unsupportive. Reflecting her experience, the advice she'd give to newcomers wasn't "life goes on" or "it's the other guy's problem," it was "give up your self-respect":

> Take the initiative. Be willing to make the mistakes. Just kind of
> resign yourself to the fact that you could quite possibly keep this job
> for a number of years until you've made most of the major mistakes
> and are not making them anymore. Especially someone who has no
> firefighting background. You're coming into a situation where this is a
> different type of life. This is nothing that you're familiar with. And
> give up your self-respect—you don't have any. And it's really hard if
> you have some. You know, if you have feelings and you have pride—
> that's the biggest issue for me. There's times when I've almost taken a
> swing at somebody, just because they'll make me look like a fuckin'
> asshole. You know, if you've got pride, this job's gonna be tough for
> the first couple of years.

Marianne understood quite clearly that her own sensitivity made it harder for her to develop as a firefighter, but this understanding didn't make it any easier to succeed.

> [My] weakness would probably be sometimes not doing something
> because I don't want to fail at it. 'Cause not all the time am I willing—
> you know, if I think I can get away with it, and I'm not feeling like it,
> maybe I won't do something that'll make me look stupid in front of a
> lot of people. . . . We had a fire the last shift, and I was doing some
> overhaul, and I had a chance to get in some axe work, but it was in
> front of a crew that I had never worked with before, and so if I was
> gonna make a mistake, I didn't want to do it in front of these people. I
> didn't know 'em, and so I kinda blew it off, and you know, I shouldn't
> have. I should've just bit the bullet and said "Fuck it, you gotta learn."

So [chuckles] I'm kinda eatin' myself up about that. You know, I need to learn to let this stuff go—OK, you didn't do it that time, you do it the next time.

Marianne's remarks reveal just how much of a handicap any sense of insecurity can be for a newcomer in field training and how either insecurity or confidence is self-reinforcing. In doing the work, firefighters learn both the techniques of their trade and the critical lesson of their own capacity. The sooner a firefighter gains experience, particularly in fighting structure fires, the sooner she can believe in herself; and when she believes in herself it becomes less important what others think. Caring less about what others think in turn makes it easier to take the initiative required for both proving oneself and learning.

THE MORE YOU KNOW, THE BETTER YOU LEARN

Putting the initiative on newcomers advantages not only those with self-confidence but also those with relevant prior experience or knowledge. Paula might have been able to hang onto the nozzle if she had been an exceptionally assertive woman, but she wouldn't have needed so much bravado if she'd been a little more comfortable with the task itself, a comfort that comes with exposure.

In addition to increasing one's self-confidence, prior exposure is also a technical advantage in the learning process because it provides a framework for information processing. When asked about what and how they learned, most new OFD firefighters described a kind of self-instruction. Sometimes this meant reviewing calls in their minds, thinking about what had happened and what they might have done differently. Or it might mean watching and listening to the veterans (or to the paramedics if it was a medical call) and filing away what they saw or heard, perhaps using the information to stimulate a later conversation. Many newcomers commented on the unevenness of explicit instruction and the need to "pick up things" on their own. Although new firefighters sometimes gathered "nuggets" from the old-timers in the sharing of firefighting lore, they often had to hone their skills through unguided observation and self-critique[5]—for which a framework based on prior knowledge was extremely helpful.

Several men talked about how much could be learned by watching a good crew in action and seeing how they worked together without saying a word. But fires are chaotic events, and making sense of what you see requires a mental framework within which knowledge can be organized. Without that framework, learning is much more haphazard. For an inexperienced newcomer, such questions as "What could I have done differently?" or "Why did it happen this way?" had to be answered by the veterans, who weren't always accessible and interested and who might be inclined to harass you for your lack of knowledge. Leonard pointed out that the culture could be daunting to learners, saying, "This is a difficult job to ask for help. It's one of those jobs where people will let you screw up before they stop you. Just to see how far you'll take it."

The more experienced newcomers could answer the basic questions for themselves, and when faced with more difficult problems could demonstrate enough knowledge to induce the veterans to help them. Experienced new kids also got to do more, and do it earlier. Ray Montoya was on a roof cutting holes during a fire by his fourth month, while many of his classmates hadn't done so by the end of eighteen months' probation. As in the process of proving oneself, those with prior experience—generally, the traditional white and Hispanic men—could make the most rapid progress.

ACCESS TO OLD-TIMERS

These traditional newcomers also had at their disposal the resources available to those with strong social connections to the department. The son or younger brother of an OFD veteran would always have someone he could go to with a question, a mentor available for consultation and advice. Newcomers with respected family members in the department also often found veterans a bit more welcoming and inclined to help ("your dad helped me when I came in").

When Tony wanted to talk over his questions or concerns, he went to his uncle, an OFD lieutenant, who could help him learn from his experiences. In thinking about a difficult basement fire in which his crew had gotten separated, Tony had been impressed initially with the officer's aggressiveness, but after talking it over with his uncle, he realized he should have been more critical. "I discussed it with him later, and in hindsight I had a problem with what had happened, but at the time I saw nothing." His uncle told him that in a situation like that, an officer always keeps his team together and keeps an eye on them. "He kinda was upset, 'cause the officer shouldn't do that . . . and that's when I started kinda waking up a little bit." This discussion was a lesson in what to look for—or look out for—in an officer, and it provided Tony with the kind of insights that might have been harder to come by without a mentor.

Ray also had connections through friends and family members and he felt a warmth from the old-timers that few newcomers described. On his first day he worked with Captain Quinn, an unapproachable man reputed to be the department's best truck officer. While still in the academy, Ray had had an opportunity to work with Quinn at an overhaul. "I was very impressed by him; and then that first shift I worked with him, I'm studying and he says—he put his arm around me and he says, 'Come on, son, let me show you the truck.' And we spent a good hour, hour and a half, talking about the truck, and he said he was looking forward to working with me. So here is this old-timer from the old school, a well-respected officer in the department, takin' time out to show a new kid around. And I thought that was really nice."

Personal ties to the fire service did not guarantee a newcomer's success in field training, but they provided a significant advantage. At this point in the history of the fire service, the advantage belongs primarily to white and Hispanic men, although a growing number of African American men have older family members in the department. Women firefighters rarely have a close family connection to the department; traditional firefighters don't encourage their daughters to enter the profession. Women may have less immediate ties, however, and on occasion do benefit from these. The connection may offer a kind of protection—that is, women with relatives or close friends in the department may be tolerated more readily than other women—but they aren't welcomed the way a son or brother would be.

THE FEMALE "ADVANTAGE"

Though women tended not to fit the OFD community's expectations of newcomers, and the community's instructional style was itself foreign to the women, being female was not always disadvantageous. There were times when a veteran would go out of his way to help or train a woman, perhaps in part to compensate for the perceived mismatch between women's technical/social training and the requirements of the environment. Jane Macey noticed that although she was often ignored while a male classmate would be given attention, there were moments when an officer or engineer would take her "under his wing." At those times she sensed that "some of the guys are more willing to talk to me and help me than they are the guys." Marla sometimes heard comments about women's inability to do the job, but then she also met with encouragement as well, and reflected, "You know, I feel that some of *that* is because I'm a woman, that the officers are makin' an effort to be encouraging and be supportive, and to make sure that I'm getting this experience that I need, and keeping up with the drills that I need to do, and keeping up with learning what I need to learn." And Marianne commented that the additional scrutiny she received at one station was sometimes beneficial because it meant extra training.

This perception was shared by some men. John, for example, noticed that being stationed with a woman from his class meant that "I can become quite invisible when she's in the room. Being the pretty little girl, I think, she attracts a lot of attention. That's got its blessings and its menaces. She's had more coaching from the others than I have had. I think they expect a little bit—not so much expect, but take for granted—that I will know things she does not." Some veterans also recalled with amusement that certain of the most vocal opponents of women in the fire service "fell all over themselves" to help the first women firefighters.

It is important to put this special treatment in perspective. First, it was not the rule and certainly not something that the women could count on. Second, and perhaps more to the point, the treatment is chivalrous and not equal: it reflects the veterans' own social conditioning, which is to treat women as "ladies" rather than peers. One captain displayed this kind of feeling—and vividly illustrated the problem—when he said he couldn't understand all the confusion about what constituted appropriate behavior around women firefighters: "You just act as you would if your mother or wife were visiting." He thought it was fine for women to be firefighters if they didn't mind the work, but he wouldn't want his wife and daughter subjected to the kinds of traumatic conditions that firefighters frequently encounter. It was his job to protect the women in his life from such things.

When the motive for assisting a woman is chivalrous rather than collegial, the women most likely to benefit are young, attractive, feminine (to a degree), and probably white. A black woman veteran described this kind of assistance as the "Miss Scarlett thing," in which male firefighters, both black and white, would go out of their way at times to help a white woman, sometimes stepping on a black woman in the process. When John spoke of the attention his female classmate received from the veterans at their station, he referred specifically to her feminine appeal, and he wasn't the only one to make this kind of observation. In addition, this kind of attention paid to women can be irritating to the men who observe it and further divide them from their female coworkers. The occasional assistance women received because of their sex, then, as helpful as it might have been in the moment to an individual woman, tended to heighten rather than diminish the importance of gender and may have worked to the disadvantage of women as a group.

The Effect of the Crew

We can see from the experience of the OFD newcomers that in most respects, firefighter field training follows an apprenticeship model in which testing is as common as teaching, a model that assumes self-confidence and assertiveness in newcomers, builds on their prior exposure to the community and its practices, and advantages those with personal ties to members of the community.[6] Because these are not unrelated, idiosyncratic features but qualities associated with certain cultural (race and gender) backgrounds, this form of apprenticeship systematically advantages some groups over others. Traditional newcomers (white and Hispanic men with ties to the fire service) are clearly much better positioned to take advantage of the standard apprenticeship process than are those who lack experience or connections (most black men) or are extremely uncertain about their place in the fire service (most women).

In addition, the relationship between newcomer and veterans, which varies with race and gender, can have a decisive effect on the novice's professional development, though it is often obscured by the focus on newcomer initiative. Despite the requirements of a general probationary plan that applied to all new firefighters, veteran OFD crew members and officers exercised considerable discretion over the newcomers' development, through variation in task assignments, instruction, and moral support. Although some veterans were accessible and even-handed instructors, many were not. As a result, the benefits of field training were unevenly distributed, often widening the skill gap between novices.

The influence of veterans was apparent in both the mastery of technical skills and the development of firefighter character, including the matter of confidence. Firefighting is a performance job in which the ability to act the part is central; competence includes a posture of assertiveness and self-confidence. Though we may think of such qualities as inherent in individuals, they can be profoundly situational: a newcomer's self-assuredness reflects his relationship with his coworkers, including the faith he has in their eventual acceptance of him. Traditional firefighter culture "tests" for such qualities in many ways, but veterans also take an active hand in building the newcomer's self-confidence by conveying a sense of trust in him, letting him know that "we know you can do it," and giving him the necessary opportunity and support.

GETTING THE PRACTICE THAT MAKES PERFECT

The OFD newcomers' field training experience reveals that, while all new firefighters had their station preferences, the variation in crew styles was far more problematic for some newcomers than others. Self-confident, experienced traditionalists maintained that a new firefighter made his *own* opportunities to learn and could do so in any station with a reasonable level of activity. But the least traditional newcomers—particularly some black men and all women— were sensitive to how the different levels of openness, support, and communication skills found in different stations could affect the success of one's training.

Traditional white and Hispanic men preferred placements with the most experienced, highly skilled crews—working with these veterans meant learning from "the best." A favorite spot among the traditionalists was Station 112, known for the incredibly smooth, tight quality of its senior crews. But other, somewhat less experienced newcomers, while they might respect the veterans at 112 for their knowledge, were less sure that these men were the best trainers. Qualifying a classmate's enthusiasm for this station, Stanley Okada commented that "as a new person in that situation, you feel like you're the odd link in a fine-tuned chain." Though he admired the crews at 112, Stanley was always a little uneasy there; they might have a lot to offer, but most of them weren't really interested in seeking out the new kid for instruction. He contrasted these men to the crew on his shift at 122—another downtown, relatively senior station—where the engineer and officers approached him to ask which drills he wanted to do and everyone made it clear they were willing to help.

African American men tended to prefer the less senior, more racially diverse crews of the east end. At Station 103, for example, Tom Armstrong found that the crew seemed to develop confidence fairly quickly in their probationary firefighters and "just let us do what we're supposed to do." This, together with the competence of the crew, made for an advantageous learning situation. "It's just an attitude. They keep us sharp, they always drill us . . . asking questions. They'll take us out and let us drive. Last day they let me drive the truck around. So we're gettin' to do a lot of things here. It's because we have officers . . . like the captain, he's not scared to take chances. And then guys like Mulvaney and Johnson, they'll talk to the captain and say, 'Hey, let's let him do this, and let him do that.' "

Tom was inexperienced but relatively self-confident and comfortable with himself; newcomers with less self-assurance were even more sensitive to station differences. Men like Marcus Everett, another black man, found that there were times an officer or crew didn't trust you or wasn't interested in working with you, and it could be hard to get the practice you needed. Marcus felt that favoritism, sometimes racially motivated, shaped the informal aspects of probationary training, and he noted that in some places he had to ask repeatedly for certain kinds of training and assistance with drills that other people received more readily. In one station, he said, his repeated requests for tiller-training were ignored, while "outside people who aren't even a part of this department will even get the tillerin'."

His assertion was not that all white officers were less cooperative than all black officers, but that the system was far too informal and relied too heavily on interpersonal factors and luck. Marcus's observation was echoed by some other black men, including Hugh Thompson and Tom Armstrong, both of whom commented that it seemed "ridiculous" that the truck experience of new firefighters was so uneven; they didn't believe that such matters as whether and when a newcomer learned to tiller should be left to chance (or worse, to discrimination).

A PLACE TO BE A BEGINNER

The women noted even more dramatic differences in the quality of training by station.[7] They agreed with the black men that some crews took a more active interest in teaching and were more willing to see that the new kids got into the action, but they also were sensitive to the supportiveness of the learning environment. For the women, field training was most effective and enjoyable when veterans were encouraging, would share responsibility for the process, and offered active rather than passive guidance. In a sense, the women wanted places where it was acceptable to be a beginner, where learning the work was not just another way of proving yourself.

Tom Armstrong, a black man, had found the truck crew at Station 103 to be an unusually receptive group; for Laurinda Gibson, it was a negative contrast to the more encouraging atmosphere of Truck 116. Even if Laurinda had received the explicit opportunities to try things that Tom was given, which she hadn't, it wouldn't have been enough. For she also needed an environment in which she felt *comfortable* asserting herself, taking opportunities and chances:

> When I was on the truck at 103, I felt like I was *all* by myself. 'Cause those guys, I mean they are *fast*. They are really fast. . . . They know their job inside out. I mean so do these guys [at 116], but they wait around. They let me try things, and then . . . if I can't figure something out, then they do it. But I didn't get much hands-on there because [snaps fingers], I mean a snap of the finger. It's really gung ho. So I never felt like I was part of the team when I was on the truck. I always felt like if they need help, I guess they're gonna ask, [laughs] 'cause I don't know what they're doing. But they know how each other think and everything, which all *these* guys are in synch too, but they know that you have to learn. Of course, the captain kinda tells them, you know, "Let her try this, let her try that, let her do this." But that's partly my fault. I'm supposed to jump in and say, "I'll do that, I'll do that," but that's where my confidence isn't so high [laughs]. Bringing attention to myself [laughs] . . . I feel that I do that with certain people. I mean I'll just—I'll trip and stumble and fall, and I don't even care. . . . Here I'll jump in and do most anything. I mean I've done things I didn't do anywhere else. . . . Like I said, I do things, before they even called orders. Which I would have never done before I came here.

In talking about their officers and crews, the women mentioned with pleasure those who were "supportive" and "encouraging" of their efforts to learn, in contrast to the veterans who seemed to look for opportunities to belittle them. Certain crews established a positive learning environment in which it felt safer to take risks and make mistakes, where there was "no shame" attached to being a beginner. This difference in climate was far less of an issue for the men: when a man got "chewed out," he did his best to shrug it off by either viewing the incident as a learning experience or telling himself it was the other guy's problem. But to the women, abusive criticism was a message that it wasn't all right to make a mistake. Their initial reaction often was to internalize the criticism and question their own abilities—a counterproductive strategy but one in which women tend to be well versed.[8]

Elena felt a distinct difference between those stations where her every move was negatively scrutinized and those where it was all right to make a mistake in the process of learning. Carrie noted how important it could be to find a climate in which you could make mistakes and ask "dumb" questions. She learned most easily from those people who "give a lot more positive feedback than they do negative feedback, and when they give negative feedback, it's more in a tone . . . that tells me, 'Well, we do care about what happens to you' . . . givin' me more feedback as to how I can *fix* problems rather than just say 'This is messed up.' "

Working with a good crew in a busy house was not only a pleasant experience in itself, but it also had a lasting effect because it enabled a woman to take what she'd learned, including her self-confidence, into other more difficult settings. For Laurinda, working at 116 was a critical step in her development as a firefighter, "because working with them, as opposed to a couple other houses I've been to, they show confidence in you and make you feel like you can figure things out on your own. And they give you a chance to answer stuff. . . . They'll let us try out anything. If we're wrong, they'll tell us, but they won't harp on it. They won't bring it up a hundred times after we do something wrong."

A related distinction that women drew between good and bad learning environments was in the sense of responsibility that the officer and crew took for training. Though the women agreed with their male classmates that it was almost always *possible* to get a drill done or to obtain information by asking directly, they appreciated those veterans who didn't wait to be asked, who were motivated to take a more active role in the process. The women initiated drills and training activities as newcomers were expected to do, but they sometimes felt guilty or uncomfortable asking for time and attention, and were thankful when a veteran was easily approachable or—better yet—would initiate training without being asked. When Carrie would go by herself to look over the truck or engine, removing equipment and starting power tools, a crew member would usually join her for the reason that "they always want to come out and see . . . what you're doin' wrong." She found them "willing to do it, but you kinda have to prompt too much, and feel guilty about asking 'em to take time out" to share information. She would have preferred an environment where the veterans took a little more responsibility for the training rather than the onus always being on the newcomer to ask for it:

> Because, see, most people they'll just go in their rooms, sit down, shut the door, and it's like when you shut the door, what that means to me is "Don't come in, I'm busy," "I'm busy watching TV" or reading or sleeping or something. Or "I got paperwork" or something—that kind of thing. . . . There's been some stations I've gone to where I haven't really talked to some of the people at the stations at all, really—if they don't take an interest in what I'm doing. . . . [When they do take an interest] I don't feel like I'm taking away from their time by going and asking them, "Do you mind doing this with me?" . . . They should know their responsibility to do it, and then I go ask 'em. That's what I'd like to see.

Marianne agreed that a lack of interest from the old-timers made learning difficult. She felt the crew at 114 liked her well enough, but with perhaps one exception, "they just really were not that interested in training or teaching me anything. I mean we played around with the saws a couple of times, taking them apart and, you know, I'd have to chase after the guys, go in the kitchen and get 'em, you know, it's like 'It's your saw, do you want the fucking thing back together?' . . . it's just . . . almost the feeling that you think that they don't feel like it's worth their while to train you." These moments stood in unpleasant contrast to those occasions when officers and crew members did take an active role in the training process, as Carrie and Marla both found with an engineer at Station 116. Carrie explained that "I wouldn't have to ask him to show me how to pump the water or how to do pump tests and that kind of thing, he would say 'Let's do this.'" She said he was "tremendous" to work with, always wanting to show her things that she needed to know.

Valerie also found it frustrating that learning from the work was such a haphazard process, with minimal and generally quite informal post-incident instruction. The teach-yourself method worked fine for her in EMS calls, where her own theoretical knowledge gave her a basis for understanding what was happening and a structure for later self-assessment. But with respect to the firefighting, she was disappointed in the lack of follow-up. Without much prior training, it was harder for her to figure out on her own why things happened as they did, and what she could have done differently. Such information "is very valuable, and hard to get." By way of a counterexample she mentioned an officer to whom she'd complained about the lack of clarity in most information on pumps. He called her off-duty to recommend that she visit a local department where they had a two-stage pump that had been cut away and suggested that she call him to discuss it afterwards. Rather than spoon-feeding her, he "gave me the tools by which I could assume the responsibility for my own learning."

When an officer gave clear instructions at an incident, Marianne noted, things "just worked out really well." But when your officer simply disappeared without a word, "it was like, OK, so what now?" Being a newcomer at one of your first fires and really not knowing what to do was "a horrible feeling." As Laurinda said, "With guidance, it seems a lot easier to get something done. Somebody's telling you what to do instead of [you] just trying to figure it out on your own." At her first structure fire, she happened to be riding the truck, for which most newcomers were ill-prepared. Thankfully, she was accompanied by two helpful crew members, who "never left my side, the whole time." Their presence was critical because "I really didn't know what to do—I was just lost. And people were just runnin' around—chaos everywhere."

In summary, the women were seeking a nontraditional form of apprenticeship—one in which teaching came before testing. Finding a supportive crew was critical for the women's development as firefighters in three ways: (1) it reduced or eliminated the tension that made it hard for newcomers to practice and learn; (2) it signaled to the women that they could in fact be firefighters; and (3) it provided a model of firefighter identity to which the women could aspire.

Differing Images of the Good Firefighter

The process of apprenticeship achieves both skill development and identity transformation through practice, a practice that requires access to work and to elements of identity, but such access can be uneven. For many reasons, newcomers are not equally well positioned to engage in the work, either because they are denied opportunities or because they feel unable to take the stage before a hostile audience. Additionally, the traditional occupational identity—as reflected in dominant cultural norms and as enacted by most veterans—is not one that is equally attainable by, or even desirable to, all newcomers. What, then, did the apprenticeship process teach different newcomers about being a firefighter?

After twelve months in the field, each newcomer was asked, "Can you tell me about a firefighter, officer, or engineer that you particularly admire?" In responding, participants articulated the qualities they associated with a good firefighter and talked also about the kind of firefighter they themselves hoped to become. Their answers revealed striking and important distinctions between groups.

White and Hispanic men focused strongly on the performance of firefighting work, whether in the role of officer or firefighter. Several highlighted physical skill, admiring veterans who went at the work in a "nice and easy" manner, retaining their calm, but knowing the job so well and being so physically efficient that they could readily accomplish what they needed to do. As Glen put it, he wanted to be "a smooth worker," like a Michael Jordan who could make everything look easy. "That's kinda like the way I [describe] . . . a good firefighter, is he can just—you know, almost like he's not breakin' a sweat." Andy admired a veteran who made no unnecessary trips between the scene and the rig: he could take a look, see what was needed, grab it, and go, in part because his unusual size and strength allowed him to carry several heavy pieces of equipment at once. And Ray couldn't say enough about the physical skill of his favorite veteran, a man who was "an incredible worker" despite his many years with the department: "I have never seen anybody take out the side of a house with an axe as he did. Unbelievable! He was a machine! He knew exactly what to do. . . . I've never seen anything like that. . . . He was a surgeon."

Other key aspects of smooth performance for these men were encyclopedic knowledge of firefighting, familiarity with the tools, and an aggressive attitude toward the job. Tony's most respected officer was widely known to be capable but abrupt and occasionally very rude. Though Tony was himself much more mild-mannered and respectful of others, he excused the officer's personal shortcomings because he was such a "*great* firefighter." "I probably respect him a lot more than most of the other officers I've come across. . . . You can tell if somebody's dealin' with it [an emergency] well, just from their demeanor, their control, the respect that they gather. This particular officer is an outstanding firefighter. . . . He's one of the few officers that you were together as a team—you went in as a team, and he kept an eye on you the whole time. . . . Also very aggressive . . . loved to beat people into stills [calls] in their district." Tony described a fire they were called to in another company's district, at which they arrived first. The officer assessed the situation, a structure fire with people inside, and quickly gave his assignments for the attack and simultaneous rescue effort. It was a low-intensity fire at that stage, and they went in—without masks—and put it out. When the other company arrived, Tony thought to himself, "The party's over."

Asian American men tended to somewhat less traditional views, appreciating veterans who were capable but not so intense. George's favorite veteran was an exceptionally knowledgeable man who had happily remained a firefighter rather than fight the political battles seen as necessary to promote. At an incident, his demeanor was confident but relaxed: "his first motion is his two hands wavin' down like this, like 'Just relax, just slow down. We need to figure out what we need to do here.' And then . . . he takes over. The captain doesn't have to say anything to him, 'cause he's done it all before, and he takes over." Rodney, going a step further in highlighting attitude and perspective, appreciated veterans who didn't take the job too seriously and didn't get worked up over the issues—like women in the fire service—that often agitated other men.

In the context of this interview question, none of the white, Hispanic, or Asian American men said much about interpersonal qualities. By contrast, the black men, though they also admired knowledge, skill, and composure, looked for these in *combination* with teaching ability and a sense of respect for others, including the community. Tom cited the example of an engineer whom he admired not only because he was "so thorough" but also because he was "real patient with you. . . . He makes sure that when you're with him that you get somethin' from him. . . . There's a lotta guys that have a lotta knowledge about this job, but they don't have the temperament to teach a person that doesn't know." He compared his favorite lieutenant to a good coach, someone who could actually boost your confidence. Leonard made strikingly similar comments about the officer he admired: "I mean . . . when you go on a truck with Ronnie, you can learn anything. I don't care if you're just goin' off for a mailbox fire, you'll learn somethin'. . . . He's good with the communication part—'cause . . . there's a lotta guys you can learn things from, but they're not good at teaching. . . . And you got a lotta guys who know things, and they just don't tell nobody!"

While the more traditional newcomers talked about *firefighting* abilities, at least two black men mentioned their appreciation for officers who took *medical* calls seriously. Marcus enjoyed working with a particular captain in medical situations because this officer would "roll up his sleeves" and get into the incident, not separate himself from it. Another officer he admired for showing "genuine concern" for even the poorest of citizens; speaking of this man, who happened to be white, Marcus said, "I hate to bring in race, but I look at it like . . . this . . . to me, from my perspective, he's like a color-blind-type person. He does a job, and it seems like it's regardless of color. And I appreciate that about him, you know?"

Hugh also admired officers who treated all citizens with respect and who saw medical as well as fire calls as an important part of the job. He believed firefighters were there "to render a service," not to play the "smoke-eatin', axe-swingin', firefightin', macho" role to which many traditional firefighters apparently aspired. He identified with men who looked at the job "as a good way to improve your personal situation" and felt that "you should do it [your job] the best way you can, but you should also get somethin' in return."[9]

Several men—black, white, Hispanic—mentioned that the firefighters or officers they admired were "well respected" by others in the department, a sign that these individuals embodied generally valued qualities. But to Eddie, being respected was also a mark of dignity, a quality that he particularly admired. "I'll tell you," he said, "in this department, they base a lot on physical stature, but one of the guys I admire the most is Hank Lawson. . . . He's a black man, he's small, but that doesn't stop him. And no one makes small jokes to him. . . . There's a certain respect there. . . . He's so strong in other areas that . . . they can't use that. . . . I'd like to be just as knowledgeable, I'd like to be proficient as he is, I'd like to have the same confidence with this that he does." Hank was about to be promoted, and Eddie thought that it would be "a transition with respect, and no one second-guessin' that he should not be there, and I'd like to make that transition, I'd like to go and become an officer, and not have people try to undermine me or second-guess me and I think that comes with being confident in yourself and knowing what you're doin'." Eddie distinguished Hank from those veterans who built up their own self-confidence by diminishing others. If you were really a man of character and ability, he asserted, you didn't need to do that.

Interpersonal support and respect—themes largely absent from the comments of the white, Hispanic, and Asian American men, and present in the observations of some black men—dominated the responses of the women. *All* the women referred to interpersonal qualities in talking about veterans they admired, and they spoke more about attitude, toward both the job and other firefighters, than about knowledge and skill. When they did mention ability, it was often in conjunction with mentoring skill, as when Marla noted that she admired officers who were "helpful and supportive and encouraging" who also "know what they're talkin' about."

It wasn't simply that more considerate people were more enjoyable to work with, it was that supportiveness and receptivity had such a powerful effect on the women's ability to learn and develop self-confidence. When Carrie talked of a favorite engineer, she mentioned that he "*cares* about you and what you learn." Jane immediately thought of an exceptionally knowledgeable and motivated young veteran who "wanted to teach me everything." Elena described another young firefighter who "praises you when you've done something good. . . . And deep down, he's trying to help you out, he's not trying to hang you." If he saw something wrong, he'd pull her aside to make a suggestion, rather than embarrassing her in front of the rest of the crew. Finally, Laurinda enjoyed her whole crew because "they're just so open-minded that you're willing to try things that you wouldn't normally try." Her officer, in particular, was always positive and encouraging, and she admired his willingness to retain these qualities even in the face of aggressive, judgmental firefighter culture. In this context she told the story of Paula losing the nozzle to an impatient veteran and her officer's critical reaction. She admired him for that, she said; "Bill always seems to stand up for things he thinks are right, and he doesn't really care what anybody thinks."

As noted, the women talked a great deal more about attitude, both toward the job and toward other firefighters, than they did about knowledge and skill. In contrast to the traditional men, who admired an *aggressive* posture, the women seemed to appreciate a *conscientious* attitude. Most women singled out veterans who were "motivated" and who "knew when to take it seriously." Marla respected those who wanted to "work hard . . . do a good job . . . do it right and not just kick things under the carpet." And Valerie looked up to veterans who had retained a commitment to the job and a healthy perspective despite the years of exposure: "Somebody who has seen so much and has done so much and has not lost their compassion and has not lost their interest in the job. . . . I've talked before about the sense of alienation . . . of . . . missing a connection . . . but every once in a while I'll come across somebody and they'll just have that [real but not cynical] perspective, and it's an invaluable experience for me. . . . And these are people that I would follow into a fire in a second! Because they're not hotshots, they got nothin' to prove, they're who they are, and they're *good* at what they do."

Valerie's comments seem to reflect a more general feeling among the women: they clearly admired competence, but they saw it more as a matter of intelligence, levelheadedness, and strength of character than of bravado. In answer to the question about admirable veterans and their qualities, no women talked about toughness, aggressiveness, or physical strength and skill (though they occasionally mentioned these things in other contexts). Their emphasis on attitudes, mental ability, and social skills probably reflects both their own perceived strengths and limitations and their recognition that there is more to firefighting than brawn—that, as one of the more liberal chiefs was fond of saying, "you can't bench-press a fire out." They are less willing than some men to accept the traditional definition of a good firefighter and far less inclined to express the kind of hero worship that some men displayed. When Marianne was asked to name someone she admired, she initially couldn't come up with anyone. After a lengthy pause she mentioned a couple of people about whom she had mixed feelings although they were good at some things. Then she thought again and said: "No, there isn't anybody that I, that just strikes me as being like [pauses] the God of Fire or something. [Chuckles.] . . . And it would probably be easier for me also to identify with a woman firefighter who I thought was really good. But . . . I haven't really worked with the women so there would be no way for me to make that [call]—to judge how this person was—you know, [to say] 'Oh, wow, I want to be like her.' "

Group Differences and What They Reflect

To a considerable extent, these images represent the model of professional competence to which the newcomers aspire; in a few cases, individuals clarified that they admired someone they realized was unlike themselves, but for the most part they acknowledged that they aspired to the qualities they saw in the veterans they described. In this context, their varying answers most likely reflect different personal values as well as different perceptions of their own strengths and weaknesses.[10] With respect to the women in particular, an awareness of their own generally lesser size and strength, along with the higher value most women put on skill in personal relationships, could be expected to produce a very different set of aspirations. Similarly, given their backgrounds, it is not surprising that some black men noticed and approved of those officers who demonstrated respect for the citizens of Oakland and that they also admired veterans who were personally successful.

But most black men also highlighted the coaching capacity of the veterans in much the same way that the women did, pointing out that simply being knowledgeable wasn't enough: a veteran had to be able to communicate his knowledge in a way that facilitated a newcomer's own development. This parallel between the black men and the women, as contrasted with the comments of the white men in particular, probably reflects a common experience in their field training rather than similar prior values. Specifically, the supportive training attitudes of veterans were of greatest import to the black men and the women because these groups were both less well prepared to learn independently in this setting and were less assured of veteran interest and support.

It is also probable that the newcomers' differing levels of concern for respect influenced their responses. In the context of fire service history, white men are generally able to assume that they will not be excluded from the occupational community for their race and sex; if they can do the job and get along reasonably well, then they will pass the test. Black men, and even more, women of any color, who lack this assurance, are much more likely to be sensitive to their treatment by the veterans. In some cases, their sensitivity may be counterproductive or ill-founded, but in other cases it is quite reasonable. Such concerns influence their evaluations of other firefighters. If the white male veteran who was most admired by several white and Hispanic men is, as a black female veteran said of him, one of the most racist, sexist people in the department, he is unlikely to earn the admiration of black men and women.

As they neared the end of probation, OFD's 1-91 class members had very different ideas about their own identities as firefighters, as well as widely varying levels of exposure to certain important activities, including truck work, tillering, nozzle time, acting-officer assignments, and specialized training sessions. Defenders of traditional firefighter apprenticeship would say that anyone who has difficulty learning in this environment probably doesn't belong in the fire service, that the training norms are entirely appropriate because they select for those best qualified for the job. This process clearly favors some newcomers over others: it works best for the self-confident, aggressive, experienced, and well-connected. But the argument in favor of this model ignores the extent to which such qualifications are socially constructed, inside as well as outside the fire service.

Chapter 7

Becoming an Insider

*I think my probation's been probably as smooth as it
could be. . . . The only thing that I didn't think was good
is that I never was stationed anywhere to get the kind of
attention that some people have gotten because they were
stationed [in one place]. But you know, I haven't been
mistreated anywhere. . . . It's just a people game, and
your experience is gonna come from the people you're
around; how much they let you get involved. So you
know, you've gotta be just open to everybody. They may
not be open to you, but don't make it be your fault.*

—TOM ARMSTRONG

*A lot of times there were situations where you just didn't
know and no one was really tellin' you . . . [that] this is
the way things are done. And if no one's tellin' you, and
if it's an unwritten thing or you're expected to behave or
conform a certain way, I mean, unless you're a mind
reader, then you're not gonna know. So that adds stress.
And a lot of stress on this job is not the actual work itself,
it's I would say 90 percent is dealing with the other people
around you, that's where the stress comes from, and it's a
very, very mentally draining type of thing.*

—MARCUS EVERETT

As Tom said, it's just a people game; your career withers or flourishes according to the relationships you build. Social acceptance fosters professional development in many occupations,[1] but it is particularly critical in firefighting. From a recruit's first weeks in the academy, the support of others can mean the difference between passing and failing: classmates can assist someone—whispering reminders, taking up the slack, covering up when a mistake is made and before it's observed—or leave him hanging.[2] Problems of uneven social integration are even more prominent in the training and development process that takes place in the field, where so many opportunities for learning are discretionary. And social acceptance influences the quality of a firefighter's daily work experience directly. Any job is easier and more pleasant if done in the company of reasonably sympathetic coworkers, but when the job involves living with a close-knit group for twenty-four-hour periods it can be almost intolerable to be socially excluded.

Professional success can depend on the uncertainties of social acceptance even if impartial personnel policies are in place. But in addition, as the struggle for equal employment opportunity in the fire service demonstrates, it can be extremely difficult or even impossible to develop and implement reliable, non-discriminatory formal policies. The process of screening candidates for hire or promotion is far from scientific; when it results in significantly disparate impact, as has often been the case in firefighting, sorting out legitimate standards from improper discrimination is anything but straightforward.[3] It is hard to see, then, how the goal of nondiscrimination can be reached in the absence of stronger progress on the informal level of intergroup relations and acceptance. In this chapter I focus explicitly on the how and why of social acceptance, beginning with the newcomers' early expectations and interactions and moving forward with them as they make or fail to make connections and gain acceptance.

Early Days, Expectations, and Strategies

New firefighters entered the field with different expectations about and different challenges to their social integration. Most men understood that getting along—after the initial period of slamming and practical jokes—would be relatively easy, and they didn't look for anything more in their first few months. In his initial station assignments, Steven Brandt, a white man, felt like an outsider whose presence was barely acknowledged by the old-timers. Over the first six months, with his growing exposure and skill he noticed a slight increase in acceptance, but he didn't expect more, believing that real acceptance "takes years. . . . I don't even worry about it. I make sure I don't sit in anybody's seat, and I don't insult anybody, propagate the rumors and what not. And that other stuff, it'll come down the road."

Leonard Bentley, a black man, agreed; he described the senior veterans at 112 as forming a tight huddle when they saw the new kid coming. "And that's just the way it is, I mean, eventually, in time when you prove yourself, and you know, you've stuck around—of course, when a station's as senior as this is, you have to stick around a *long* time. These guys'll probably retire by the time I get enough time in to be accepted as one of them." Other male newcomers agreed that "it just takes time" to fit in, and traditionalists even felt it was wrong to seek acceptance too early. As Frank Cross explained, the sense of being a complete team member early in your career would be "almost a deficit because now you're feelin' too comfortable . . . you know, you'll be playin' practical jokes with 'em when maybe you shouldn't be quite playin' those jokes yet. . . . And then it's time—when I see it, hey it's time for me to move to another station 'cause I'm gettin' too comfortable here."

As Frank's remarks suggest, even in these early assignments, a degree of familiarity was often attainable, either through personal ties to the department—an advantage enjoyed primarily by men with traditional backgrounds, or by assignment to crews with common interests—a benefit potentially available to all the men. After six months in the field, many men—white, Hispanic, black, and Asian American—felt that despite their status as learners, they were treated "like one of the guys" in the stations where they were best known. Growing acceptance was reflected in such things as inclusion in house social activities, a relaxation in the level of scrutiny, and the opportunity to get extra training. For those who experienced it, this acceptance came with time and exposure—"a lot of action and interaction" in which they showed their ability to act like good team members.

GOING ALONG TO GET ALONG

In theory, simply behaving in the "proper probie manner"—being pleasant and helpful, showing deference to others, and avoiding serious friction—should be enough to gain a newcomer a working tolerance if not the respect of veteran coworkers. And this strategy worked for the men. But for the women, even the most appropriate demeanor could not guarantee that they would meet with a basic level of tolerance in every house. Furthermore, the women faced a dilemma that did not confront the men: some measure of social integration was essential, but at the same time, the wrong kind of social assimilation could become a kind of trap, a substitute for professional acceptance. In short, they had to play along in much the same way the men did, but the cost was often higher and the reward less certain.

Though all newcomers were expected to keep their opinions to themselves, doing so could be most uncomfortable when the talk was racist, sexist, or homophobic—especially if one happened to be a member of the group being slandered, a common experience among the women. Speaking up could alienate you from the group, but not saying anything felt to some women like a violation of one's principles.

Marianne Grant believed that the women and minorities assigned to her station were selected on the basis of their ability to "blend in and not really be distinct people." Though she had strong feelings about the social atmosphere of this station, she planned to keep those feelings to herself at least during probation because to do otherwise wouldn't be worth the hostility she

would evoke: "They could make my life hell here." By keeping quiet and doing her best to get along, she might earn enough acceptance to have the veterans take an interest in working with and training her. "They're all very
friendly to me and very nice, and I think that they do like me at a certain
level. They know that they have to have a woman at the station, and I think
that they feel that I can get along all right, and that's really all they're looking for." Marianne recognized what the cost would be of making her opinions
known, but she also felt uncomfortable holding back. "Some of the things that
I hear these guys say are really just appalling. And nobody would ever say that
in another work environment and get away with it." As long as the comments
were general rather than personal, she remained silent, but she feared that
this would be confused with consent. She had seen women who "went along"
by "trying to play into it" and was deeply bothered by this, but sometimes wondered if "maybe I'm just as bad because I'm not saying anything at all."

In certain situations and for some women, the price of basic acceptance
didn't seem so great. A woman like Laurinda Gibson, for example, was less
offended than Marianne and chose to see her own behavior not as a compromise, but rather as the positive attitude that new kids were expected to display. She also came to interpret her own ability to get along as a significant
part of her own job performance and observed that women firefighters were
often judged on this basis. When asked about good women firefighters, she
responded:

> I haven't worked with that many women, but I can say that as far as
> personalities go, I've noticed the women that have gotten along have
> been—like I said, the ones without chips on their shoulders, like Liz
> Cahill, and April Hadley, and . . . Allison Banks—people just get
> along with them really good, and you never really hear any bad stuff
> about 'em. And I think as far as how they act at fires, I don't really
> know anything about that, [because] you usually don't see that many
> women when you're on a shift, unless you go to a class or somethin',
> but as far as firefighting goes, you never hear anybody sayin', "Oh,
> yeah—she was great at that fire! She, you know—"
> C: Kicked ass.
>   Yeah, you never hear that, and I don't think I ever will! [Laughs.]
> So, I think attitude is the big thing.

Laurinda explained that in bull sessions after a fire "usually you hear about
who the good firemen are. Then on the other hand, you hear positive things
about women like, 'Oh, she gets along great with her crew,' and stuff like that."

There is no question that an indulgent or easygoing attitude could enhance a woman's ability to get along with coworkers. But Laurinda's remarks
clearly reveal the difficulty: that women would be judged on the basis of friend-

liness rather than competence. Elena Cochrane's case is an illlustration; she looked to interpersonal success to balance her insecurity about her firefighting abilities. At a high-rise fire she ran into a familiar crew and accompanied one veteran on a search of the building. Uncomfortable with the task, she just held onto him and felt "sure I was nothin' but a nuisance to him." But when they returned to the street, she was delighted with his friendliness. "Wally went up to all the guys here [her current crew] and he goes, 'You takin' care of my girl?' You know, 'You takin' care of her?' And they're like, 'Oh, get on! She's ours now!' " She laughed. "But anyways, that made me feel good, 'cause Wally—there's quite a few women that he don't care about, and he lets people know about it! So I'm fortunate that, you know, that he feels that way."

But even Elena, a woman who worked hard to be liked, still understood that her acceptance was limited and unreliable, and the experience of women like Elena illustrates how social acceptance could be a substitute for more serious acceptance as coworkers. She openly acknowledged her own reservations:

> I mean you can get accepted a little bit, I still think it probably takes a long, long time. Like these guys ever since I wasn't gonna . . . be here anymore, everyone in their own way has gone, "Oh, it's really too bad—you do good here, you fit in well, we feel comfortable with you here" . . . but see, then again, I know not to trust 'em too much. . . . What I feel is, you know, Nancy—she was here for a while—she had trouble here. . . . They really didn't like her . . . and so now, Marie's coming here . . . and you know, she's . . . gay. . . . [And] I think these people don't really approve . . . and so . . . so that's why they want me to stay, because they figure—they all know that the chief wants them to have a woman here. I'm just the lesser of the two evils! [Laughs.] It's not like it's me . . .

These descriptions illustrate that the experience of social acceptance could be circumscribed for women in two important ways. First, it was often grudging and untrustworthy; and second, it could become a substitute for serious acceptance of women as contributing team members. Women often heard and saw other women firefighters evaluated in terms of their social skills, and in some cases they adopted these standards for themselves. In doing so, they were tacitly acknowledging the inability of women to be taken seriously as firefighters.

It should be noted that although a problematic kind of acceptance was the rule for women, there were exceptions, times when a particular woman would establish a good working relationship with a particular crew. At Station 113, Valerie Dickinson felt like a "viable, necessary part of the team," teased by her crew but also appreciated as a contributing coworker. When a relationship like this could be established—through a combination of the crew's receptivity and a woman's conscientious effort to cooperate—it not only made the immediate job more rewarding, but it could ease the burden of work-ing in colder, more hostile environments.

DEALING WITH HOSTILITY

Women were by no means the only newcomers to encounter animosity; most if not all new firefighters at one time or another confronted some kind of hos-tility, from being pointedly ignored to being verbally attacked. But the mean-ing of such behaviors was subject to varying interpretations according to race and gender.

Traditional newcomers, particularly among the white and Hispanic men, tended to interpret episodes of unwelcomeness or open animosity as unusual or idiosyncratic, even pathological. If they felt it necessary, such men were capable of standing up for themselves and had little hesitation about doing so. Resistance would be expressed in response not to the standard razzing by senior veterans, but to what felt like unwarranted harassment by less respected coworkers, as when a particularly difficult veteran yelled at Tony Escobar for no good reason, and Tony decided he'd had it:

> That was it. . . . I'd had my limit. I just looked at him, I said, "Who the fuck are you talking to?" Excuse my language. And he just, he just looked at me, he goes, "What!?" And I said, "Who the blank are you talkin' to?" And then he came, just steamin' out, and like runnin' at me like he wanted to fight. . . . And he's just yellin' and screamin', "You blank blank new kids! I got ten years on this job! I tell you what to do, you do it!" And I'm talkin' about a firefighter here, this guy is not an officer. "I tell you what to do, you do it!" And I'm pretty much lookin' at this guy, and I'm not sayin' a whole lot at first 'cause I'm tryin' to analyze what's goin' on. . . . Am I gonna have to respond to this guy physically? . . . So then . . . I told the guy, I said, "Look, I don't care who you are, you don't talk to me that way."

Confident of his ability to be accepted virtually anywhere on the basis of his abilities, Tony interpreted this kind of episode as an atypical, interpersonal difficulty and responded to it accordingly. The hostility was directed at him as an individual, not as a member of a group. But animosity that reflected an element of racism or, more commonly and openly, sexism could be more prob-lematic because of its potentially systemic nature.

Some African American men had been warned about racist attitudes ex-isting in some stations or held by some veterans and they would occasionally pick up racist "vibes," but most felt that the problem wasn't as great as it once had been. Nevertheless, at least two men felt their paths to acceptance at times seriously blocked by race. After enduring a difficult assignment in a tension-filled station, Marcus Everett had been pleased to be moved to a friendlier locale, where he began to build his self-confidence and hoped to establish a good working relationship with a crew. But even here, he said he couldn't feel like a full team member because of "things that [have] happened here that I overlook, but I can't keep overlookin', because I mean everybody sees it goin' on." He felt he was experiencing a "double standard" of treatment—denied training opportunities afforded others, grilled in a way that appeared unusual— but he only became convinced that race was behind these differences when fellow firefighters remarked on the problem.

Marcus acknowledged that being a probationary firefighter meant taking some ribbing, being the first to jump to do things, being tested. "But as far as the other part, about being black, it comes up in certain, like, haunting ways. It's like, we have a saying, 'being haunted by the plantation ghost.' So, heh, there's this ghost that comes in . . . and I say 'Oh, there it is,' and I try to ignore it, but it's there." He didn't feel racial prejudice from fellow firefighters, but he did see it in one or two officers, and those men could not only directly affect his training, but they could also foster an unwelcome climate within a station of otherwise accepting people.

For Hugh Thompson the problem was one of trust; he wasn't convinced that he could count on all white firefighters to make the same effort on his behalf that they might for a white brother. He knew some of the history of racial conflict in the department and was wary of its effects: "There's a lot of rednecks, a lot of racism in the department, a lot of personal conflicts, so I try to keep my personal conflicts to a minimum. I mean, everybody talks about how on the fireground, you put everything behind you, but a lot of these guys seem to be pretty unstable," he chuckled. "Like when you're thinkin' in terms of whether or not they'd have your back [covered], you don't know whether they're lookin' at it as they lose a firefighter or it would be just another nigger gone . . . big deal, it's just a black person or whatever. So you don't really know how they're lookin' at you."

Whether the hostility was racial/sexual or interpersonal, the newcomer was usually best off simply ignoring it, particularly if its expression was indirect. This strategy was appropriate for all newcomers, but particularly important for women and to some extent the men of color, who were likely to be seen as having "a chip on the shoulder" or branded as "political" (or in the case of women perhaps as "bitchy") if they objected to something like a derogatory remark or sexual innuendo. Even crew members who disapproved of the insult or innuendo would more readily close ranks around their own than sympathize openly with the offended outsider.

It could be hard for people who sensed that their exclusion was race- or sex-based to shrug off such prejudice. However, this strategy was—at least in terms of immediate social acceptance—more effective than confrontation, though the latter might at times be unavoidable.[4] Particularly for members of marginal groups, the ability to define a hostile episode, however inaccurately, as individual rather than racial or sexual and to remain open to connections with others eased social integration.

Not surprisingly, the two women who were most satisfied with the job reported hostility as the exception and supportiveness as the rule; this view reflected in part the way they chose to interpret coworker behaviors. Marla Harrison, a self-confident woman with an independent style, tended to interpret hostile episodes as the other person's problem; Laurinda saw them as the stuff all new kids get.

Marla noted that, although she had heard from some female classmates that "there's still a lotta shit going on," she hadn't experienced much of it herself and was "very thankful for the women who have been in the service for a long time because it's a much different story now. . . . My biggest complaint is if I feel somebody doesn't like me, you know, I haven't gotten any harassment—that I've noticed—I can't say what they're sayin' behind my back, but to my face or around me, from what I've heard . . . All my officers have been great, and very supportive and helpful." Of a man known to be hostile to women, who met her greetings with stony silence, she said, "I don't like people who do that, and I don't care what his reasons are, if it's because I'm a woman, or 'cause of what, I just think he's a rude shit!" Such encounters felt "personal" rather than systemic in the sense that "it feels like it was that particular person's viewpoint." Overall, Marla felt she'd received a high level of support and was able "to count the times" she'd been made to feel uncomfortable because of her sex. She couldn't be sure how people felt about *women*, but she thought they were accepting of *her*, believing her to be a good firefighter, a good learner, someone who was doing a good job.

Defining hostile encounters in a personal or idiosyncratic way—as opposed to seeing them as an expression of widespread sexual prejudice—which they may well have been—allowed a woman like Marla to remain receptive to other coworkers and to enjoy her work. Some African American men employed a similar strategy and felt it paid off in their relations with all coworkers. As Tom Armstrong explained, "there's some people that will not talk to you at all. Well, I don't get a vibe—I don't start dislikin' them because they don't talk to me. . . . [If] they talk to everybody else and they don't talk to me, then I think well, something's wrong. But if they're that way, don't let that be a problem for you. Just, you know, you just be yourself."

Eddie Gibbs felt his openness enabled him to enjoy the mentorship of both black and white officers: "I'm really versatile. . . . I kinda stay on the fence . . . I guess leanin' more toward the black side, [but] I don't separate myself from an individual. . . . I can get helped by a lotta different people, actually." He knew that he could be excluded for reasons of racial prejudice, but he didn't see much to be gained by dwelling on that possibility, and he tried to keep his energy focused on the things he could control. "I don't have control over your opinion, but my first impression . . . or what I'm tryin to get across to you—I have some control over that. . . . If a person has a prejudice toward me, hey, that's their shit, and they need to handle it."

Eddie, Marla, and Tom were not necessarily denying the existence of prejudice (though others did), but they were choosing not to emphasize it as a daily personal concern.[5] This approach would be naive and counterproductive if it lulled the individual into an unrealistic level of trust in others, which could happen, but in most cases, the strategy was successful.[6] It is worth noting that the strategy was most likely to succeed for people who had other things working in their favor, such as personal charm or attractiveness, exceptional skill, and connections.[7] Watching the probationary firefighters at a phase check, a female veteran commented that women like Marla and Laurinda received some "protection" as a result of nonsexual affiliations with respected veterans in the department,[8] which they both came by somewhat accidentally. She contrasted their experience to that of a female classmate who, lacking such protection, became a kind of magnet for hostility and responded to the environment in a relatively unforgiving way; in turn, her response had produced more harassment and alienation.

Making Connection

In their early months on the job, OFD newcomers concentrated on getting along well enough to obtain the essentials of training and achieve a tolerable working environment. But as time went by, many men began to move beyond this stage, to stronger interpersonal connections and a sense of belonging. Although some men had an easier time establishing themselves than others, in general, a sense of membership among the men was usually achievable *simply* given enough time with a crew. For the women, social connections were much more elusive, both because of differences in background and social style between the women and most veterans *and* because a defining aspect of firefighter solidarity was its masculinity.

From the outset it was clear that social interactions could occur much more readily between men (of any color) than between men and women. In addition to the relative exclusion of women from the hazing and practical joking that test and bond firefighters, male newcomers simply had much more in common with the veterans than did the female newcomers.[9] Even those men without personnel ties to the department were more likely than the

women to share veteran interests such as fishing, hunting, golf, and other outdoor activities, drinking in local nightclubs, and moonlighting work in the
trades.[10] And similar interests could provide a critical starting point for developing relationships with coworkers.

Casual conversation in the firehouse often covered sports, military experience, prior blue-collar work, and sex.[11] Probationary firefighters were usually quiet in their first months, but as the environment warmed up they began
to feel freer to contribute to the conversation, particularly if they could offer
something on a topic other than firefighting, about which they were presumed
to know nothing. But someone whose interests differed significantly from those
of the other crew members could have a hard time finding anything to contribute and would sit silently—as I sometimes did even in familiar houses—
through a two-hour dinner session. The kinds of conversational ploys that
might work effectively in a one-to-one interaction with a stranger—asking
questions and expressing an interest in the other's experiences—couldn't easily be used in the context of a boisterous group meal.[12]

A battalion chief told me that he had himself begun to understand this
problem when he found himself stationed with a group of much younger
firefighters. Their conversation at the dinner table—what he called the "fo-
cal point" of social activity in the house—consisted of a limited number of
topics in which he had no interest. Both the chief and the female probationary firefighter were quiet throughout the meal. Afterward, she would sit silently for a few minutes and then excuse herself. The others interpreted her
behavior as a sign that she didn't want to be part of the group, but the chief
could see that she simply had little in common with the rest of the crew and
no way to participate in the conversation. He understood, he said, because
he had come to feel the same way; the difference was that if he said nothing
or left the table there was no assumption about his motives.[13]

Common experiences, such as an interest in sports or past blue-collar
work, were more characteristic of male newcomers, but they could in theory
at least be shared by women. However, the important bond of maleness was
one from which the women were by definition excluded. This fundamental
boundary between "us" and "them" was communicated to most if not all of
the male firefighters very early in their field assignments, as they heard the
veterans disparage the women's skills, gossip about their personal lives, raise
questions about the women in the class, and test the loyalties and trustworthiness of the new men by making such comments. Eddie felt he was being
accepted by his crew when they expressed an interest in his background, talked
with him about something besides work, and would run an off-color joke by
him. "I don't think that you're accepted if they can't say certain things around
you." He specifically noted that this test would involve talk about the women,

"kind of like a trusting type of thing, to see what they can and can't say around me. . . . I think that's part of it. I think part of it is they want to see how *you* perceive the situation, if you're part of how they believe or not."

The men were all privy to conversations that wouldn't have occurred in the presence of women, and more than one probationary firefighter described the social environment of the firehouse as being like "fellas' night out." As one of the black men explained:

> It's funny—a lot of the guys—the older guys will say that they come to work to take a break from home. I can see how it gets to be that way, because—like, I was talkin' to one firefighter, and he was—well, he's a total womanizer, and he's married, but—[laughs] which it seems a lot of these guys are—but he was saying you know, "You can have problems at home and you can come to work and, and sit down with the guys and they can make you laugh and cheer you up, and at least you're away from the bullshit for twenty-four hours." So, it's kinda like fellas' night out.
> C: Yeah. I would think that having women in the fire stations would make it less appealing to people who are looking at it that way.
>   Yeah, . . . that's pretty much what it is, is breaking up the boys' club. You know—well, some—a lot of them really feel that women can't do the job as well, but I think the majority of it is, is more so the socializing, you know. They can't do the *macho* stuff anymore.

The gendering of firefighter identity is also evident in the relationship between firefighters and civilians: male firefighters hold an appeal for the opposite sex for which there is no female analogy. This asymmetry produces a role—that of the Don Juan—that can be shared by male newcomers and veterans but from which female newcomers are by definition excluded.[14] A story from Hugh's early experience illustrates how this process can work to the male newcomer's advantage: "Like at 105, I call it the womanizing station. We were out getting ice cream one day—all of us got phone numbers—it was pretty funny. We were at the ice cream parlor, and I got a phone number first—'Way to go, new kid!' . . . I went from 'new kid' to 'Hugh.' "

At the same time, encounters between female civilians and male firefighters can put female firefighters in a strange position, as became clear to me in one of my firehouse visits. On this occasion, the crew members, including one woman, were sitting around the kitchen table when a very dressed-up woman entered the station and asked for one of the firefighters by name. He happened to be sitting in the room but was on the phone. When he got off he looked at her blankly, and she asked with some impatience if he didn't recognize her. It became clear during their conversation that he had flirted with this woman on the street at some point and had encouraged her to visit the firehouse. She became increasingly embarrassed by the encounter and turned to leave, whereupon the firefighter jumped up and followed her out of the room. I asked the rest of the crew how often this kind of thing happened and was given the half-joking response, "every other shift." The young woman firefighter present treated the encounter in the manner of a sister indulging a favored brother, which she was able to do in the context of her rapport with this particular crew. Another woman firefighter, however, might well have felt a sympathy for the visitor and an emotional distance from the men in the room. In many small ways, women who accommodated to the male culture had to distinguish themselves from other women, as the young female firefighter in this case was doing.[15]

Her model of accommodation was to play the role of the sister, one of the more effective strategies for women seeking acceptance in nontraditional environments.[16] Particularly in a setting like the firehouse, from which women have been so conspicuously absent, there are no real models of male-female peer relationships. Though some women firefighters have worked previously in male-dominated or mixed settings, most male veterans have had extremely limited exposure to women as coworkers. Their models for male-female interaction are taken from the social sphere, in relationships to lovers, wives, daughters, mothers, sisters. Of these, the most favorable roles for women firefighters are those of the sister (usually "kid sister") or daughter, neither of which necessarily reflects a relationship of equality. Furthermore, such roles are available only to those women, primarily attractive and youthful in appearance and personality, that men could imagine having as sisters or daughters. Of course, male newcomers may also assume familial roles in relationship to other firefighters, but they are less restricted in their choice of roles; they can be "buddies," for example, and their familial roles are either equal (brothers) or transitional (the son will inherit the father's position).[17]

For all these reasons, it was clearly easier for male newcomers than female newcomers to affiliate with their crews. At the same time, the men may also have looked for less in these relationships than did some women. One metaphor for the firehouse crew is that of a "team," a particular form of social relationship with which men tend to be more familiar than women.[18] In team relationships, a bond is created through joint participation in external events or activities rather than primarily through direct interpersonal connection. Team members can enjoy each other, feel comfortable together, and have a sense of group cohesiveness without necessarily having much in common as individuals. People who are comfortable with this type of social interaction are more likely to feel at home in the fire station than are people who look for a stronger interpersonal connection. Consider the different ways in which Glen and Valerie described their most recent firehouse experiences: Glen was happy to "hang out" with the guys, while Valerie was frustrated by the lack of connection. When I asked Glen to compare the job to others he'd had, he said:

> Um, this job, I would, would think it would be more along the terms of a team, like a football team I was on, in high school. Where you practice, you train, you go to school together and stuff, and you go out together and have fun together and it's kinda like you hang out together. [Pauses.] Pretty much, I guess, like a professional team too— I've never played any pro ball or anything like that, but the same type of thing, where you kinda go on road trips together, and you're hangin' out together. [Pauses.] I'm sure there's a certain amount of hanging [criticizing others] they do amongst themselves, kidding around, the jokes. So that's kinda unique, and it's kinda, kinda nice.

He didn't find it hard to find things in common with other firefighters: "They always like to eat, they always like to go out and have a good time, and most of 'em either—there's a lot of 'em that aren't golfers, but there's always somebody that enjoys goin' campin' or somethin' or even if they don't do that, you end up runnin' across them socially at a retirement dinner or something like that. Everybody likes to tell stories and jokes and things."

By contrast, Valerie looked for a stronger personal connection and for serious conversation that was *about* something. The meal table was especially hard, she said. "It's kinda this time where you just sit there and you think about something else. . . . And the thing is because I'm still a social person, getting up and leaving . . . that's a drag, too." For women like Valerie, the quality of coworker relationships ultimately determined one's job satisfaction: the presence of personal rapport was not an "extra," as it was for most men, but a central, defining quality of the work experience. Marianne was somewhat more resigned in her attitude than was Valerie, perhaps expecting less, but she felt frustrated as well. She knew she got along fine with her crew, and they accepted her as the woman on the shift, but she felt they didn't really know her or accept her for who she was. "You know, the days are so long because there's just no sense of bonding with anyone. And that's—I mean there's nothing worse than going through twenty-four hours when you're just like—I have nobody I can say anything intelligent to. It's exhausting. It makes the day exhausting."

Not all the women expressed this sense of frustration with their lack of connection to crew members, nor did all the men seem satisfied with "bullshit friendships," as one man called them, but there were tendencies for the men and women to speak very differently about social relations in the firehouse. It would be surprising if this were not the case, given most men's preparation for this kind of environment (the team, the fraternity) and women's social-ization into a concern for relationship.[19]

It seems clear that people with a strong interpersonal orientation would be at something of a disadvantage in most firehouses, expecting more from the social setting and getting less than do their (mostly) male counterparts. On some level, there may also be a more severe judgment associated with women's lack of social success: because women are expected to be social, a woman who fails to make interpersonal connections is somehow less of a per-son; a man who doesn't make interpersonal connections is just being himself.

Patterns of Acceptance

Although probation lasts for eighteen months and its conclusion is an impor-tant moment of passage, the OFD newcomers had experienced a significant shift in the social environment by the end of their first twelve months. The difference was most apparent in the way the newcomers themselves felt about the prospect of being detailed to an unfamiliar station: where once this had been a cause of considerable anxiety for most of them, by the end of a year in the field they felt far more comfortable with themselves and far less intimi-dated by the veterans. The "unknown" had been reduced on both sides: new firefighters had a better sense of what to do at incidents and in the firehouse; and the crew would often know the new firefighter by reputation, prior con-tact, or both.

REPUTATION IS INDEED EVERYTHING

After a year in the field, a new kid was known, for better or worse. When he showed up at an unfamiliar house, people already had some sense of him, and for newcomers who felt that they had performed well, this was a comfort. Glen Jarvis was assigned to the east end after spending most of his early assignments in the other two battalions, but he wasn't concerned about starting over. "People know you from . . . [other firefighters] who've worked with you for a day, or seen you at a fire or somethin', so your name comes up. . . . When my name was up here to do the route out this way,[20] they were talkin' about, you know, 'Who's this guy?' 'What's he like?' 'Who's worked with him?'—that type of thing." If your reputation is decent, "you're more quickly accepted. It's like I said, well, about six months ago, when I said your reputation's just every-thing you have or all you have, really, in the department."

Most newcomers had taken to heart the advice they heard in the acad-emy that "you don't want a bad reputation." And many men felt that the grape-vine had worked in their favor: they had successfully proven themselves and were beginning to be accepted on the basis of their work. But there were occasions when they felt themselves unjustly hindered by the gossip mill, sometimes for reasons that had nothing to do with their own performance. As Marcus explained, if someone didn't like you, he would spread the word to his friends at your next station assignment. "You know, they've already told people, 'Well, this guy—'. They've already painted a picture, so people have preconceived ideas about you before you get here." This feature of fire department life made it critical that a new firefighter work to get along with as many people as possible and that he choose his battles carefully. If you had to alienate someone, best that it be a person who was generally disliked or not trusted. Similarly, if you were friendly with someone who was disliked, that association could get in the way of your being accepted by others.

The women were also aware of the need to establish good reputations and made an effort to do what was necessary. But they didn't cite positive reputational effects at this point as often as the men did, and, when they did so, they reported having reputations as hard workers or congenial crew members, not as capable firefighters. Their increasing comfort in the field had less to do with being accepted by others than with a greater sense of self-confidence. As Valerie put it,

> I would say the biggest change has happened within myself more than
> anything else. . . . Comin' out of the drill tower, you know *nothing*!
> You know *zip*! You don't have any sense of whether you're ever gonna
> be a contributing member. You just feel that you're nothing but a
> liability, you end up being made to feel like you're nothing but a
> liability. And after a while, you spend some time working, then you
> start to see that you really can have some kind of an effect. . . . And
> you start getting this sense that I can do my job and . . . it's OK for me
> to be here without having to run around like a chicken with my head
> cut off and trying to fit in . . . or trying to play the game according to
> all these implicit rules! And then you start going, well, I mean, "To
> hell with that shit!"

Valerie was describing a kind of self-acceptance essential to all new firefighters, but her tone suggested that she had achieved it in spite of her surroundings, not as a result of becoming more at home in them.

MAKIN' BETTER MOVES

Part of being accepted was proving yourself as a firefighter, but another part was learning how to handle yourself around the firehouse. A newcomer's reputation precedes him and unquestionably affects his entry to an unfamiliar station; but the crew's reaction could also be influenced by the new kid's own sense of ease in the firehouse. After bouncing around the east end for a while, Tony grew accustomed to entering new stations: "And you kinda just learn a little, uh, rapport on how to just go in and present yourself. Actually, the transition is much smoother and faster now. . . . [Like] the first two days I was here [at 122], as I walked in, I was automatically talkin' to people, and I was . . . jokin' around . . . right off the bat. Whereas before, it was more like just quiet, get the feel of things, and now it's you know, 'Here I am, I'm gonna do my job, this is who I am, I'm here to have a good time, too.' "

George also believed that much of the veterans' increased acceptance and diminished scrutiny was probably related to the newcomers' improved understanding of how to act around the firehouse. "*I* know how to fit in a lot better. Whereas when you're first in the firehouses, you're not quite sure how to react to something, such as a phone ringing, or somethin' like that. Or you know, when to jump in and help and all this other stuff and so . . . maybe it's just because we're makin' better moves now, you know, that we get accepted much more like all the other firefighters."

MOVING TO THE INSIDE TRACK

Among the men, the quality of membership achieved by the end of the first year was in most cases primarily a function of how much time had been spent in any given station. Most men felt like team members when they worked with familiar crews and felt accepted as coworkers even in unfamiliar stations. They believed they had done what was required to prove themselves on the fireground and to get along in the stations, and for the most part these efforts had paid off.

Leonard Bentley, a black man, was able to spend much of his time in a limited number of stations, and by the time he'd been in the field a full year, was feeling very welcome and confident even at a station where he had once felt isolated and somewhat uncomfortable. "I'd say I'm inside. Everybody here, even on the other shifts, when they told me I was gonna be here, they came and shook my hand, and they trade with me and they do all kinds of stuff. . . . You know, it's like everyone's genuinely happy to have you there."

Of course, the men also had their preferences. Jonathan Lawrence, another black man, felt comfortable working anywhere, including those stations with a reputation for exclusivity, but he was happiest in the east end stations. Ray, a more traditional Hispanic man, preferred Station 112, one of the most senior houses, where he felt he was a team member. He explained that "where I'm coming from for that is, uh, Tony Mendes at dinner once told me, he said, 'There are firefighters and there are fire*men*.' He says, 'In the time that you've been here, you've become a fire*man*.' And that's what they call themselves. They're the fire*men*." Though he felt at home in this station, and the social expectations on the new kids had by this time relaxed some, he continued to maintain his new kid courtesy out of "respect, affection, and gratitude" for the veterans at 112.

Ray felt like an insider when the crew called him a "*fireman.*" Other signs of movement to insider status included being trusted with special tasks, being privy to private conversations, being included in house social activities, and being teased and joked with in a friendly way. Frank felt that having the veterans watch out for you—both on the fireground and in the house—was a simultaneous acknowledgment of your newcomer status *and* your acceptance: "I'm being accepted for my abilities, but . . . they're keepin' an eye on me 'cause they know that I'm gung-ho, and I can get myself in trouble just because of that. You know, I could get myself hurt, so they keep an eye on me for—just for that. . . . And that can be from opening my mouth at the wrong time, sittin' here at the dinner table, or you know, at a incident. But they watch out for it. So, yeah, and they wouldn't do that for everybody, so that is your way of being—you know you're on your way to being accepted."

Those men who were moved around a great deal didn't feel the same degree of comfort, but they did have confidence that acceptance would come fairly readily if they simply did what they were expected to do. Steven was bounced from one station to another and frequently had to reestablish himself; assigned to a route at twelve months, he said of entering new stations, "Well, it's still awkward, but . . . I feel confident that if I had to go work at 112 or 122 or somethin', they would give me shit for a while, and then I'd kick ass at the first structure fire, and then I'd get less shit. . . . It's not as nerve-wracking anymore. You know, you're definitely still an outsider, but I'm practiced at being an outsider now."

This feeling was expressed by the black as well as white men. Eddie, for example, felt he was "becoming a team member" in his current station assignment, but that his continual movement during probation had prevented him from developing a solid relationship with a crew. "I mean, the times I was there [in a given spot] . . . I felt like part of the crew, but I always knew I would have to pick up and leave because I wasn't a permanent person there." Though he was happier in some places than others, he hadn't really felt unwelcome anywhere.

In a few cases, men of color and especially the African American men expressed stronger reservations: either acceptance was simply not forthcoming in some stations, or perhaps its appearance couldn't be trusted. Among those who found a dramatic difference between stations was Marcus, who described a night-and-day difference between his first and second assignments: "I really felt like I was in a fishbowl for the first six months. I really felt like I was in a fishbowl. The first six months. And then that second six months . . . I think, like I say, I think it has something to do with being at . . . [a] station . . . [that] enabled me to relax, and the guys I worked with, you know, they told a lot of jokes and stuff, in fun. It was nothing like real pointed, you know what I mean? Acceptable, and it was a lot of fun, a lot of fun. And I felt more re- laxed, like I said. But the first six months I felt like I was in a fishbowl every day. And, and I was the only fish in the bowl."

Hugh felt welcome in most places but remarked on the coolness in the most traditional houses. "At pretty much all the stations I've worked at, with the exception of maybe one or two, I was pretty much goin' in feeling like I was a . . . [a full team member]. Um, some—a couple of houses make a point of makin' you feel like you're not part of the team, or reminding that you're not part of the team. . . . And . . . speaking in particular of Station 112—my background is nothing similar to anyone in that house, so you know, there's not much for us to—other than the job, and you know, maybe talk about women or whatnot—but there's not a whole lot for us to really bond on." Hugh also observed that in the peculiar social context of the firehouse, it wasn't always easy to gauge how well you were being received. "You never really know what people think of you," he said, "sometimes I'm kinda conscious of that." People could act like "buddies" to someone's face and then slam him behind his back. "I . . . get a lot less supervision, you know, people have told me that I'm doin' fine or I'm doin' good, or whatever, but a lot of people have differ- ent opinions and you don't always know what they're based on."

While men who had serious doubts about their status as team members were the exception, among the women it was unusual *not* to have such reser- vations. By the end of the first year, only two women had a strong sense of belonging, and, even for them, the quality of participation varied strongly by station. The rest were experiencing various degrees of uncertainty or dissatis- faction. Jane, in particular, was wondering how much longer she would stay with it. As good as the job was, it didn't seem worth the sacrifice she felt she was making in terms of her feelings and self-esteem. "I've been thinking about leaving. . . . I haven't been comfortable in this department from the begin- ning. I don't feel that women are welcome, I know women are tolerated, only because we have to be, but as one woman put it who's been in the depart- ment for five years, she said, 'You know, Jane, the doors are open for women here, but they're not welcome.' "

Marianne's response was more measured. She described significant differ- ences between crews in their level of openness—usually to women as a group (and sometimes to new people in general), but occasionally to an individual woman personally. Regardless of the reasons for the openness, this factor heavily influenced the quality of her experience.

Laurinda was the most positive. She'd had enough support to balance out her negative experiences and was very happy with her current placement. She reported with delight that her captain had asked to have her placed there and felt lucky to have found a home. "They just made me feel right at home the first day . . . [and] since I've been here, I've built a lot more confidence, and [now] it doesn't bother me to go other places anymore." Laurinda felt not only fortunate but proud of her ability to get along, and in looking back on her experience, she reconstructed her earlier difficulties as simply new-kid hazing and insisted that women were not treated any differently. "I think as far as the women go, I don't have a big chip on my shoulder, that's it. That's why I've gotten along here, I think. 'Cause I just act like I would around my brothers and my dad, and [it] seems to be pretty successful. Just—it seems like some people have the attitude that they're treated differently because of their sex . . . but it seems like a new person's a new person—and they're getting—everybody's getting treated the same it seems like."

By the end of probation two of the seven women in this study had left the department: one quit midway through probation because of dissatisfaction with her treatment, and the other was terminated at the end of probation for an infraction that some observers believed was no worse than the transgressions of many other firefighters.[21] This woman was reinstated some nine months later, as the outcome of a formal grievance procedure, but she was not part of the end-of-probation process described below.

Being Wanted

At the end of probation, all new firefighters were permitted to "bid" (along with veteran firefighters seeking reassignment) for open slots throughout the department. Assignments would be made primarily on the basis of seniority (in the case of classmates, on the basis of class ranking), subject to other departmental concerns such as a need for special skills in certain stations. In the past, house officers had influenced station assignments directly, but today their influence has become more informal.

Under traditional norms of courtesy, the newcomers in this group were expected to consult with a house officer before requesting a spot in his station, and to defer their request in cases where the officer and crew favored someone else who was interested in the spot. Those newcomers with familial ties to the department were aware of this system, but the informal protocol came as a surprise to other newcomers and was offensive to some, who felt that the assignment process should be by-the-book. Tom Armstrong felt it was enough to follow the formal rules; he shouldn't have to consult with house officers and didn't intend to do so. He said he wasn't "comfortable" with the informal protocol. "I think that's crap. I know that the one house put out a memo that if you wanted to put in, call the officer, and basically what he was doin' was tryin' to talk you out of coming. And I don't think that's right."

The mix of formal and informal systems produced considerable awkwardness in the bidding and assignment process for the 1-91 class, occasionally pitting friends against each other. Much of the time an officer and crew would favor a new firefighter already in their station on temporary assignment, and in at least one case, an officer specifically requested that a woman firefighter remain in a spot that had been requested by others. In two other cases, black male firefighters who had been in a particular station for some time were preferred over white women to whom the slot was potentially open. In one such case, a white woman acceded to the request of the black firefighter that she not bid for his slot, and she ended up in a station where she was poorly treated.

While it was not true in every case that men were preferred to women, most active recruitment was targeted at male rather than female firefighters, and the men also felt least constrained in their choice of stations. The great majority of them had felt accepted in most or all their assignments, and many had heard repeatedly that they'd be welcomed back. By contrast, the women felt accepted in a more limited number of stations and were wary of the treatment they would receive in others. Though some women were told it would be "fine" if they wanted to put in for their slots, active effort was apparently made on behalf of only the one woman mentioned above. Several men received invitations from more than one station to bid for their openings, but no woman reported such contacts. As Carrie put it, as a man, you'd have to be "really weak . . . a lump or an asshole for them to . . . pick a woman over you. And I think that's pretty much throughout the department."

Marianne's experience illustrates the problems some women encountered at the end of probation. She was stationed with a crew with whom she got along, but who had no commitment to training her or allowing her to try new things. When the opportunity came up to bid, she decided to put in for stations where she thought she would find more receptive crews, but because she'd been in her station for an extended period, she'd had little opportunity to develop the kind of rapport that might have made those other crews willing to have her. When she learned that she was supposed to defer to people already in those places if they were happy there and well liked, she realized she'd have a hard time getting what she needed. It seemed that every time she mentioned a spot she might want to bid for, it turned out there was someone to whom she should defer: "They wanted to stay in every place that I wanted to put in. So . . . I thought it was ridiculous and so I said it was bullshit. And I still think it is kinda bullshit. . . . 'Cause the chances are that they're gonna pick any guy over me anyway, so it's—you know? . . . I think that that whole process is just kinda—with this great number of people bidding for places, you can't do that. It's just not gonna work; it's not fair. You know, I was getting to a point where my fifth and sixth choice down the list I was told I can't put in for [because someone else wanted to stay there]. And that's when I said forget it." New women firefighters were more likely to be in a situation like Marianne's than in a place where someone would fight to get or keep them.

Among the men, the most significant racial differences were in their affinities for different parts of the city, which reflected to some degree the lingering racial divisions (and hierarchy) within the department. Stations downtown and bordering downtown tend to be more traditional; they often have older white officers and are reputedly less friendly to men of color. Some would say it is no accident that this area is also characterized by a diversity of structures and other exposures that result in a wider variety of incidents and more opportunity for learning and advancement than can be had in other areas. Black officers are more common in the east end, where structures are primarily single family bungalows, and the incidents, though more frequent, are less varied. The remaining battalion includes hill stations ("firefighter retirement homes") and some central city stations that have mixed districts; the officers in these stations tend to be white.

Of the seven white male probationary firefighters in this study, five gave as their first choice a station in the downtown area and two named east end stations. Among the black men, three of the six named an east end station first, two named the headquarters station (downtown), and one named a station in the central part of the city. The other men of color resembled the white men in their choices, with three of the six requesting downtown stations, two a central city station, and one an east end station. Consonant with their preferences, four of the seven white men were assigned downtown, and one was put on a central/downtown route; three of the six black men were assigned to the east end, two to the downtown/west end, and one to a central city station; and three of the other men of color were placed in the downtown/west end, one on the east end, and two at central city stations. In other words, there was some correlation between race/ethnicity and district in both the choices and the assignments of the men, but it was by no means perfect.

Women did not as a group prefer a particular area of the city. Of the five remaining at the end of probation, one requested an east end station as her first choice and one a downtown station, two requested central city stations, and one was reluctant to make a choice because she felt she had no real chance of getting it. Three of the five women were assigned to east end stations and two to downtown/west end stations. Roughly half of the men were assigned to their first-choice station; one woman was so assigned.

Fitting In

Among the men, a sense of team membership at the end of probation was unquestionably the rule. Landing in a spot where you had a great deal in common with the crew, having a social connection to the department, or being a truly outstanding firefighter made it easier to integrate. But even without such advantages, most men didn't feel it was difficult to be accepted, as long as you did what you needed to do.

From a rural background, white newcomer John Bowman experienced a certain amount of "culture shock" in Oakland, but felt he still managed to make himself welcome. Having been assigned to a station where he was the only white on all three shifts, he felt he could counsel other new people who were feeling uncomfortable: "My advice to those people would be to focus on your job and people will respect you regardless of what you are. That is how I approached it, and again, I think I was successful. I could tell I was being scrutinized. [The engineer told me that he saw that] I gave as much to his people, or blacks, or however he put it, as I did to everybody else, and he went on to somebody else and said, 'Bowman fits in well with our melting pot here.' . . . So I think if you feel like you don't fit in, then maybe it's incumbent upon yourself to take steps *to* fit in."

Like others, Hispanic and Asian American men varied in their fondness for different houses, but didn't feel truly unwelcome anywhere. Again, social ties and exceptional talent were a decided advantage, but a politic newcomer could make the most of almost any placement. Over time, George Alarcon came to feel like an insider at Station 114, despite the very traditional character of the house and the seniority of its crew. Though he wouldn't necessarily have chosen his coworkers as friends, he found it easy enough to get along with them. He enjoyed himself at the station, socialized with the veterans, and was encouraged to bid for the spot at the end of probation.

Among the black men, the sense of comfort varied somewhat more by station, but they had a general sense of their ability to learn anywhere and a confidence in finding a good spot. When the time came to bid for permanent assignments, most African American men were actively encouraged to put in for their current slot, and some were recruited by other stations as well. Some men were fortunate enough to win a spot that was just where they wanted to be, but others knew they'd have to bide their time and were prepared to do so. Marcus thought it might be as much as "a year or so . . . before . . . I find a place where I really fit in with the guys," but he believed it would happen.

Among the women—even after eighteen months—a sense of belonging continued to be unusual. Of the five remaining, only Marla and Laurinda were thoroughly enjoying themselves on the job. Marla didn't have a strong sense

of social connection but felt confident of her abilities and of her basic acceptance as a coworker throughout the department. Laurinda was less self-assured
but had managed to develop what she felt were comfortable relationships with
one or two crews. She was also avowedly more anxious to get along with others than to stand up for abstract principles: when a black male classmate suggested that she should have objected to an off-color dinner conversation, she
vehemently disagreed. "I felt that was totally out of line. If I want somebody's
input on something, I'll ask for it. And then if something bothers me, I'll say
so. But I've never had to say anything and I don't think I would, anyway. I'm
not into that whole—controversy, and when I go someplace I wanna be liked
and—there's a line you have to draw, but I don't think it has to be *so*—you
know, guys'll be guys and girls will be girls, so."

The other three women felt varying levels of discomfort or disconnect-
edness: some were still glad to have the job; others questioned the decision
to remain. The degree of dissatisfaction a woman felt depended on the importance she placed on social connection, her ability to tolerate its absence,
and the strength of her belief that she would eventually achieve it.

Valerie had enjoyed some of her early assignments but later decided that
these were exceptional. She found the double houses particularly hard, saying "eight men and me is a bit much." Ideally, she wanted to be in a place
where she both felt good and could learn, but she could tolerate a cool environment as long as she was developing her skills. "Failing that, I have to look
for maybe leaving the department and going and working for another
department. . . . There will be a lot of the same . . . sort of issues, but just having
talked to people in other departments, there's a [higher] level of professionalism. I think a lot of it has to do with the fact that they haven't had women
for very long, and they've had [lots of] training . . . about how to have women
in the department. . . . They're [also] more scared, so consequently it isn't
gonna be this particular kind of atmosphere where . . . it's whatever you think
you can get away with, sort of thing."

Other women were more resigned to their condition as outsiders, in some
cases because it was a familiar experience. As one gay woman explained, "I
don't think that there's any station within the Oakland Fire Department where
I would be what I consider *myself*. . . .There's a lot of my personal life that
just isn't gonna fit in anywhere. And that's OK, you know. I've learned to
adjust to that because in most jobs for me that's the case."

As the newcomers passed from being probationary firefighters into the regular force (though they would remain in some sense "the new kids" until another class came through), most of them crossed the boundary from outsider
to insider. A boundary remained, but it no longer divided all newcomers from

all veterans; now it divided veterans from each other, as there were those who had passed probation but had not been accepted as insiders. Most, perhaps all, of these were women. Will it simply be a matter of time before they make that passage, or will they always remain outsiders in their own occupational community?

	Gender and Race
	in the Urban
Chapter 8	Fire Service

Policy Implications

THOUGH MOST MEMBERS OF OFD Class 1-91 retained their badges at the end of probation, they could not be called equally successful in their efforts to become firefighters, for they varied widely in skill development, confidence, and acceptance. We have seen the ways in which gender and race were influential in this outcome, but we have also seen how these social categories were not entirely determinative. Many African American men, in a department that once confined them to only a handful of stations, achieved a membership that was not so different from what most white men achieved. Women of all races had a much harder time, but even in this group there was significant variation in experience. In our last conversation, Marla Harrison alluded to the hard, even "monstrous" times endured by some of her female classmates; but her own probationary assignments had gone smoothly, and when she looked at the diversity of her class, she felt that anyone who wanted to work at it could become a firefighter.

These differences in experience—first between men of color and women, second among the women—teach us about the nature of resistance to workplace integration and the ways in which it can be overcome, in other words, about possibilities for change. In this chapter I compare the division by gender to the division by race among men, and ask what, if anything, the experience of men of color can tell us about the future of women in the fire service. Next I look to the ways in which factors *other* than race and sex—that is, personal and situational features within and across groups—shaped the newcomers' experience. The subsequent policy discussion considers how an understanding of these factors can be used to alleviate structural problems of gender- and race-based inequalities within the context of organizations like the Oakland Fire Department.

Assessing the Impacts of Race and Gender

Both the experiences and the self-assessments of the OFD newcomers provide strong evidence that race and gender affect one's entry into the fire service, and that at least in the particular context of the Oakland Fire Department
today, racial differences are less influential than are sex differences.[1] In an earlier time, white men were "us" and black men "them," but today the line seems
much more clearly drawn between the sexes. "The gender issue has a long,
long, long way to go before it's resolved," explained white newcomer John Bowman. "It was blacks before that, and even that issue isn't one hundred percent resolved, but it's a lot farther along than the gender issue is." Other men
agreed. As an African American, Hugh felt that race did still matter in some
places, but he believed that sex mattered more, saying, "I know that I've had
an easier way to go than a woman. People just feel like women shouldn't be
here. And they feel that women can't do the job—without seein' 'em . . . perform." Though black men and sometimes other men of color recognized moments of racism, they rarely saw these as a serious obstacle to their own
professional development. Both women and men, however, tended to believe
that the fire service was still "a man's world" and that women were seriously
disadvantaged in their effort to gain admission.

Newcomers disagreed, though, on the nature of the resistance to women
and the prospects for change. A number of men argued that the antagonism
reflected the veterans' concern over the "lowering" of physical entry standards
and their legitimate questions about whether most women could do the job.
Truly capable women could eventually prove themselves, it was argued, if they
worked at it hard enough. But several women and a few men believed that a
woman's performance had very little effect on her acceptance and that her
ability to get along (to put it positively) or her willingness to tolerate an offensive environment (putting it more negatively) was a much more powerful
influence. Both views were correct to some extent: a woman would not be
respected without considerable ability and hard work, but she also had to "fit
in" socially to be supported by her coworkers. And "fitting in," to the extent
it could be done, generally meant not rocking the boat, whatever the provocation.

Fitting in may also have been easier for white than for black women,
though the joint influence of race and sex could not be examined in great
detail here. At least one white woman expressed this view, noting that although she didn't feel comfortable, she did think that "being white probably
makes it a lot easier for me. . . . I think that the black women firefighters have
it a lot harder. There are none at this station, and I think that's for a reason. . . . They're not accepted as easily." As suggested earlier, black women may
have been less able to make use of the sister or daughter role to gain accep-

tance by white male firefighters in particular and may have been less suited for the "Miss Scarlett" role that could elicit help from either white or black male firefighters. Alternatively, though, the different socialization of black women might be an advantage in this setting, if, for example, they were trained in verbal contests or had developed greater self-confidence—as appeared to be the case with some black women veterans.[2]

Whatever racial differences, or differences by sexual orientation, there were among women, they paled by comparison with the gender divide, for women as a group confronted a deep-seated and widespread resistance. They found themselves to be less welcome, subject to greater scrutiny and suspicion, and judged more harshly than their male counterparts. And even in those places where an individual woman was tolerated, there was simply no way for her to be "one of the guys." A strategy often recommended to newcomers was to work to "be part of the firehouse," but when I asked Ray Montoya if this was harder for women, he said, "Absolutely. Beyond any doubt. The women know that they're not accepted here, by the men—whether they're black, Hispanic, Asian, or white . . . I am accepted as one of them. [But] . . . it would be very, very difficult for a woman to be accepted. It's still a man's world as far as the fire service is concerned!" It was not clear when, if ever, women could expect to achieve equal status and opportunity in this community.

In striking contrast, most black men didn't feel that race posed a problem in their working relationships with other firefighters, and the presence of African American men at all levels of the department made life easier in several ways. Black newcomers noted that several stations had racially mixed crews and that even if they worked in a station where all other firefighters were white, they were by no means the first to do so. In addition, the presence of black officers meant, according to Jonathan Lawrence, that you didn't have to wonder why there weren't any. All these factors, he said, made his "path a little bit smoother. Although there have been times where I've been the only black in the station, it never really came into effect. I mean, at least it hasn't represented in my face. I've been accepted as a firefighter, regardless of what color I am."

Tom Armstrong also felt that he hadn't been treated differently because of his race, at least in a way that would be apparent to him. But he did see that the possibility was there, pointing out that if the conversation changed when a woman was absent, it might well change in his absence as well, " 'cause I tend to think if they have a problem with a woman, they probably got other problems, too. If you have a problem treatin' people equal, you don't just stop with gender." In similar ways, most black men acknowledged that individual people or stations might be racist, but they also felt strongly that this possibility wasn't something that had to stand in their way.

Racial tensions seemed more common among older firefighters—some of whom carried resentments from past political battles over hiring and promotions in the department; veterans who had been particularly prominent in these conflicts were more likely than others to hold or inspire ill feelings. In particular, just as politically active women were even more suspect than those who maintained a low profile, political men of color attracted negative comment. Whereas most men of color were judged as individuals rather than by their racial category, political activists were more likely to be subject to stereotyping. An Asian American firefighter explained that he'd heard judgments "not about blacks as a whole, but as the black firefighters [association] . . . if somebody is a Black Firefighter, one of the top guys, then he's reflecting on his whole group."

In addition to the racial sensitivity associated with political activism, certain stations were described as strongholds of racial feeling. The more traditional stations, for example, almost entirely white with white officers, were sometimes described as racist, perhaps in part because of their political conservatism. As one Asian American newcomer observed, dinner table conversation about the local community might be taken to have racial implications. "I don't think it's about black people but because of the poor people in Oakland being black, I think that's where it goes sometimes," he said. Some would argue—as did one or two of the black men in this group—that such conversations often *did* reflect racism and existed on a continuum that included disproportionately harsh judgments and storytelling about black officers as well as open antagonism to black firefighters.[3]

But there were reports of animosities and prejudices on both sides of the black/white divide. Another Asian American newcomer reported that in both predominantly white and predominantly black stations he had heard unflattering generalizations about the other group. In some cases the hostility and suspicion of African American veterans may have been directed at white newcomers who were seen as linked to the old power structure, but in other cases the antagonism was more general. One white male newcomer encountered at least two black veterans who refused to acknowledge him when he tried to introduce himself on arrival at their stations. Though this newcomer did have ties to the department, his impression was that on at least one of these occasions, the black veteran wasn't aware of these ties and that this veteran "just doesn't like white people."

A Hispanic firefighter also remarked on the racial antagonism expressed by some black firefighters in a few of the east end stations. "I've never met as many people who are prejudiced as some of the people that were out there," he said. "Even in light conversation, everything was black and white, everything was really a racial issue with them." Occasionally he was not accepted, either by unfamiliar crews or individuals, "but the minute we'd work together and got together it'd just kinda all fall away." The prejudice he encountered was surprising and disturbing, he said, because "my natural instinct was that anybody that's ever been done wrong to or thinks people are prejudiced against them, are usually very open and accepting of other people, 'cause they know what it feels like. This was turned around."

In this case, though, as in all reports of racial animosity, the point was made that the problem behavior involved one or two individuals or small groups, not the department as a whole. In the words of this firefighter, "For the most part, you know, black, white, Asian, whatever, most of it wasn't like that." In contrast to the widespread sense that women simply didn't belong in the fire service, racial tensions tended to be much more specific—revolving around political battles over resources (jobs, station assignments, promotions)[4]—or localized, centering on "racist" personalities or subgroups. Very few black, Asian/Filipino, or Hispanic men believed that race stood squarely in the way of their success in the fire department, but most of the women *and* men believed that sex was still a significant barrier.

Just a Matter of Time?

In considering why sexual differences were more significant than racial differences in this setting, two possible explanations come to mind. The first is simply a matter of time and numbers: women are today where blacks were twenty years ago. Certainly there is historical evidence of substantial progress made by African American men; perhaps with the passage of time and increasing numbers, the fire service will come to accept women as it appears to be accepting black men. According to this view, women will achieve greater acceptance as their numbers increase; indeed, some would insist that the paths of women in the fire department today are much improved over what they were for the first women who entered.

The time-and-numbers explanation implies a similarity between racial and sexual exclusion, where the latest group of "others" fulfills the same function as that served by previous groups of outsiders. As one Asian American firefighter put it, "women have really taken up the slack where race might play a role. . . . If there weren't any women in the department, or any women makin' trouble, [laughs] . . . it would be more focused in on something else. . . . And it could be race, it could be Asian, it could be black, it could be a number of things. But with the way that it is, it kinda takes the pressure off of everything else. . . . [It's as if] you're not gonna be as bad as *that*, or you can do better than or you are better than that. . . . If somebody in the department came out—like these guys that are comin' out in the Army . . . that would probably take some of the pressure off the women!" This view is consistent with one put forth by California State Fire Marshall Ronny Coleman in an article on gays in the fire service.[5] Coleman asserts that "there is almost always at least one group that is considered to be the undesirables, and the rest of the organization prejudges them. This even goes so far that people who had earlier been discriminated against might often join forces with their previous adversaries to then become biased against another new group that is attempting to enter."[6]

This perspective seems to suggest that exclusion is primarily or even entirely a function of timing and that each new group meets a similar kind of resistance. However, the socialization experience of firefighters suggests an additional possibility: resistance may be greater to some groups than others regardless of the order of entry or the proportion of representation because of differences in perceived suitability. In the view of traditional members of the fire service, there is greater similarity between black and white men than between men and women—an understanding based in part on the importance of size and upper-body strength and in part on the differing social constructions of gender and race.

It is difficult to evaluate precisely the legitimacy of the "strength argument" as a reason for excluding women. On one hand, firefighting is a physically demanding job, and there are occasions when a very unusual degree of strength is required. These circumstances would support the assertion that there is good reason to worry about the presence of women and other small-statured firefighters, both in terms of the effectiveness of the department and the safety of the crews. However, the emphasis on strength may be a pretense for the exclusion of women. For example, veterans generally do not complain about those older men who are in poor physical condition. The justification for their acceptance is that they have "paid their dues," but of course this fact doesn't address the problem of safety or efficiency. For example, some OFD veterans opposed to women in the fire service argued for annual physical agility testing of those who would be hired under a proposed 1991 consent decree, but when the compromise wording required testing of all firefighters, the union membership refused to endorse the decree. This action was generally interpreted as an opposition to both the proportion of women called for by the proposed decree and the physical testing of veteran firefighters. Likewise, treatment of men and women of comparable stature differs: small men seem to receive the benefit of the doubt much more readily than do women. Finally, men disagree about the level of strength that should be demanded for the job; some believe that the argument often used against women—that a coworker should be able single-handedly to pull another firefighter out of a hole if he falls—is an unreasonable and unrealistic expectation that couldn't be met by all the men in the department.

There is no way to conclude definitively whether the differential impact of race and sex has to do entirely with timing and numbers or is also the result of socially constructed differences that in this context highlight gender over race. There certainly seems reason, however, not to dismiss the role played by culture, even given the importance of time and numbers. When I asked a black veteran and OBFFA activist if it seemed to him that gender was more of an issue than race in the fire department, he agreed that it was, and he also believed that the reason had more to do with the nature of the gender difference than a simple matter of timing. As to the possible entry of some hypothetical new group of outsiders, he said, "You could bring in three-legged cats and dogs and as long as they were male and dominant and strong enough, they would be OK."

In the final chapter of this book I explore the idea that gender divides people in ways very different from the ways in which race does. For the moment, however, I focus on instrumental concerns—time and numbers, qualifications and preparedness, strategies for managing and surviving the work environment—in the interest of identifying organizational interventions that can enhance the nontraditional newcomers' likelihood of success.

Across Race and Gender: The Successful Making of a Firefighter

In thinking about how organizations might more effectively support diversity in their work forces, we must reflect on not only the differences between groups but also their similarities and internal variations; in doing so, we avoid the reification of race and gender categories that can distort understanding and impede efforts at social change. Within each race/sex group described here, some members were more thoroughly integrated into the community by the end of probation than were others, and this outcome can be understood as the result of both personal and situational factors.

Among the personal characteristics likely to enhance success were the following: self-confidence and assertiveness; strength, size, or athletic ability; mechanical aptitude; practical intelligence, good judgment, and an ability to think under pressure; relevant training or experience; relevant social experience; motivation; enjoyment of physical work; a "thick skin"; and an outgoing personality, charm, or attractiveness. But apart from an individual newcomer's qualities, certain situational factors were also clearly influential. Most important among these were early opportunities for action, early and/or lengthy assignments in crews with good teaching skills, assignments to reasonably supportive, nonhostile crews, and extended assignments in one station (assuming it was not hostile). Finally, sponsorship or protection from a well-respected veteran in the department, a situational factor associated with certain individuals, could promote success.

Several comments should be made about these factors. First, some are clearly more crucial than others: it is almost impossible to be accepted without an adequate level of physical ability and a demonstrated willingness to work hard at fires. Second, the presence of all factors is not necessary, for some can substitute for others. Coming in with no prior background is less of a problem if a firefighter is assigned to busy stations early on and has a moderate level of self-confidence and talent. Third, although some factors are expressed in terms of personal qualities, they are relevant to organizational policies in two ways: an organization can recruit and screen on the basis of such qualities, and it can implement personnel practices that will promote the development of those qualities.

Both the factors identified above and the discussion below are shaped in part by the setting of this study and its place in time. A similar project conducted ten or twenty years ago, or in a different organizational and cultural setting, would have produced different emphases, though most of the basic findings would probably have been the same.[7] For example, the importance of visible top-level commitment to diversity is mentioned but not emphasized in the following discussion, simply because it is present in the Oakland Fire Department and its effects are more striking in cases where it is absent. Similarly, station assignment strategies are highlighted here because assignments were so powerful in the experiences of those who participated in this study; in a department with greater similarity between stations this factor would be less significant. It should also be noted that although the discussion that follows is directed primarily at employers, successful implementation requires the active participation and in some cases initiative on the part of organized labor as well.

As a Practical Matter: Organizational Policy Implications

BRINGING IN THE "RIGHT STUFF": RECRUITMENT AND SELECTION

A successful diversity program begins with the recruitment of people who have the potential to succeed. A woman veteran made this point nicely when she talked about the reality of the work and how it could feel to those who were unprepared for it:

> I mean, women do not get their fingernails dirty; they don't have calluses. They're not used to working so hard that their heart's

pounding out of their chest, their legs are ready to crumble under-
neath 'em, and their arms are ready to fall off. . . . I mean, there aren't
very many women that are exposed to that. . . . Sometimes I just
think, "Oh my God! [Laughs.] Can I really do this?" You know, when
I'm hangin' off a ladder on a roof, and I'm tryin' to operate the chain
saw and my arm's shakin'. . . . But then . . . I hear other people talking
and, and they kind of have the same experiences, and a lot of 'em are
men. So I think, "Well, maybe I'm just not alone out there!" But you
really feel alone when you're [laughs] up in the smoke and the heat
and you're trying to do something, and you know, your body just is
saying, "*Why* are you here?! What are you doing?" But that's the
challenge of it too, you know. I mean, that's what's real appealing
about the job, is the testing, testing yourself. And . . . my athletic
background . . . has really helped me in this because that's what you
constantly do when you're athletic, is you're pushing yourself to a
limit and trying to get beyond, and that's what this job does. . . . Just
pushing yourself beyond, beyond the limit that you think you can go.

The personal qualities to which this woman alludes—self-confidence, a commitment to the work, and physical aptitude—were among those that distinguished successful OFD newcomers. One other important quality that she does
not articulate but we may infer from her background is that of appropriate
social skills and orientation (such as might come from participation in competitive athletics). Recruitment, screening, and selection processes must pay
particular attention to these qualities, for they are crucial for performance and
acceptance and relatively unamenable to organizational influence. There are
of course other essential qualifications—physical health, for example—but this
discussion focuses on those just enumerated because they appear to be less well
understood or to be given insufficient weight in the current screening process.[8] With respect to relatively uncommon qualities, such as physical strength
among women candidates, it should be noted that *targeted* recruitment is likely
to be more efficient than broad-based recruitment with an effort to winnow
the candidates through selection.

Self-confidence. A constellation of personal qualities is envisioned here,
including self-esteem, a comfort with risk-taking, a reasonable level of
assertiveness, and a relatively thick skin. The importance of these qualities—
so apparent in the experiences of the OFD newcomers—should be acknowledged in the recruitment and screening process.[9] Self-confidence facilitates
learning by prompting people to ask for attention, to put themselves forward
in work situations, to deal with criticism, and to recover easily from mistakes.
Socially, self-confident (as distinct from "arrogant") people are better able to
deal with difficult coworkers, not take comments too personally, and ride out
the emotionally stressful aspects of the job that derive from both the work

and the social environment.[10] There also appears to be a reinforcing effect of confidence: a more self-confident person is able to behave in ways that garner respect from others, which in turn enhances self-esteem.

Appropriate social skills and orientation. The matter of social skills must be approached from two perspectives: the first takes into account the qualities desirable in female candidates, and the second, the complementary qualities desirable in their male counterparts. Among women, some familiarity with the cultural processes of this kind of setting, including an orientation toward group- and task-related bonding rather than interpersonal connection in the workplace, is helpful; these may develop out of experience with competitive athletics or prior work in blue-collar settings. For their part, male candidates ought to have some exposure to women as colleagues or coworkers and an ability to relate to women in roles other than social. This means not only agreeing that "it's OK to have women in the fire service as long as they can do the job," but also having an understanding of how to work with women and a respect for women as people.

The goal in emphasizing these qualities in the selection process is two-fold: to select appropriate candidates and to communicate something about the culture to men and women who are interested in joining. Because the culture will not change overnight, nor should it necessarily, it is both ineffectual and cruel to admit people who are socially unprepared and have false expectations about the environment. At the same time, however, certain aspects of the culture are not only disadvantageous to women but may be counterproductive in other ways, and in the interest of change the department can select for people who have less traditional attitudes and experiences.

Strong commitment to the work. Not only is a commitment to the work desirable from an organizational perspective, but this quality heavily influences coworker judgments of new firefighters as well. Veterans repeatedly express impatience with people who don't seem interested in working hard at a fire, and newcomers often observe that credit is given for a good effort, even if the performance isn't perfect. Commitment to the work includes both an appreciation for and a desire to do hard physical labor. People who are unhappy pushing their bodies to the limit will be neither comfortable in this job nor accepted.

Physical aptitude. It is impossible to say too much about this issue. Firefighting involves physical work, and in the culture of a traditional urban fire department coworkers are judged to a considerable extent on the basis of their perceived physical ability. In this setting, the common belief that standards have been lowered to admit women increases whatever resentment and suspicion would otherwise accompany their entry into a male-dominated occupation.

At this point, the question of appropriate screening standards is far from settled.[11] The earlier entrance examinations of most urban fire departments had a dramatically disparate impact and their job-relatedness was unsubstantiated; test scores sometimes even rewarded behaviors that would be counterproductive on the fireground.[12] However, the invalidation of older tests has not been followed by a consensus on appropriate standards. And in the absence of such consensus within a department, it becomes difficult or impossible for firefighters of smaller stature and lesser upper-body strength, particularly women, to prove themselves and to develop self-confidence, even though they may be capable of satisfactory performance. Furthermore, trust among coworkers is weakened and resentment against affirmative action policies is unnecessarily heightened when a department's screening and evaluation procedures are not widely respected.[13]

Resolving conflicts over physical testing issues will not be easy. There is no absolute standard to which appeal can be made, particularly given the circular relationship between a department's physical agility standards and the design of its equipment and procedures.[14] Such difficulties notwithstanding, greater movement toward consensus is critical, and it should be possible for various interest groups to arrive at agreement on basic aspects of the physical agility entrance test with disputed areas left to the discretion of a mutually acceptable outside expert.[15] In addition, concerns for both fairness and organizational effectiveness demand that incumbents also be periodically evaluated and required to meet appropriate standards of physical agility—a goal that many departments, including Oakland, have not yet been able to achieve.

The importance of physical ability for both performance and acceptance suggests that this quality should be emphasized in the targeted recruitment of female candidates in particular. In the short term, active recruitment through such venues as college athletic programs, gyms and fitness centers, military bases, women's sports leagues, and organized athletic events such as runs and powerlifting competitions should be emphasized. Such recruitment might also facilitate the hiring of women with appropriate social skills for this environment. In addition, as OFD has recognized, it is important to encourage young women to begin to think in terms of preparing for a career in firefighting, and visits to high schools and junior high schools should be part of the long-range recruitment program. With more resources, fire departments might work with schools and other community groups to establish physical training programs for young women.[16]

ALTHOUGH THESE QUALIFICATIONS are important, I reiterate that sheer numbers do make a significant difference in alleviating the pressure on all women and on men of color,[17] and over time greater numbers may have a salutary effect on the occupational culture as well. The experience of new firefighters in Oakland demonstrates that neither quality *nor* quantity of hirees can be safely ignored. For integration to be successful, members of previously excluded groups must be both undeniably qualified and sufficient in number to constitute a critical mass and avoid the negative effects of skewed group composition. In achieving this goal, numerical targets such as those found in many consent decrees can be necessary and unhappily counterproductive. Without quotas, the urban fire service would in all likelihood continue to be almost entirely white and certainly all male. However, where historical patterns of exclusion have resulted in an uneven distribution of qualifications (e.g., women less physically and mechanically prepared than they might have been under conditions of greater equality), departments must engage in a more concerted effort to locate and prepare the best candidates. Failure to do so while simultaneously implementing quotas can result in hiring unqualified candidates, as undoubtedly happened with the nepotistic hiring practices of the past.

In this context Oakland and a number of other departments have achieved some success in establishing organized programs that provide for minority and female candidates what has been provided by the informal networks of white men in the past: advance preparation for the tests and job. With the cooperation and assistance of the department, black and other minority firefighter groups and to a lesser extent women's groups offer outreach and support, including preparatory classes.[18] Oakland allows candidates to preview its physical agility test and offers hirees a pre-academy physical training class (discussed below). Some departments also offer preexamination physical training designed especially to prepare female candidates. In concert with efforts to improve fairness in the testing process, such programs have significantly increased diversity in the firefighting work force.[19]

At the same time, though, more traditional recruitment patterns can also be useful. For example, as the proportion of black firefighters increases, incumbent firefighters are an increasingly important source of referral for black candidates. For different reasons, women are sometimes recruited by veterans as well. It is interesting to note that a number of Oakland's "old-timers" spoke of having recently recruited and prepared women to enter the fire service. Clearly, some of these men are coming to accept the facts that, like it or not, the occupation is being sexually integrated and it is in their interest to encourage qualified women to pursue this career. While recognizing that there can be significant problems with the "old boy network," the idea of at least some recruiting through current personnel is valuable: it can promote familiarity with the work, sponsorship, and a sense of investment in newcomers on the part of veterans. Moreover, it occurs to some degree though not always in the ways that would be most productive for integration purposes.[20]

MAKING THE "RIGHT STUFF"

Organizations not only screen for the qualities they seek in members, they also influence member behavior, intentionally and unintentionally, through training, reward and opportunity structures, and a variety of other internal policies and practices.[21] This type of intervention can be particularly important when an organization is dealing with the entry of previously excluded groups. For example, women's educational and social experiences rarely prepare them for blue-collar work, but they can adapt to such work given proper opportunities and encouragement.[22] The strategies suggested here are based in part on the experiences of OFD's Class 1-91 and in part on research concerning organizational change.

FIREFIGHTER ACADEMY TRAINING. Departmental firefighter academies face a difficult challenge in their efforts to train classes with a wide range of backgrounds and levels of skill development. To address unevenness specifically in physical preparation, Oakland offered a pre-academy training that was attended by most of the women; in addition, OFD included a rigorous physical training program as part of the regular academy. Both efforts were important in preparing people with less physical backgrounds.

But in addition to physical differences, the 1-91 class included recruits with a range of expertise in firefighting and medical services. Such variation can have both positive and negative effects: some of the more experienced recruits were an important source of additional help to their classmates, while others were a source of intimidation or confusion. In this kind of setting a cooperative-learning approach, if properly managed, can be quite successful, and in the 1-91 academy, a cooperative approach was promoted to some extent through the assignment of recruits to six-member squads, which on occasion received group awards. Additional incentives for cooperation could be provided through a mixture of group and individual evaluations, where the latter included an assessment of teamwork efforts.

The need for staff diversity in curriculum design and implementation has been recognized in Oakland, and cadre diversity has had some positive effects. The involvement of women instructors or aides in a physical training program is particularly important because effective physical techniques are often different for women (or smaller men) than for large men. In other aspects of the academy, minority and female instructors not only provide role models for minority and female recruits, but they also send a signal to more traditional recruits that a department is culturally diverse. However, it is not enough for the staff to be heterogeneous; it is also important that instructors be effective trainers who are respected by their coworkers. For example, a female instructor who is not well regarded will not only be an ineffective role model, but she may also be a source of discomfort to female recruits; by contrast, a capable and respected woman can be a powerful influence. The presence of respected instructors in the academy also increases the trust that veteran crew members have in the new firefighters when they enter the field.

Another factor in this trust is the belief that trainees are held to appropriate standards of performance. The relative infrequency with which recruits in recent Oakland classes have been separated from the department, either in the academy or during probation, coupled with a lack of confidence in the current selection process, heightens the veterans' suspicions about newcomers. In Class 1-91, from an initial group of fifty-three people, one person resigned, and no one was terminated in the academy; two people resigned, and one was terminated during probation. Many veterans observed that for everyone in a class that large to be qualified to pass the academy seemed highly improbable, and this concern raised suspicions that people might have been retained for the wrong reasons, increasing the barrier to the acceptance of some newcomers.[23]

Establishing clear, job-related performance standards and enforcing them consistently is necessary for organizational effectiveness generally. It also demonstrates a commitment to procedural fairness, which in turn can mute opposition to affirmative action and resistance to some newcomers.[24] In developing such standards, attention must be paid to all aspects of job performance—not simply structure firefighting, the feature of greatest concern to most veterans. For example, in departments like Oakland where EMS calls constitute the lion's share of activity for all firefighters, medical training and performance should be taken as seriously as firefighting.[25] (Alternatively, the department could institute a strict division of labor in which paramedics replace some firefighters.) Similarly, other aspects of the work, such as hazardous materials management, should either be done by specialists or constitute a serious part of firefighter training and evaluations.

SOCIAL PREPARATION FOR THE FIELD. Some time in Oakland's 1-91 academy was devoted to discussions about life in the firehouse and firefighter culture, with a good deal of advice offered to the recruits. In addition, the technical training of the academy also included many socializing elements (see chapter 2 for examples). Some recruits have the advantage of having been "ride-alongs" through their community college firefighter programs, and others know something of the department through friends and relatives. All of these aspects of social preparation are important and helpful to some degree.

In view of the tension around gender in the fire service, however, some additional social training might be useful in preparing people both to survive and to support each other in the field. Women and men might be required to participate in both separate and combined sessions, with different agendas. The separate women's training, for example, could have the goal of promoting their assertiveness and giving them practice in verbal contests.[26] A separate men's training might be an opportunity for men to voice without censure their feelings and concerns about having women coworkers; this discussion must proceed with the clear understanding that male behavior toward the women remains subject to department regulations and legal standards. Joint sessions could be used to bring about more open communication between men and women; for example, a series of vignettes or role-playing exercises could get people talking about what kinds of behaviors should be considered illegal harassment and why. Such a discussion would not only begin to clarify some of the genuine confusion around what constitutes illegal harassment, but it might also be an opportunity to set a tone for later discussion and possible low-level conflict resolution, emphasizing the need to listen to other people and to clarify one's own communications. These goals would be relevant in ongoing training of incumbent firefighters.

STATION ASSIGNMENTS AND FIELD TRAINING. The importance of early exposure to action, particularly for inexperienced probationers, cannot be overstated. While doing the actual work new firefighters not only learn but also develop confidence in their own abilities. Of course, placement in a busy house does not ensure that newcomers benefit from exposure, if the environment is openly hostile or the veterans are reluctant to work with the newcomer. People perceived as "outsiders"—whether because of sex, race, or other personal characteristics—are particularly vulnerable to the vagaries of the learning environment.

Although the new firefighters in this study were sometimes assigned on the basis of their training needs, the department's actions were seriously constrained by such factors as the unwieldy size of the class and the seniority rights of veterans. In addition, when several women were assigned to double houses to facilitate their truck work, some male classmates expressed resentment. Such constraints notwithstanding,[27] fire departments would do well to recognize the overwhelming importance of appropriate early assignments for newcomers and the benefit to the entire department of effective training.[28] The Oakland practice of designating some double-house positions as training slots might be elaborated by taking into account also the special qualifications of the crew members as instructors. Some officers and veterans are clearly more motivated teachers and more effective trainers than are others, especially for inexperienced or unself-confident newcomers. It might be appropriate to formally recognize such abilities by giving primary responsibility for field training to those who do it best and even rewarding these positions for the additional work.[29] Guiding the professional development of new firefighters is obviously an important and necessary function of veterans, but it tends not to be formally recognized as such.

In designing a more formal approach to field training assignments, departments should consider certain implications of firefighter culture. First, if the training station crew members are not respected by other veterans in the department, then the newcomers they train will not necessarily be seen as having proven themselves. Second, although some newcomers are more susceptible than others to field training differences (recall that the white men here felt they could learn almost anywhere), a policy of assigning only certain people to special training houses would obviously tend to create a subclass of individuals seen as requiring remediation. The message would be damaging but also incorrect; it implies that the "problem" involves the newcomers' lack of qualifications, whereas in fact the difficulty arises from a lack of fit between some newcomers and some veterans.

MANAGING THE SOCIAL ENVIRONMENT

All organizations exist within a larger social context that shapes interactions and interpretations of behavior, particularly in the areas of race and gender differences. Power inequalities as well as differential socialization can cause men and women, whites and people of color, to have very different interpretations of shared events.[30] To a great extent, organizations must take such differences as given, but they are not entirely without leverage. For example, social categorizations—the delineation of in-groups and out-groups—do influence our perceptions and evaluations, but these categorizations are subject to redefinition:[31] groups can be constituted (by design) on a variety of dimensions other than race or sex. In addition, situational factors, including working conditions and opportunity structures, have a powerful effect on individual behaviors and tend to be more predictive of behavior than are individual dispositions or personality traits.[32] The following discussion attempts to consider both constraints on and opportunities for organizational interventions. It focuses on those that address gender differences because this study found them to be so salient; however, with some qualifications, much of this discussion could be generalized.

Sensitivity training. The widely recommended cultural sensitivity and antiharassment trainings have been instituted in Oakland and many other fire departments. These programs receive mixed reviews from participants, who report limited gains or sometimes even negative consequences, especially when the program emphasizes *blame* by making certain people or groups "wrong" and others "right," an approach more likely to promote resentment than understanding.[33] If designed and implemented effectively, sensitivity training programs might be more consistently useful, but alone they are unlikely to bring about dramatic change. In particular, the programs cannot change attitudes, and they are most likely to backfire when this is their aim. By contrast, if the purpose is simply to supply information to and answer questions for employees, as in a recent series of antiharassment trainings in Oakland, such sessions may be necessary and useful. Similarly, training sessions designed to assist supervisors by clarifying their responsibilities and offering practical strategies, such as for informal conflict resolution, are important.

To say that diversity trainings by themselves will not change attitudes is not to say that organizing discussions about diversity issues, including harassment concerns, is pointless. Given the level of confusion and anger around the problem of sexual harassment not only in fire departments but also in many organizations, some dialogue on this subject outside the courtroom seems necessary. Men and women alike need an opportunity to explain their positions and feelings in a setting in which neither group is made to feel right or wrong. This kind of exchange rarely seems to occur in antiharassment trainings. More commonly, a videotape purporting to demonstrate impermissible behavior is shown, and the reaction—as in a training I attended at an IAFF human relations conference—is laughter, jokes, and murmurs of discontent from the audience, with no real engagement. Men leave feeling aggrieved at what they often believe is special treatment required by women, and women leave feeling that the men "still don't get it." The confusion is compounded by a cultural setting in which some degree of hazing has traditionally been part of the social initiation process. Men can claim with some justification that they *are* hard on each other, not only on the women, but there are clearly differences in behavior.

An aspect of the problem can be illustrated with a dirty joke that resulted in an OFD officer's short-term suspension when he told it under particularly strained social circumstances (a woman crew member had recently returned from stress disability leave after being subjected to some harassment). As the episode was explained to me, the officer had heard the joke from a woman firefighter and intended to "break the tension" at his station by repeating it. After hearing about this event I asked a group of firefighters at another station to tell me the joke, which they did after some hesitation. The "joke" as related to me was: "Men who like women with big tits and tight pussies have big mouths and small dicks." When the joke was repeated for me, several of the men agreed that it was a lousy joke and expressed their amazement that the officer who told it could have thought it would ease the tension at the station. But they also didn't see how it constituted sexual harassment. In this fairly typical conversation I noticed that male firefighters realize many women are uncomfortable with this type of remark but lack understanding about *why* that is the case.[34]

Given the sensitivity around the topic of sexual harassment and the resistance to women in settings like the fire service, any kind of antiharassment training may provoke the more traditional firefighters and consequently increase the discomfort of some women. However, the depth of cultural differences and degree of misunderstandings that exist between men and women suggest that efforts should be made to bring about some discussion, preferably in the context of nonconfrontational, regular training sessions.

Policies and practices dealing specifically with sexual harassment. Much attention has been paid recently to the subject of antiharassment policies, and the City of Oakland was in the process of redrafting its policies at the time of this research. Specific suggestions as to formal policies will not be offered here because such policies are constrained by state and federal law, and detailed recommendations require specialized knowledge. However, I can make certain observations relevant to implementing organizational policies and perhaps, on a broader scale, to how this problem ought to be framed in governmental policymaking discussions.

To begin with, special features of the organizational or occupational culture must be taken into account, however difficult this may seem. While it may be desirable for all workplaces to be free of harassment and it is legally required that they be free of racial and sexual harassment, the expectation that generic rules of behavior can be formulated and implemented without negative repercussions is unrealistic. A number of norms in firefighter culture complicate this matter. First, the use of verbal harassment and practical joking for testing and initiation has already been mentioned; an effort to eliminate these practices or to restrict their use is clearly disruptive to the community—though not a uniformly unwelcome change—and fuels resentment. Second, strong norms prevail against complaining about a fellow firefighter, particularly about going outside the chain of command to do so; people who take such action invite reprisals, which may be illegal in the context of sexual harassment but can be controlled only to a limited degree, and disrespect, which cannot be controlled. If an OFD woman lodged a harassment complaint against a male coworker she would almost invariably be criticized and ostracized, regardless of how inappropriate the coworker's behavior was acknowledged to be. In listing examples of women who "do things to undermine their position" John Bowman, a relatively nontraditional newcomer, mentioned a woman who had formally complained about her coworkers watching a pornographic movie in the firehouse. He agreed that "they were outta line, they shouldn't have been doing that, but still, by the act of writing them up, she now has cast a pall of suspicion over her. And people aren't gonna trust her."

Fear of repercussions is of course a major reason for the nonreporting of sexual harassment in all contexts,[35] but the intensity of social ostracism that is likely to result in a fire station exceeds the likely scenario in many offices and is also harder to control. One woman in this study commented that she had heard about a classmate filing a complaint about a serious incident of harassment (exposure with threatening physical behavior and sexual touching); she saw what the woman went through following the complaint and was unsure *what* it would take for her to speak up:

> So she must've been pretty pissed off at this particular guy for doin' that, but I'm just tryin' to think of how—me personally, I wouldn't try to prove the point. You know, I—because it's not worth it! You know, unless, [pauses] unless you're—unless—I don't really know what limit I would go to. . . . I mean if someone was to grab me like that, I don't know what I would do [pauses].
> C: Really?
>   Yeah! . . .
> C: Even with, even with something like that?
>   I don't think I would. . . . I might tell my officer, but then I think once you tell your officer, he's obligated to [do something and] . . . it escalates. . . . [And] it's just not worth it. Like Ronnie [the woman who complained] had to go through so much, and she will for a long time . . . 'cause the majority of the people stick together. . . . I wouldn't wanna go through that. I wouldn't wanna put other people through that! But I don't know what I would do. I would *really*—it would have to be really something extreme. But then, who knows? Maybe I guess at a certain point, you know, you put up with some crap from some people that—you're just like, I don't have to! But it's just . . . the repercussions. . . . And you have to think of that, too. Not just your rights.

This story is told, not to suggest that a complaint should not have been raised in these circumstances, but to convey how costly it can be for a woman to speak up in this setting. The underlying policy question is how best to create an environment in which women will feel able to complain about serious harassment and men will not side with a coworker who engages in clearly reprehensible behavior. One line of argument emphasizes the continuum linking general sexual comments and *Playboy* magazine on one end with *quid pro quo* sexual harassment, physical intimidation, or assault on the other and suggests that tolerating the less intense forms of "harassment"—that is, a sexualized work environment—promotes an atmosphere in which more serious forms can occur.[36] An alternative view is that these behaviors, while related, are not the same thing and that lumping them all together under the general category of "sexual harassment" trivializes the more serious acts by linking them too closely with less serious behaviors.[37] Among firefighters, the result is a magnification of male-female conflicts that may feed the men's resentment and decrease their sympathy toward women who suffer truly hostile and threatening forms of harassment.

If we consider the comments of the women who participated in this study, it is clear that "sexual harassment" is defined contextually and a key aspect of the context is the *attitude* that the other actor conveys to the woman herself. Most women were relatively unconcerned with sexualization of the workplace—in the form of sexual language or jokes, for example—as long as it was not directed at them *and* they personally were treated with respect.[38] With borderline behaviors in particular, a coworker's *intent* was significant to the women: if the goal seemed to be to make a woman feel uncomfortable, threatened, or out of place, the behavior was harassment; if there appeared to be no such motive, the behavior could be treated as an act of stupidity. In some cases, a pattern of behavior, as when one man was discovered to have made unwelcome advances to numerous women, was itself suggestive of a problematic attitude. It should also be noted that women sometimes desire simply that the negative behavior stop, not that the perpetrator necessarily be punished, but the formal procedures may inhibit this level of resolution.

Yet this perspective on the problem—taking into account context and nuance—poses a dilemma with respect to organizational intervention. In general, such interventions are better suited to control of behavior than to changing attitudes,[39] but this is clearly a situation in which attitudes should not be ignored. Policies and enforcements that focus on behavior without considering attitudes or motives may have the unfortunate consequence of overstructuring interactions, reducing warmth and spontaneity, and provoking additional paranoia and hostility.[40] Furthermore, because the legal definition of sexual harassment includes the element of unwantedness, identical behaviors can be considered harassment in some contexts and not in others; this discrepancy leads to additional confusion and anxiety.

The centrality of attitude in the problem of sexual harassment suggests a need for organizations to proceed along two tracks: (1) establishing and communicating standards of behavior, and (2) simultaneously addressing attitudes. The goal is not to convince people to change their beliefs, but to strengthen their ability to deal with each other as peers, instead of relying on stereotypes.[41] This goal can be addressed in several ways, including the following: selecting candidates who have this ability; addressing the concerns about procedural fairness that may aggravate prejudice;[42] providing opportunities for open communication and dialogue; and setting examples of appropriate behavior.

As noted, high-level commitment to equal opportunity is critical for both practical and symbolic reasons, but more immediate and powerful effects can come from such commitment at lower levels of authority:[43] a respected officer can set a positive or negative tone for an entire crew. Increasing diversity in the officer ranks can itself enhance intergroup relations *if* officers are carefully selected, trained, and supported.[44] In general, diversity is well served in organizations that establish and retain a high level of professionalism in which training is ongoing, personnel throughout the organization are involved in planning and policymaking, job performance is monitored and rewarded, and a commitment to fairness as opposed to favoritism guides practices. In addition, it can be useful to bring people together in ways that cross traditional group boundaries. For example, task forces, training sessions, or other group activities that facilitate contact between individuals from different stations—as opposed to whole crews—can provide an alternative to the traditional categories of identification that sometimes foster exclusivity.

Physical privacy, equipment, and work-family policies. Many fire departments began the process of sexual integration with little consideration given to modifications that might be required to accommodate a two-sex work force.[45] Failure to devote more significant time and resources to these questions probably exacerbated integration difficulties for a number of reasons.[46] The absence of more systematic arrangements creates situations in which individual women have to negotiate their own accommodations with varying degrees of comfort and success. When conflicts or difficulties arise, they tend to be focused on the woman instead of the policy or administration. The underlying message is that women are not regular members of the department. As one Oakland woman observed, the absence of women's bathroom facilities in some stations as late as thirteen years after the first women were hired was "a message right there to the firefighters that hey, 'We're not acknowledging women here so we're not demanding that of you either.'" The suggestion that women are getting "special treatment" if changes are made to facilitate integration assumes that the historical conditions are sex-neutral, which, of course, they are not.[47]

Even the most positive OFD women pointed out that the physical environment of the stations set them apart unnecessarily. In many cases, the privacy problem was resolved by women deferring their physical needs. When Laurinda arrived at Station 103, the captain told her that to avoid awkward encounters with the men on the shift, she should announce to the crew anytime she was going to use the bathroom; she felt ridiculous doing this and would put off relieving herself for extended periods of time. Most women didn't feel free to shower at the station because it meant closing off the bathroom to the others. As Marla put it, "If I wanna take a shower in the morning, I need to get up before anybody else gets up in order to not utilize *their* space. You know, it never feels like *my* space in the bathroom." Another woman solved the problem of not having access to the bathroom in the morning by brushing her teeth at the hose outside the station.[48]

The lack of separate rest-room facilities, a source of needless discomfort and divisiveness, may well contribute to the problem of sexual harassment by facilitating the invasion of privacy. Male firefighters have been known to walk in on a woman in the shower, to block a woman's exit from a bathroom stall, and to engage in other acts of intimidation and invasion. Even if the problem is more one of awkwardness than hostility, the effect is to set women apart.

Like the stations, firefighting gear and equipment were also designed for a single-sex work force. Though more appropriate gear is now manufactured, it is not always readily available to women firefighters,[49] and ill-fitting uniforms, gloves, boots, and masks continue to make the work not only more uncomfortable, but more difficult and dangerous. In addition, much equipment in older departments is disadvantageous to firefighters of smaller stature. While those joining the fire service today must be able to use the equipment currently available, modifications can be made as equipment is replaced so that strength and height requirements are not exaggerated. Some of these changes will benefit all firefighters by reducing physical strain and injury.

Problems with gear, with equipment, and in balancing work and family responsibilities were not the most salient issue for the women in this group during this period (though they did arise), but they constitute a potential source of difficulties and are certainly a concern to other women in the department and in the fire service more generally. Here again, when a fire department is slow to develop formal policies pertaining to maternity leave, fetal protection, firefighter marriages, and other issues that arise in a two-gender workplace, it directly handicaps female employees in their work and conveys a message about their second-class membership.

THIS DISCUSSION OF POLICY and practice has focused primarily on issues relating to gender integration because of the salience of gender differences in the occupational community of firefighters. It seems clear that the question underlying the uneven integration of women and problems like sexual harassment is whether women can be accepted and respected as coworkers in this environment. At this point I extend the discussion of organizational concerns to a broader perspective, for the shaping of gender relations in the fire service is not unrelated to the construction of gender relations in the society as a whole.

The organizational policy discussion has of necessity been shaped by a concern for implementation difficulties, including costs and political constraints. As a result, some of the policy suggestions discussed above may seem inappropriate when viewed from a perspective that emphasizes social justice over pragmatism. The final chapter of this book is an effort to give the justice perspective its due.

Chapter 9	Questions of Identity, Community, and Social Justice

And then [when] the Oakland Fire Department . . .
started letting the blacks get into the department, oh, we
came in here like [a] mad plague. So therefore, you
know, they couldn't stop that. They could not stop that.
But the old guard network truly hated to have women in
the department. You know, they've had this thing. White
males have always had this thing of placing the white
woman on the pedestal anyway. And they didn't feel like
it was a position for them to be here, workin' side by
side. They're supposed to be at home in the kitchen.
Somethin' of that nature; secretary. Those type of jobs.
Workin' in the bank. Even the bank president. But—
firefighting?

—JONATHAN LAWRENCE

TOWARD THE END of my fieldwork, OFD firefighters often asked me about my conclusions. In response I would usually describe the cultural conflicts I saw, and particularly the lack of fit between the male-oriented occupational culture and the life experiences and expectations of the women firefighters. On one occasion a white male veteran, an early contact, asked if I had found much in the way of racism and sexism in the fire department. Having earlier heard my cultural analysis, he seemed somewhat surprised when I said that yes, I did think there was racism and sexism in the fire department. I went on to say that fire departments like other organizations exist in a society in which racism and sexism are prominent, and it would be quite surprising for such organizations not to reflect those influences.

Two forms of discrimination are commonly described in the literature on equal employment opportunity: personal prejudice, whether conscious or unconscious, and institutional discrimination.[1] In the latter case, apparently neutral organizational practices systematically disadvantage certain groups with the result that rewards are allocated in part on the basis of ascribed characteristics, such as race or sex, that are unrelated to performance. Probably the most obvious example of institutional discrimination is setting entry standards that have a disproportionate impact on certain groups and are unrelated to job requirements. Institutional behaviors can range from the most egregious practices in which the injustice is obvious and indefensible, to situations in which the line between legitimate standard-setting and illegal discrimination is much less clear, as in the physical testing of firefighters.

Although occupational culture is not usually analyzed for its discriminatory potential in the way that organizational practices are—presumably on the assumption that culture is not an appropriate subject of policy concern—its influence can be as powerful as that of an organization's formal procedures. When people do not fit comfortably into an existing cultural framework, their outsider status is highlighted, their unfamiliarity and discomfort with behavioral norms and underlying assumptions disadvantage them, and they are encouraged to doubt themselves and their suitability. This effect is sometimes intensified by a kind of boundary-heightening activity in which the dominant culture is exaggerated in response to the entry of outsiders.[2] One new black firefighter noted, for example, that when women came through a traditional station, the veterans "went out of their way to be macho and kind of vulgar . . . out of their way to prove that they're men."

Such boundary-heightening gestures may involve a conscious effort to exclude. More often, however, the influence of culture seems both less conscious and more legitimate. A shared system of meaning has evolved out of the needs of workers to adapt and survive within a specific context of physical and social conditions.[3] This system functions to ensure reliability in coworkers, so that if people fail the cultural tests, they are probably not well suited to the work. If a particular group of people, such as women, tends to fit less comfortably than others, that may be unfortunate, but is not necessarily the result of a conscious attempt to exclude such groups. Furthermore, culture is not something that can be easily changed to suit the goal of integration.

Setting aside for a moment the problem of policy intervention, let us consider both the inevitability and functionality of the occupational culture of firefighters. If this culture is understood as an inevitable result of the work context and it is clearly functional in that context, then the argument for not merely accepting but honoring the culture is strong. However, if the culture is seen as contingent—a product of the historical dominance of a single group rather than the occupation per se—and its usefulness uneven, then it should be approached more critically.

One clue to the contingency of traditional firefighter culture on male dominance is its similarity to cultural forms found in other male-dominated environments regardless of structural conditions. For example, the use of ritual insults, practical jokes, and even physically threatening behavior to test character and establish and maintain group solidarity can be found in a wide range of settings, from blue-collar work environments to junior high school and even elementary school playgrounds.[4] The appearance of similar cultures in disparate settings suggests that firefighter culture is shaped by not only working conditions but also the work force itself.

Another way of examining this relationship poses a different question: would a different group, specifically women, produce a similar culture under comparable conditions? It is difficult to answer this question empirically given the historical exclusion of women from occupations like firefighting. Studies of women entering other types of male-dominated occupations have generally found women acquiring many values of the occupational culture,[5] but this is not the same result as women independently producing the same culture. Furthermore, the acculturation is not complete: gender differences within occupations remain.[6]

Some anecdotal information suggests that given the opportunity to create their own culture, women might respond to the demands of a particular work context differently than would men facing the same conditions. A powerful illustration of this phenomenon is offered by Judith Foster, a truck driver who learned her trade within a women's trucking collective.[7] She notes that her coworkers "created an environment of support for each other so they could learn a male-dominated trade in a noncompetitive atmosphere."[8] When Foster returned from a training run in which she had committed a major and costly mistake she found that instead of being lambasted by the others, "the women in the collective shared their own stories to let me know I was not alone in my experience, that in the learning process, no one can be expected to be perfect."[9] The culture of the women's trucking collective provides a striking contrast to the dominant learning environment of the fire service,[10] in which people are "chewed out" for mistakes and the veterans often give the impression that, as one black firefighter put it, "Nobody was ever new. Everybody broke in, they were [snaps his fingers] solid. You know, nobody ever made a mistake when they first got in. They were all ready to go."

The variation among firehouses in Oakland and the unconventional attitudes expressed by some veterans, particularly black men, also demonstrate that the traditional culture is not an inevitable product of the working conditions. In my visits to Oakland fire stations I occasionally met people who explicitly disavowed such norms as the harassment of newcomers and questioned the usefulness of these traditions. Sensitive newcomers found such houses a welcome relief from the customary rigors of the social initiation process, but other firefighters were sometimes critical or suspicious of the professional skill of these companies.

The defenders of traditional firefighter culture assert that it is well suited to the work environment. On the fireground, for example, norms of rough treatment are believed more efficient than polite communication. The abuse of newcomers is justified as a test of composure and the lack of active instruction as a way to assess the learner's enthusiasm and aggressiveness. In general, the rigors of the initiation process are believed to strengthen those who can take it and discourage those who cannot; this results in a more qualified, reliable work force. In our gendered society, this approach is consistent with the dominant form of masculinity.[11] If one were to imagine a firefighter culture shaped in accord with the values we commonly think of as feminine, it could look different in some respects. Instead of *testing* for the presence or absence of desired qualities such as aggressiveness and composure, for example, there might be an effort to elicit, develop, and support such qualities. On-the-job training would probably rely less on newcomer initiative and more on the active involvement of veterans. There might well be more disclosure of feelings in response to extremely traumatic incidents.[12]

It is an open question whether such a culture would be more or less functional than the traditional culture of a male-dominated fire service. It is certainly possible to see potential benefits of modifying this culture.[13] The traditional emphasis on untempered aggressiveness may put firefighters in needless danger at times, particularly if they are inexperienced. The reluctance to wear masks at outside fires undoubtedly increases toxic exposure and probably shortens life expectancy among firefighters. The inhibition of emotional responses may result in stress-related disorders that might be avoided by handling such responses differently. And the emphasis on conformity may discourage the creativity and enhanced problem-solving skills associated with heterogeneity in work groups.[14]

Of course the possibility that a different culture might be preferable implies neither that changing the culture is an appropriate policy goal nor that practical intervention could accomplish this. Because the culture is embedded and serves legitimate functions, direct attempts to change it would be inadvisable and probably failing. As an intellectual exercise, one could imagine dramatic alterations in the structure of work that would result in cultural changes—moving to eight-hour shifts, rotating station assignments for all veterans, and so forth—but such actions would meet with extreme resistance, and their effect would undoubtedly entail some negative unintended consequences. More gradual cultural transformation will result from changes in personnel, though as illustrated here, a balance must be struck between hiring radically different people who will not be accepted and continuing to hire people who will perpetuate the traditional culture. It is also possible that changes in the nature of the work will produce cultural transformation, though the experience of the last twenty or thirty years suggests that the process will be evolutionary at best.

Individual Rights in the Community of Firefighters

People who live and work in groups face a tension between individual autonomy and group cohesiveness; this tension can be particularly great in an occupation like firefighting where the pressures for solidarity are unusually strong. All firefighters have to give up something of themselves to get along, and newcomers especially are expected to conform to group standards. The entry of nontraditional groups into such an occupational community inevitably raises questions as to the legitimacy of community standards and what constitutes a fair level of accommodation. In a context in which all newcomers are expected to put up with a certain amount of harassment and subjugation, it becomes difficult to define precisely which behaviors are illegitimate because they exclude people on the basis of race or sex.

In a community of equals the problem of drawing boundaries is resolved informally: for example, an individual may simply refuse to put up with a coworker's abuse. Ultimately, this approach relies on an assumption that the resistance will be respected by the community—as opposed to provoking extreme anger, ostracism, sabotage, and the like—and in some cases that the protester will stand up for himself physically if necessary. In circumstances of inequality—as when unwanted groups enter the community—these conditions do not necessarily pertain, and the alternative regulatory or legalistic approach may be invoked to protect the members of the previously excluded group. An example of this approach is the increasing specification of policies pertaining to sexual harassment, clarifying the kinds of behaviors that are and are not tolerated by the organization.

Here as in many other contexts, reliance on a legalistic approach raises its own set of problems,[15] some of which were noted in the earlier discussion of sexual harassment policies. The structuring of human interactions by rules can lead to misplaced emphases and distorted incentives in which the behaviors that can be specified become the focus of concern, rather than the frequently more important but less controllable attitudes and actions. With sufficient enforcement, a fire department may be able to eliminate nude photographs from the lockers of firefighters, but will this effort ensure that women are fairly and effectively trained and evaluated? Some advocates argue that it will because eliminating pornography fosters a more positive working environment for women. An alternative and equally plausible scenario is that the effort will create a backlash of anger at the loss of freedom and resentment of the apparently "special treatment" accorded women, an attitude that results in a reduced willingness to accept and work with them.

If the latter result occurs, then the need for rules and enforcement becomes even greater, and external regulations begin to supplant the social norms of the group. People no longer interact as members of a community, but as independent individuals whose behavior is regulated strictly by rules. Under these conditions, interpersonal discretion and spontaneity are limited, while paranoia and distrust increase. Ironically, as some feminist legal critics have pointed out, an emphasis on individual rights in a white male-dominated society can result in decreased responsiveness to the needs of those who do not fit the traditional model of a citizen or worker.[16] Furthermore, this emphasis ignores the importance of community and the ways in which we as individuals are constituted by our interaction with others—a concern of many feminist social theorists.[17]

The unreliability and cost of conflict resolution through adjudication of rights can be seen in a recent case in the Los Angeles County Fire Department (LACFD).[18] In 1992, the department issued a policy prohibiting "sexually oriented magazines" such as *Playboy*, *Penthouse*, and *Playgirl* in all work locations, including dorms, rest rooms, and lockers. In response, the ACLU and the publishers of *Playboy* filed a lawsuit on behalf of a captain in the department, contending that the policy was a violation of free speech; a U.S. District Court agreed and struck down the policy.[19] Interestingly, at least one advocate of women in the fire service has criticized the ACLU on the basis of its concern for "the interests of one . . . over the greater good shared by all,"[20] an argument that one could imagine being made by the opponents of the LACFD policy.

The point here is that an appeal to rights cannot always be expected to protect the interests of the subordinate group, and such an appeal can damage the community. At the same time, the community cannot itself be relied on to treat its members well and fairly in the absence of mutual trust, respect, and power-sharing,[21] which appear not to be accorded to at least some members of the urban fire service. To avoid a destructive choice between the protection of subordinate group rights and the maintenance of community, we must reexamine the nature of the conflict. What concerns us here appears to be something beyond the "normal" tension between individuality and group solidarity because it reflects broader inequalities and cannot be readily resolved through the self-regulating mechanisms used by most group members (drawing one's own boundaries). Why is it not possible to achieve a community that will generally honor and protect the interests of its members, independent of their race or sex? What is the source of unresolvable conflict in this particular situation between the individual and the group?

Rethinking the Questions of Gender, Race, and Identity in the Urban Fire Service

In this group of urban firefighters, sex differences within race have proven more problematic than racial differences within sex. This finding is intriguing because most literature on employment discrimination tends not to draw analytical distinctions between racism and sexism.[22] The implication is that these phenomena operate in very similar ways and the situation of women of color can be understood as one of "double disadvantage" as though the effects of sex and race could simply be added (or, at most, multiplied) to arrive at an estimate of their joint influence.[23] The separate literatures on race and gender do clarify some distinctions,[24] and also a few writers have compared the problems of racism and sexism on a theoretical level,[25] but it is unusual to see the different workings of race and gender displayed in a single empirical setting.

In this context, the resistance to gender integration differs from the resistance to racial integration. Racial divisions among men have for some time been focused on the allocation question: Who is to receive fire service jobs and promotions? The conflict has been intense and ongoing, magnified by a combination of declining opportunities in blue-collar occupations and the particular appeals of firefighting. Gender divisions, by comparison, have centered more on the fundamental question of identity: Who belongs in the fire service? With women, the issue is not how many positions they should have, but whether they should be present at all. I could argue that this distinction is primarily an artifact of the particular time and place of this study: that is, the attainment of a critical mass by men of color in this department decisively answers the question of who belongs, at least as far as race alone is concerned. However, the results of this study and the literatures on race and gender more generally indicate that *in a context such as the urban fire service, the issues that divide black and white men are different from those that divide men and women.* Given this condition, the process of sexual integration differs from the process of racial integration and may be a good deal more problematic. Furthermore, because sex and race are not perfectly analogous factors, their joint effect in the case of women of color is complex and ambiguous. In brief, these women experience the socioeconomic disadvantages and the prejudices associated with their racial and sexual categories, but they may also derive some benefits from their familial and cultural backgrounds.[26]

DIFFERENCES IN RACIAL AND SEXUAL INTEGRATION
OF THE FIRE SERVICE

Black men have been part of the professional urban fire service for much longer than have women of any color. For at least half a century, these men have been struggling for increased access and opportunities, while women have been excluded altogether.[27] As late as 1976, a survey of California fire chiefs found that a majority of the respondents did not believe that women were physically capable of performing the job and that in fact almost a third would have refused to hire a woman *even if she were physically and mentally qualified.*[28]

The charge of incompetence has been part of the argument against both women and minority men, but changes in physical testing standards seem to have generated longer-lasting and more intense controversy than changes in academic standards or written tests. The physical aspects of the job have been heavily accentuated and the intellectual requirements deemphasized; as several men commented to me, "You don't have to be a rocket scientist to be a firefighter." According to one veteran, part of the reason the male firefighters show such lack of interest in EMS is because it's an activity at which women can excel. Similarly, truck work is glorified, although the engine crew generally puts out a fire. The pervasive importance of physical stature in this environment is illustrated by the sentiments of a black veteran expressing his disgust at the elimination of the height requirement. "A five-foot-tall person isn't good for *anything!*" he said emphatically, and it took a moment before he added the qualifier, "as far as the fire service goes."

The social experiences of men of color in the fire service have also been different from the experiences of women, regardless of color. Black men have been ostracized and harassed specifically over efforts to improve their circumstances, as when the Oakland stations were desegregated, but on the whole their experience seems not to have had the same quality of social distance and isolation felt by many women.

THE PARTICULAR MEANING OF *SEXUAL* HARASSMENT
IN MALE WORK CULTURE

Although both women and minority men have been subjected to special harassment as a way of signalling their unwantedness or in retaliation for political action, in many ways sexual harassment and the sexualization of the workplace have no racial analogs. As diversity trainers often observe, there is a greater understanding and consensus about the illegitimacy of racial harassment than sexual harassment: people often joke about "wanting to be sexually harassed" but don't suggest that racial harassment would be fun. Use of sexually explicit language and material is commonly defended, but very few white firefighters would assert a right to read white supremacist literature in the firehouse or to put up photographs depicting black men in dehumanizing, stereotypical poses. Even the telling of racist jokes is less frequent and more self-conscious than the telling of sexist jokes.

The more extensive confusion and outcry in response to anti-sexual harassment policies reflects three interconnected problems in gender relations not present in racial relations: the apparently greater social acceptability of sexism than racism,[29] the link between heterosexuality and sexual oppression that is part of women's experience but not generally acknowledged or understood by men, and the importance of sexuality to the male work culture.

The greater legitimacy of sexism probably derives primarily from our cultural conviction that constructed gender differences are based on biological sex differences.[30] While we are increasingly reluctant to accept racial or ethnic stereotypes, at least openly, we continue to apply and assume the rationality of sexual stereotypes. This feature of our culture becomes particularly clear when we stop to consider the omnirelevance of gender:[31] our sexual categories are considered relevant in virtually every aspect of human interaction, regardless of how little that interaction relates to the actual biological differences between the sexes. To illustrate the contrast between racial and sexual categorization, consider the fact that primary school teachers often address their students by sex: "Let me have your attention, boys and girls." Imagine how artificial the phrase would seem if it highlighted racial identity instead of gender.[32] Our taken-for-granted assumptions about sexual differences are expressed and fortified in the occupational world, where sex segregation, though declining somewhat, is still a prominent feature of life.[33]

A concomitant of sex segregation in occupations is the transfer of stereotypical sex roles from family or private life into the work setting.[34] In theory, this process could apply equally to men and women, but the inequality between the sexes results in an asymmetrical effect. Men are more likely than women to work in environments in which members of their own sex dominate,[35] and even in occupations numerically dominated by women, men tend to hold positions of power and authority.[36] They are therefore likely to be more influential in shaping the work environment, with the result that women are seen as women and men are seen as workers. The uneven effect of sex-role stereotyping in the workplace is magnified by the different roles of men and women in heterosexual relations: men are expected to be active, to make choices, to pursue, while women are expected to be relatively passive recipients or objects. As sexual objects, women are often dehumanized, their individuality submerged within a classification that emphasizes common body parts and physical functions. This treatment reaches an extreme in episodes of sexual violence, the fear of which is a defining feature of many women's lives.[37]

In a male-dominated environment like the fire service, then, the sexualization of the workplace that is enjoyable to many men can be threatening and demoralizing to women.[38] For them, continual reminders of their sexuality—including references to other women on the basis of sexual attributes—can signal disrespect because these actions emphasize a woman's sexual identity instead of her work identity. Most women recognize that this is not necessarily the intent of every man who makes a sexual comment, and they try not to overinterpret such actions. However, it should be noted that even the most tolerant women can eventually become weary of a general atmosphere in which sexuality is so prominent.

And sexuality appears to be a central feature of masculine work cultures.[39] Language, humor, and artifacts all suggest a preoccupation with sex and with women as sexual objects. Although some observers maintain that this humor and language constitute no more than "a pleasant diversion,"[40] others believe that sexual joking serves important purposes for male bonding,[41] which by definition excludes women. Sexist joking is particularly effective because it separates intimacy from (hetero)sexuality: women as objects do not threaten the male bond the way women as intimates might.

"WOMEN" DON'T BELONG IN THE FIRE SERVICE

The vehemence and the pervasiveness of opposition to women in the fire service and other masculine preserves,[42] such as military combat, suggest that there is something more at issue in these situations than either concerns about qualifications or threats to group cohesion. At stake is the meaning of gender as a category and, more specifically, the definition of masculinity. Psychoanalytic theories of gender identity posit that masculinity is achieved through the rejection and denial of femininity: as psychiatrist Robert Stoller puts it, "The first order of business in being a man is: don't be a woman."[43] The basic argument is that both sexes generally begin life with an attachment to a female care giver, with whom girls may continue to identify as they develop a sense of femininity, but from whom boys must separate to become masculine.[44] Masculinity, then, is achieved with some effort and is always vulnerable, whereas femininity is simply a matter of being female.

Whether or not psychoanalytic theory is an adequate explanation, there does appear to be a pronounced asymmetry reflected in many aspects of gender identification. For example, the notion of proving and defending one's *manhood* has only very weak female parallels. Similarly, a man can be insulted with the suggestion that he is behaving like a woman, but women are often complimented by being told they do something "like a man." Male homophobia and the exclusion of gay men from certain masculine environments can also be understood as a manifestation of the need to repress the feminine.[45]

It is not difficult to see how occupational segregation, particularly the association of higher status and rewards with men's work, bolsters the gender dichotomy and the meaning of masculinity. The entry of women into fields not only numerically dominated by men but traditionally thought of as masculine proving grounds poses a threat to this distinction, for the fewer the domains from which women can by definition be excluded, the less evidence we have for the validity of a gender distinction.[46] Because the distinction is fundamentally justified by the physical differences between the sexes, work that requires strength is a particularly critical area of contention. As Susan Martin found with police officers: "The objection to patrolwomen on the basis of their physical characteristics is 'the bottom line' and therefore, can be expected to be staunchly upheld. In jobs requiring some physical exertion, such as policing, the pressure to exclude women is based not only on men's desire to preserve their superior social and economic status but, more importantly, to preserve the meaning of 'manhood.' If the physical differences which are visible, measurable, and the traditional basis of the division of labor are irrelevant, how can other, less tangible differences be significant?"[47]

The exclusion or marginalization of women in such occupations serves not only the immediate interests of the men in those positions but also male dominance more generally, by sustaining a cultural ideal of masculinity.[48] At the same time, though, the aggressively masculine culture of many blue-collar settings also reflects tensions between gender and class hierarchies: the forms of dominance available to working-class men are different from those available to men in positions of greater political and economic power. The "anti-feminine" cultures of blue-collar male occupations, then, can also be read two ways: as a compensation for lack of material rewards,[49] and as a rejection of upper-class forms of masculinity.[50]

On the Question of Social Change

The cultural analysis of racial and sexual integration in the fire service reveals significant differences in the way race and gender operate in this particular setting. Gender appears more divisive here because of its centrality in the occupational identity—and the importance of this identity both for those in the occupation and for men in general. In another occupational culture in which different dimensions of identity were highlighted, race might be more problematic than gender—that is, the cultural similarity between white women and white men might seem greater than that between white men and men of color. In such a situation, it is likely that white women would be integrated more rapidly than men or women of color.

In either case, immediate policy prescriptions would include, as suggested earlier, an awareness and understanding of cultural differences and an effort to select people with strong cross-cultural skills. In time, achievement of more numerically balanced environments attained within a context of procedural fairness will also make a difference. However, both the feasibility and the effectiveness of such interventions are likely to be limited as long as the underlying opposition of identity, whether it be gender or race, is unresolved. That is, in situations where one group defines itself by denying its affinity with another, ongoing resistance to integration and equal opportunity can be expected. This problem is as likely to reflect racial opposition as gender opposition,[51] but because the present study has highlighted the latter, the remainder of this discussion is devoted to that question.

The experience of women in the fire department reflects the more general experience of being female in American society, for in many settings a girl or a woman is viewed by boys and men as "the thing not to be." Particularly dramatic evidence of the male disparagement of femaleness is found in studies of gender identity and values among adolescent and preadolescent boys and girls. Myra Sadker and David Sadker, for example, asked upper elementary and middle school students to write about the question "Suppose you woke up tomorrow and found you were a member of the other sex. How would your life be different?"[52] Among girls, the results varied; some were comfortable with their sex and would find the idea of changing it to be confusing, but others found the idea intriguing and were attracted by the greater power and possibilities associated with being male. Most telling, however, were the responses of the boys, for whom "the thought of being female is appalling, disgusting, and humiliating; it is completely unacceptable."[53] Many of them responded with elaborate suicidal fantasies.

In another Sadker study—this one involved nearly 1,100 children—42 percent of the girls found positive things to say about being male, but 95 percent of the boys saw nothing to look forward to in being female. Sixteen percent of these boys wrote about ways to escape their female bodies, including, most frequently, suicide.[54] In their essays, "boys took imaginative, desperate measures to get out of being girls."[55] The Sadkers summarize their own response to these findings: "Although we have read hundreds of boys' stories about waking up as a girl, we remain shocked at the degree of contempt expressed by so many. If the students were asked to consider waking up as a member of a different religious, racial, or ethnic group, would rejection be phrased with such horror and loathing?"[56]

Similar findings have emerged in other studies. In Cynthia Mee's work, two thousand middle school students were asked to complete open-ended statements on a variety of topics, including gender. In response to the incomplete statement "The best thing about my gender . . . " girls had quite a difficult time answering: in classroom discussions their body language conveyed withdrawal, and their most common written responses were "I don't know" and "Nothing," followed by comments about hair, makeup, shopping, and clothes. The boys responded enthusiastically, and their offerings fell into two general categories: "we can do more things" and "not being a girl." Conversely, the boys found little to say when asked "the worst thing" about their gender, whereas girls readily responded, focusing on physical appearance and biological issues.[57]

A number of ethnographic studies of gender construction in children have also found in some cases an incipient sexism and gender inequality, on occasion quite virulent, which mirrors that found in the most male-dominated spheres of adult activity.[58] These studies reveal early divisions of activity and power, but also opportunities for the development of greater equality and mutual respect.[59] The message is not that gender divisiveness is inevitable but that it is actively constructed early in life, and conscious intervention is necessary to counter this construction.

Various propositions have been offered to explain the process of gender differentiation and its vastly unequal results. A number of researchers highlight the importance of the social elaboration of physical differences as they emerge: the developing female body represents heightened sexual identity, decreased physical activity, and increased vulnerability, while the developing male body represents greater strength, athletic prowess, and increased independence.[60] Within the context of the present study, this differentiation is clearly relevant: the systematic discouragement and active exclusion of girls from organized sports greatly magnifies biological differences in physical ability and reduces the number of women inclined toward and capable of performing physical jobs such as firefighting.[61] This disparity in experience also creates cultural differences that advantage men and disadvantage women in this kind of work environment.

Some gender theorists, particularly those writing in a psychoanalytic framework, point to child-rearing practices and the asymmetry of gender identity development that results from single-sex care giving.[62] Others emphasize the construction or "doing" of gender in which we all participate, through collaboration and resistance, from childhood throughout our adult lives.[63] And some have concluded that the very creation of dichotomy produces inequality and that our best hope lies in an alternative social construction that does not define gender as a dichotomous category.[64]

The question of how to address these concerns, though well beyond the scope of this study, is not irrelevant to it. The experiences of women firefighters are shaped by a much larger context of gender conflict. Until and unless there is a more fundamental and equitable resolution of this conflict, social issues such as the sexual integration of the fire service will remain unsettled.

A Comment
Appendix on Method

A<small>NY ETHNOGRAPHER</small> will know that the outline of my research presented in chapter 1 is a minuscule fraction of the story. Although a more complete accounting of how this book came to be must be reserved for another time and place, I can offer here some additional details about my sample and logistics and, more important, a brief reflection on the challenges and quandaries inherent in this type of research.

OFD Class 1-91 included fifty-two recruits at the time I began observation (one had resigned before I arrived); of this group, thirty-eight expressed an interest in participating in the study and I was able to conduct interviews with thirty-two of them before the academy concluded. These initial interviews covered personal and familial background; the individual's path to the fire department, including motives and actions taken; expectations about the work; and experiences within the academy, both academic and social. Most interviews ran forty-five to sixty minutes and took place in a conference room at the academy whenever the recruits had a break—during lunch hour, immediately after the day's training, or occasionally during training downtime. Several members of the cadre graciously assisted me in arranging interviews around the academy schedule—for example, pulling a recruit out of the yard when it was clear he wouldn't be needed immediately and telling him to see his "debriefer."

I continued to observe both classroom and fireyard training for the duration of the academy, moving freely around the facility, talking with instructors and recruits, and meeting members of the companies when they visited the Tower to assist with training. Most people were curious about the study and readily shared information about the occupation, the department, and their own experiences. At the conclusion of the academy, I attended both the graduation ceremony and the party the recruits had organized to celebrate.

The department agreed with my request to follow recruits into the field and to conduct follow-up interviews with them over time. Subject to the approval and discretion of the company officers, I was permitted to visit the fire stations for observation and interviews and to attend incidents either in my own car or in a department vehicle if an extra seat was available. From among the initial group of interviewees I selected for follow-up some twenty-six recruits (described in chapter 1), a group that was small enough that I could get to know the members, but large enough to provide reasonable variation within subgroups (of race/ethnicity and sex). Some of this variation is shown in Table A–1, which gives ages, education levels, and firefighting backgrounds for people in these subgroups. Probably the most striking feature of this table is the relatively high frequency of firefighting experience and social connections to the department among the white men.

During the next eighteen months—the probationary period for Oakland firefighters—I reinterviewed the members of my sample group four times. In follow-up interviews, we discussed their experiences with different firehouses; details of important or memorable calls such as the first structure fire or difficult medical; lessons learned; leadership styles of different officers; interactions with veterans; differences between experience and expectations; sources of enjoyment or discomfort about the job; and general impressions of the work. These interviews ran between forty-five and ninety minutes and almost always took place in fire stations—usually in the lounge or officer's quarters to allow privacy.

Over the course of the study I visited every fire station in the city, making extended and repeated visits to some. As I have explained, these visits as well as my attendance at emergency responses gave me an opportunity to meet and talk with veterans and to observe firefighter work and life. In addition to partaking in many informal discussions with veteran firefighters, I conducted a handful of more formal interviews with certain individuals—leaders of the union and the OBFFA, members of the administration, and women who had entered in previous classes. These interviews were intended to address gaps in my understanding and to provide background information on the department that would supplement what was available in public documents.

This methodological narrative does not do justice to the difficulties of negotiating access in a study like this. Before approaching Oakland, I had talked with firefighters in this and other departments as well as people employed by the City of Oakland administration and had been repeatedly advised that official access would be next to impossible to obtain. It was, thus, with some trepidation that I approached Chief Ewell, and with considerable

Table A-1
Characteristics of Study Participants

Age	Education	Firefighting experience	Firefighting education	EMT education or experience	Immediate family member in OFD*
White Men					
24	some college†	no	yes	yes	yes
27	BA/BS	no	no	no	no
27	some college	yes	yes	yes	yes
28	some college	yes	yes	yes	no
30	some college	yes	yes	yes	yes
33	some college	yes	yes	yes	no
38	BA/BS	no	yes	no	yes
Asian American, Filipino, and Hispanic Men					
30	some college	no	no	yes	yes
31	BA/BS	yes	yes	yes	no
32	high school	no	no	no	no
32	high school	no	no	no	no
34	BA/BS	no	no	no	no
36	BA/BS	yes	yes	no	no
African American Men					
25	some college	no	yes	no	no
26	BA/BS	no	no	no	no
26	some college	no	yes	no	yes
34	some college	no	yes	no	no
41	BA/BS	no	yes	no	no
41	some college	no	no	no	no
Women					
23	some college	no	yes	yes	no
24	some college	no	no	no	no
26	BA/BS	no	no	no	no
28	BA/BS	no	no	no	no
34	BA/BS	no	yes	yes	no
35	BA/BS	no	no	yes	no
36	some college	no	no	no	no

Notes: *Several more people had family members in other departments or extended family members in OFD. †"Some college" includes attendance at community colleges, which in some cases is limited to fire science and EMT classes.

amazement and delight that I learned that he and certain other high-ranking officers were not only willing to participate but interested in the research. They are to be credited for their generosity and open-mindedness.

This, of course, was not the end but the beginning of the story. As any ethnographer knows, the process of entry is continual, renegotiated with each encounter. Rapport does build over time when one has repeated contacts with the same respondents, but in my case the department was so large and the movement of my participants so frequent that it seemed I was constantly entering unfamiliar settings and introducing myself to officers and veteran crew members. For the most part, these people were remarkably accepting of my presence, but it was difficult under the circumstances to establish the comfort level characteristic of good ethnography. There were a few places in which I came to know the crew reasonably well over many visits, but even in these cases it happened that almost every time I showed up at the station there would be an unfamiliar face—someone trading in for the day or working overtime for an absent crew member.

Despite signs of their growing acceptance of and fondness for me—people teasing me, treating me like a mascot, showing pleasure at my arrival—I was always conscious of my outsider status. I was not a firefighter, nor did I have any other kind of official role in their world. I was there only by the grace of their forbearance, and I never forgot that. My practical need to be accepted paralleled in many ways the needs of new firefighters to be accepted, and I was confronted with some of the same dilemmas. I had to interact as a real person in the environment, and yet I could not be myself. I made the compromises all new firefighters make to some degree—smiling sometimes at jibes that seemed cruel or prejudiced, and more often, remaining silent when in different circumstances I might have spoken up in disagreement. My sex added another dimension to the complexity and ambiguity of the work; clearly, I could be more readily accepted if I made an effort to make myself attractive and appealing, but at the same time I sometimes felt I was betraying the women firefighters by doing so, for this is not ultimately a healthy basis on which to build male-female work relationships of equality.

My entry was also complicated by the need to develop and sustain rapport with a number of sometimes opposing groups. In many ethnographic studies, the researcher must be accepted by others who more or less constitute a single group—the workers on the factory floor, the members of a single urban gang, the people living in a homeless shelter. There are always the delicacies of negotiating one's way around interpersonal jealousies, but these are not the same as structural oppositions and, in any case, are orthogonal to the research question, not coincident with it. By contrast, although I needed to establish relationships and rapport with participants, I could not risk a closeness that would identify me with a particular set of interests or I would lose my access to others.

Many other ethnographers have debated the effects of research and writing from the outsider versus insider perspective; it is difficult to fully understand the subjects' world without becoming one of them, but if a writer becomes an insider, she can no longer see what is visible from an outside perspective. Sometimes the handicap of my outsider position was pointedly brought home to me, as when a veteran demanded angrily how I could hope to understand firefighters if I wasn't prepared to run into burning buildings. I also felt my disadvantage when I stood outside a fire and tried to make sense of the activity taking place before me. I took solace at these times in the knowledge that even the participants wouldn't have a complete picture, as I often heard in my interviews. I tried to overcome my distance from the subject of firefighters by spending as much time as possible with them, by asking people to review an emergency scene for me, and by always listening with great care. Toward the end of my fieldwork, I would try out my ideas on insiders and invite their responses.

In this context, I should also mention that I am uncomfortable with the frequent use of the phrase "participant observation" to describe the kind of work that I have done. To me, the phrase implies that one is a full participant in the constructed world of the subjects, and this I was not. I was a participant in our shared world—that of human beings talking and interacting across occupational boundaries—but I was not a firefighter. I have thus consistently referred to my firehouse and incident activities simply as "observations," with only minimal reference to "participation."

There are many moral and emotional dilemmas in this work. Most researchers are admirably concerned with meeting rigorous intellectual standards, but I am sometimes shocked by the level of arrogance and nonchalance often displayed in their approach to moral and emotional questions. Perhaps I swing too far in the opposite direction, but I am regularly troubled by the implications of my own choices and behavior. For example, if I were confronted with a woman firefighter who was struggling to do the work and who shared her self-doubts with me, how should I respond? As a researcher and an outsider, I might also have doubts about her suitability for the work; should I express these? As a feminist and a woman, I might deeply admire her for even trying, and especially for succeeding as well as she did under conditions that would have defeated me; should I say this? As a human being who grew to care about this person and who felt her pain, should I simply comfort her? And what were the implications of these alternative courses of action?

Furthermore, what should I do with such *information*—as a researcher and a human being in relationship with individual participants? How much ought I to reveal, and in what context? Perhaps the most talked-about dilemma for research of this kind is the need to balance respondent confidentiality with faithfulness to the story. There are no easy answers for those who take this problem seriously; meeting the challenge involves constant and sometimes troubling compromise.

Finally, there is the problem of deciding when the work is finished. At the end of a book, in an effort to provide coherence and a satisfying conclusion, a writer may give the false impression that the last word of the story has been written. In two senses, this is not the case. First, the action continues. Shortly after I completed my fieldwork, a number of sexual harassment charges were being investigated and different features of the problems of gender and race were being revealed, which I could not pursue. Second, with respect to what had already taken place and been observed and recorded by me, there will always be other layers of interpretation that could be offered. Though not necessarily contradicting what I have written, they could highlight an entirely different set of issues and concerns. As a wise captain in the fire department said to me of his approach to investigating harassment complaints, "You start by telling yourself that you won't make a decision until you get all the facts. Then you gather the facts, you assess the situation, and you make your call. Then you remind yourself that you don't have all the facts. And you never will."

Notes

Chapter 1 After the Door Is Open:
Finding One's Place in the Community of Firefighters

1. Urban fire department training facilities generally include a drill tower—an empty building of several stories that is used for practical exercises—and the training division itself may be referred to as "the Tower." In Oakland, the drill tower is five stories high, with an outside stairwell, a fire escape, a basement, and standpipes (pipes installed in the building for firefighting purposes).
2. It is often difficult to find racial/ethnic designations that are both accurate and objectionable to no one. The term "Hispanic" is used here because it was the choice of the men themselves when asked to identify their own race/ethnicity.
3. Names, station numbers, and certain other identifying details have been changed to protect identities.
4. I am aware of the linguistic practice in which the term "sex" is used to refer to biological categories and "gender" to cultural constructions. I use the terms more interchangeably because I agree with Kessler and McKenna (1978) that the differential use of the two terms suggests that the biological dichotomy is not socially constructed.
5. Reskin and Roos (1990).
6. Ibid.
7. See Jacobs (1989). He notes that if all women who aspire to traditionally masculine occupations were to enter and remain in such work, sex segregation would be much less pronounced than it is. Jacobs argues that while early socialization and educational tracking contribute to segregation, the "revolving door" of women into and out of male occupations can only be explained by gender-based social control in the workplace itself.
8. According to an NAACP lawyer cited in Sullivan (1988), more than one hundred jurisdictions at the time were under court order to integrate police or fire departments. Political scientist William Muir agreed that the public safety departments became "a major focus of civil rights groups early on" (cited in Sullivan, 1988:3). Rockwell (1989) asserts that the International Association of Fire Fighters is unsurpassed as an organization in the number of "reverse discrimination" lawsuits it has activated.

9. The impact of structural changes in the American economy is discussed in Wilson (1987).

10. For example, in 1992 the annual starting salary for a New York City firefighter was $30,939 for a forty-hour week; it was $41,864 in San Francisco for a forty-eight-hour week, and $46,086 in Richmond, California, for a fifty-six-hour week (see Kapalczynski, 1993, for a list of many American and Canadian departments; note, however, that Kapalczynski's figure for San Francisco happens to be in error).

11. In a survey of New York City firefighters, more than 90 percent of the more experienced respondents felt that firefighters have a "special bond" (Center for Social Policy and Practice in the Workplace, 1988). When I asked an Oakland veteran what made the job so great, he answered, "Working with the guys." He went on to ask how many good friends I had. I said, "A small number, maybe half a dozen." He nodded and said, "I have five hundred—five hundred guys that would go through that wall for me if I needed it."

12. A survey of New York City firefighters found that substantial majorities of the respondents saw themselves as part of an elite, felt that firefighting had a special tradition, felt that firefighters had a special bond, and felt great pride to be firefighters (Center for Social Policy and Practice in the Workplace, 1988). Reflecting the gender divisions in this occupation, such feelings were stronger among men than among women in the department. The public may not hold firefighting in as much awe and respect as do its members, but they do have a very positive view of the occupation. In an opinion poll conducted by the firm of J. Walter Thompson, Americans were asked to rank seventy-three occupations according to their honesty and integrity; "fireman" was at the top of the list (Patterson and Kim, 1991).

13. During this study I frequently heard this phrase or variations of it from firefighters and recruits, particularly those with a traditional orientation.

14. The first person to climb this particular rock face without mechanical assistance was Lynn Hill, who made the free climb in September 1993.

15. Rockwell (1989) uses this term to describe the period between enactment of the 1964 Civil Rights Act and the first court settlements of antidiscrimination lawsuits—roughly 1965 to 1975.

16. U.S. Bureau of the Census (1970).

17. Riccucci (1990:109) states that a "comparison of the various uniformed services indicates that the occupation of firefighting may be the most protected male bastion and, hence, the most resistant to the entry of women."

18. Note that police and firefighter work force compositions are compared here to the composition of the employed labor force. It should be noted that minorities—African Americans in particular—are more likely to be unemployed than whites, so that if the denominator (comparison group) included all workers, black representation would be farther from parity than it appears.

19. Noting the over-reliance on organizational analysis in studies of the workplace, Van Maanen and Barley (1984:289–290) suggest "the notion of an occupational community as an alternative to an organizational frame of reference for understanding why it is that people behave as they do in the workplace." Among the features they associate with an occupational (as opposed to organizational) framework are: an emphasis on the meaning that work has for the worker rather than for others; an understanding of work and career derived more from the work itself than from movement in the organization; and the primacy of work and the work group as explanatory concepts.

20. For purposes of this book, "culture" is understood to be the social context that structures and gives meaning to human actions. Rothman (1987:40) argues that work cultures "reflect a collective adaptation to . . . social and physical working conditions,"

while Schein, writing about organizations, formally defines culture as a "pattern of shared basic assumptions that the group learned as it solved its problems of external adaptation and internal integration, that has worked well enough to be considered valid and, therefore, to be taught to new members as the correct way to perceive, think, and feel in relation to those problems" (1992:12). Cockburn offers a slightly different perspective, alluding to her informants' beliefs as "what Gramsci called 'common sense,' or what a more recent tradition of cultural studies terms 'culture.' They are ideologies in the little sense of the word, the thoughts and feelings that arise from daily experience" (Cockburn, 1983:212). The working definition used here is also informed by the essays of Charles Taylor, who does not define culture *per se*, but who argues persuasively that the proper subject of social science is in fact "common meanings," or shared descriptions of social reality (see Taylor, 1985, especially "Interpretation and the Sciences of Man").

21. Louis (1980; 1990) explicates this process of "lay ethnography" in which "surprise" gives rise to "sense making." His model, drawn in part from phenomenological sociology, calls to mind the practice of ethnomethodology or the discovery of implicit rules of normality through incongruity, contradiction, or breakdown (see Garfinkel, 1967).

22. In firefighting, the leather-lunged, smoke-eating, Marlboro-man image is becoming a thing of the past, though a nostalgic appreciation for it remains.

23. A more detailed discussion of method is presented in the appendix.

24. The one other woman of color in the class, a Latina, did not volunteer to participate actively in the study.

25. Louis (1990:104) proposes "that newcomers affect their own acculturation processes, in that differences in newcomers' entry situations draw out different resources and assistance from organizational agents." He mentions self-confidence and cognitive complexity as characteristics that may advantage a newcomer in the acculturation process.

Chapter 2 *Work, Culture, and Identity in the Urban Fire Service*

1. Ross and Nisbett (1991:170) allude to this circularity when they note that "ethnic, racial, religious, regional, and even economic subcultures are in an important sense the distillates of historical situations, as well as powerful contemporary determinants of individuals' behavior. They are, at the same time, important sources of the particular subjective meanings and construals we place upon the social events we observe."

2. As in other urban fire departments, the OFD's early history may have been somewhat less than dignified. According to a report by the department historian, a predecessor of the department was disbanded in 1855. "The official reason given was for inefficiency and lack of funding. The newspaper accounts at the time imply that the firefighters may have been too drunk—on more than one occasion—to perform their duties adequately" (Honeycutt, 1994:3). Uncouth early behavior was not unique to OFD; in describing the history of inner-city violence in New York, Foster (1986) recounts at some length the activities of the volunteer fire brigades that preceded the New York Fire Department. He characterizes the volunteer companies as "an odd lot" and details their "ongoing physical and violent conflicts," their occasional thievery, and their relationship to urban gangs (Foster, 1986:87–89).

3. Data on OFD are taken from departmental summaries. The figures cited here for OFD are current as of December 1992. Twenty years earlier the department had a uniformed force of 658 and total staff of 700, with twenty-eight stations (including eight trucks, each with five or six men); on-duty staffing was roughly 180.

4. In a 1992 survey of U.S. fire departments conducted by American Fire Services and reported in *Firehouse* magazine, Boston reported 46,563 incidents and 1,984 structure fires (Kapalczynski, 1993). OFD was not among the departments included in this report, but a comparison of its internal data with the survey responses suggests that Oakland is among the top thirty departments with respect to total incidents and among the top twenty with respect to structure fires. Because of possible differences in reporting conventions, however, it is difficult to make precise comparisons.

5. Kapalczynski (1993).

6. With reference to the American Fire Services 1992 survey, these figures would suggest that OFD's top engine companies are among the twenty busiest EMS engine companies in the country (Kapalczynski, 1993).

7. It should be noted that OFD's trucks do respond to medical calls: in 1993, roughly 17 percent of Truck 18's responses were for emergency medical services. While there is a trend toward the use of trucks for medical responses, this is not occurring in all cities, and the American Fire Services 1992 survey did not distinguish between truck companies that do and do not respond to medical calls (Kapalczynski, 1993).

8. Early data on the composition of the department's work force are hard to come by, but some information is available from newspaper reports, court documents, and the recollections of veterans. For example, a flier distributed by the Oakland Black Fire Fighters Association (OBFFA) reports that at the time the Association was founded in 1973 there were 47 black members of the department, which would be 7 percent of the total uniformed force of 658. Observers recall few if any other minority members of the department at the time. The trial court judge's Post Trial Brief in the case of *Hull v. Cason* indicated that in 1975, the 622-member force was 87 percent white, 10 percent black, 2 percent Spanish-surnamed, 0.6 percent Asian, and 0 percent Native American (a total of eighty minority firefighters). Another document in the case indicates that some thirty of the department's minority firefighters were hired between 1972 and 1974 (Supplemental Brief of Respondents Re: Exhaustion of Administrative Remedies and Request for Judicial Notice, Exhibit A, *Hull v. Cason*, 1974).

9. Figures are current as of 12/17/92. No new firefighters have been hired since that date, but there have been separations and promotions that would affect these percentages slightly.

10. Figures are for 2/1/94 (from SFFD Management Services Report). As of April 1992, the New York City Fire Department was reportedly 93 percent white male (Myers, 1992). The City of San Jose, similar to San Francisco, reports a sworn force in November 1993 that was 69 percent white and 96 percent male (from City of San Jose affirmative action statistics). Figures reported in RAND (1993) indicate that the fire department forces of Chicago, Houston, San Diego, and Seattle are slightly less integrated than is Oakland's: Chicago is 4 percent female and 28 percent minority; Houston: 0.6 percent, 27 percent; San Diego: 8 percent, 28 percent; and Seattle: 7 percent, 24 percent (recall that Oakland is 8 percent female and 43 percent minority).

11. It should be noted that intergroup alliances and participations have been fluid. Women, Hispanic, and Asian American firefighters have at different times been allied with or had their interests represented by the OBFFA, but not consistently. Not all blacks have been active and invariable supporters of the OBFFA. Finally, the OBFFA's training sessions are open and have on occasion been attended by whites.

12. McKinney and Soennichsen (1979).

13. Firehouses had common bathrooms with open shower stalls, urinals, and toilet stalls

with doors. One male observer said the department dealt with the entry of women by buying "two-bit plastic shower curtains" for the stations.

14. There was concern on the part of city and fire department administrations that sexual harassment complaints be avoided, so firefighters underwent mandatory training in which they were made aware they would be held personally accountable for unacceptable behavior, which included the traditional hazing of newcomers. Some firefighters miss those traditions, but others were just as glad to see them go.

15. One of the first women commented that the toughest part of this stage of her career was "never being accepted," and she noted that a particularly conservative officer actually refused to work with women, claiming it "a sin and an abomination against God for men and women to work together." She reported being totally ostracized in some stations, coming to blows with another firefighter, and at times fearing for her life. She had such a hard time finding people willing to work with her as a new firefighter that she concluded simply that "there was a conspiracy to get me to fail."

16. Population estimates given here are from the 1980 U.S. Census. In June 1985 the department's uniformed force was 0.8 percent Native American (compared to a 1980 census figure of roughly 0.7 percent), 1.7 percent Asian/Pacific Islander (compared to 8 percent), 5.2 percent Hispanic (compared to 9.5 percent), and 68.6 percent white (compared to 35 percent in the city). Women were 1.7 percent of the uniformed force (compared to 53 percent of the city's population).

17. See *Petersen, et al. v. City of Oakland, et al.*, USDC ND Cal. No. C-89-2784 WHO (1989).

18. Urban firefighters also frequently engage in other types of firefighting tasks, being called on to extinguish fires in automobiles, trash bins, and the like. These events, though an integral part of the urban firefighter's work, are not thought of as "real" firefighting by members of the profession. A wholly distinct though equally demanding type of firefighting is wild land or forest firefighting, in which urban firefighters may occasionally participate (either through mutual aid calls or—as in Oakland in 1991—because of the increasing wild land–urban interface area).

19. An effort has been made to use transcript conventions that will maintain both accuracy and readability. Conventions include the following. Any text in brackets—[ ]—represents something other than the interviewee's own words, including a phrase used to clarify the speech, but within the flow of the narrative; a nonverbal response; or a clarifying reference. Parenthetical words reflect uncertain transcriptions; spaces in parentheses are inaudible portions. Ellipses indicate segments of the response that have been deleted, but ellipses have been omitted at the beginning and ending of quotations as follows editorial convention.

20. McCarl (1985:157) notes the role of unspoken emotional support and bonding among coworkers in this job: "Each inch crawled down a superheated hallway pushes a fire fighter farther and farther away from our reality toward a situation where instinct must give way to conditioning. The only thing that allows a person to do that more than once is knowing that others who you trust will share your fear and still do what has to be done."

21. Figures cited here are from OFD Summaries of Company Work for 1993.

22. A July 1988 report in *The Oakland Tribune* cited a figure of 60 percent EMS false alarms (Newbergh, 1988). Many firefighters would probably put the proportion even higher today.

23. See Rothman (1987) for a discussion of the relationship between working conditions and occupational culture, including the functions served by such cultures. Evidence of this relationship may be found in McCarl's (1985) study of firefighters,

Haas's (1977) ethnography of high steelworkers, and Gouldner's (1954) description of the culture of gypsum miners.

24. Other descriptions of firefighter work and culture may be found in McCarl (1985) and Smith (1972), both describing urban fire departments. A sense of wild land firefighting can be found in Enarson's (1984) book on women in the U.S. Forest Service and Maclean's (1992) story of USFS Smokejumpers in the disastrous Mann Gulch fire. Brown (1994) describes a smaller fire department—that of Oxford, Mississippi—that seems to have a big-city style.

25. The testing and other functions served by abusive verbal exchanges are confirmed in McCarl's findings from the District of Columbia Fire Department. "These insults and put-downs . . . are mock battles in which the solidarity of the group is reinforced by verbal parry and thrust. This is a permissible type of verbal expression, which informs the group of individual emotions and serves as a gauge to an individual's reaction under pressure. . . . If the individual cannot exchange this kind of abuse with equanimity, then his opportunities for acceptance as an equal in the culture are severely limited" (McCarl, 1985:177).

26. Both McCarl (1985) and Smith (1972) describe macabre firehouse conversations and humor. These forms of expression are also common among emergency room staffs and other groups who must distance themselves emotionally from their working conditions.

27. McCarl (1985:38) notes that "firefighters retain and pass on a tremendous amount of their information in story form." Firefighter stories deal with events and social concerns, job concerns, "bullshitting," and tales of unusual, strange, or bizarre incidents.

28. Stuhlmiller found the commitment to the team to be a defining characteristic of firefighters she interviewed regarding their rescue work following the 1989 Loma Prieta earthquake (Stuhlmiller, 1990).

29. McCarl (1985) notes that practical jokes and ragging are used to signal insider status and exercise social control, ease work tensions, and simply pass the time.

30. Rothman (1987) discusses the role of rituals in work cultures generally; McCarl (1985) describes the meaning attached to ceremonies in firefighter culture.

31. McCarl (1985:58) discusses the traditional importance of dinnertime in the firehouse and notes that everyone is expected to participate. "There is only one other faux pas worse than not helping in any way with the meal and that is not to eat it, or 'be counted out.' "

32. Upon a change of status as in graduation or promotion, various artifacts are conferred, including special badges or other insignia. In Oakland, ride-alongs (interns of a sort) wear yellow helmets; firefighters, black helmets; officers, red helmets; and chiefs, white helmets. Helmets have a shield with an identifying number on it, but in the academy the recruit shields are blank. On graduation, recruits receive the badges and numbers. Clothing and badge decorations and color vary by rank, with the officers having more decorated uniforms than the firefighters, and the chief officers the only ones to wear white shirts (in the field) and gold badges. Oakland is in the process of recalling older badges that say "fireman" instead of "firefighter," a bone of contention with some old-timers.

33. Many features of firefighter culture bear a striking resemblance to the cultural elements of other male settings, including elementary and middle school boys' groups (see Thorne, 1993; Everhart, 1983) and other male-dominated work and social settings (see Schroedel, 1985; Martin, 1988; Walshok, 1981; Fine, 1987; Lyman, 1987). See also Weston (1990) for an excellent analysis of blue-collar work production as a "metaphor for maleness."

34. Others have written about domination and exclusion through culture. Epstein (1990:94) gives an example of the construction of an occupational identity among

cable splicers that is a source of solidarity for some but excludes others, as its "solidary relations come at the direct expense of other workers—especially women—who are discouraged from entering the fold. While splicers and other craft workers suggested in conversation that women would be welcome in their trade, they infuse their work with an ethos of manliness that is an all but physical barrier to women. Their occupational culture emphasizes the physical strength, endurance, and toughness required to deal with dirty and dangerous work. The splicers have taken the ethos of manliness well beyond what might reasonably be viewed as natural in manual work, and it serves to defend their craft against potential interlopers." Jones (1986) suggests that the problem of "cultural racism" compounds the structural disadvantages of black people in white-dominated society. "In this view, the maintenance and functioning of opportunity structures . . . in this country is predicated on certain values of individuality, future-orientation, written and material approaches to accomplishment which define appropriate inputs. If a person does not or cannot operate within this framework, he or she is either obliged to operate within another opportunity structure . . . or is at a disadvantage within the majority context. If a group has evolved from a cultural legacy and tradition at variance with this framework, it too is at a collective disadvantage or must develop alternative routes to the mainstream opportunity structure" (Jones, 1986:293). See also Henley and Kramarae (1991) on the notion of "cultural dominance" as opposed to "cultural difference."

Chapter 3   Newcomers at Entry: Reflecting Back, Looking Forward

1. There were one or two African American men in the recruit class as a whole who did have prior firefighting experience, but they did not happen to be part of the group that was followed.
2. Those referred to as "Asian Americans" in this study included men of Filipino descent; the distinction between Filipinos and other Asians is not analytically important here.
3. Interestingly, Leonard was somewhat mistaken in his impression that all class members would graduate with the same seniority. As the more traditional newcomers were aware, seniority would be based on people's ranking in the final exam, with ties broken by test scores on a subsequent probationary exam. Still, he was probably correct that the competitive drive had less to do with concrete gain than with personal style.

Chapter 4   Initiation: Swimming in the Shark's Tank

1. More than one old-timer insisted that today's newcomers have a mild initiation in comparison to what it was. Twenty or thirty years ago, they claim, newcomers were expected to be silent for their first several weeks or even months, gradually being acknowledged as they began to prove themselves at fires. One officer recalled being put on watch—in the days when the watch person really had to pay attention constantly—for the entire twenty-four-hour shift. Another claimed that it was common to hang probationary firefighters upside down in the hose towers.
2. Goody (1989:249) observes that the tensions that characterize the relationship between craftsman and apprentice are like those "affective tensions between a man and the first-born son destined to replace him." Coy (1989:4) comments on the economic implications of training new members: by qualifying newcomers in a trade, the masters lose some of their own control; "apprenticeship is at one time the means of perpetuating the craft and the means of destroying its power."
3. Abuse of the newcomer is commonly noted in studies of blue-collar work cultures.

See, for example, Haas (1977) on the derogatory treatment of apprentices by journeymen among ironworkers; Cockburn (1983) on the menial tasks of compositor apprentices; Walshok (1981) on the observations of women in blue-collar jobs about the need for a thick skin. Somewhat surprisingly, Van Maanen noted that police recruits were welcomed into the patrol division with no hazing, but this may have been because the humiliation and degradation of the academy were so great (Van Maanen, 1973). Studies of working-class women's cultures rarely if ever report this sort of phenomenon; see, for example, Lamphere (1985) on garment and electronics workers; Sacks (1988) on hospital workers; and Westwood (1984) also on garment workers. Westwood's workers clearly had a joking, prank-playing culture but she doesn't mention newcomers being singled out for special treatment.

4. Raphael makes the point that although initiation rites include the threat of failure, there is every expectation that the initiate will succeed; they are not really designed as screening procedures (Raphael, 1988).

5. Many urban fire departments have been the subject of antidiscrimination lawsuits, and the consent decrees from these lawsuits have given rise to a wave of "reverse discrimination" cases. In fact, Rockwell asserts that "no organization in the United States has activated more 'reverse discrimination' suits than the I.A.F.F." (Rockwell, 1989:714). He details the efforts of firefighters to resist affirmative action in Miami, Boston, Toledo, San Francisco, and Oakland. Affirmative action struggles have also taken place in Washington, D.C., New York, Birmingham, Detroit, Newark, Chicago, St. Louis, Memphis, Gadsden, and Cincinnati, among other cities. Discussions of two cases may be found in Norris and Reardon (1989) and Spiegelman (1985).

6. In the San Francisco Fire Department, where my interview data suggest that race is a much more divisive issue, the proportion of African Americans in the total uniformed force is roughly 9 percent.

7. Foster (1986); Majors and Billson (1992).

8. Majors and Billson (1992); Foster (1986).

9. Foster (1986):178-79. See also Majors and Billson (1992) on the relationship between masculinity and games like the dozens. Foster cites a number of researchers who have elaborated on the game's function "as part of the masculine struggle against female domination" or "as a puberty ritual leading to manhood" (Foster, 1986:219).

10. For example, Miller (1986) notes that conflict has been a "taboo area" for women in particular, partly because of their lesser power. Brown and Gilligan (1992) describe the extreme lengths to which private-school adolescent girls go to deny or avoid open disagreement with peers. In Sheldon's study of predominantly white preschoolers, the suppression of confrontational talk in girls results in the use of "double-voice discourse"—attending simultaneously to needs of the self and the other—by girls attempting to resolve conflict in play. Boys in conflict more frequently use single-voice discourse, a direct, self-oriented approach (Sheldon, 1991).

11. Fictional portrayals of aggressive women illustrate this point. The "catty" characters of a play like Boothe's *The Women*, for example, rarely insult each other as a form of bonding or verbal play but generally because they despise each other and they themselves are nasty people (Boothe, 1937; see especially her "Foreword"). In my own experience, women often marvel at the ability of men to engage in aggressive, open conflict with, to all appearances, no hard feelings attached.

12. For example, Goodwin's observational study of black children's neighborhood play found that girls exchanged ritual insults with boys but not with each other; girls' play also tended to be less competitive and to involve somewhat less hierarchical structuring. Girls' conflicts were more indirect, making use of "he-said-she-said" disputes in which one girl would charge another with having gossiped about her:

"Among a group of individuals for whom it is culturally inappropriate to insult, command, or accuse another person openly, the confrontation provides an event—a political process—through which complaints about others may be aired and character may be generated" (Goodwin, 1990:219). In a study of predominantly white girls, Eder found that ritual insulting, while not a frequent occurrence in all groups, "was a common activity in certain groups of girls who came from working- or lower-class backgrounds" (Eder, 1990:74). Eder also notes that studies of conflict in black girls have not always arrived at consistent findings, with some noting ritual conflict among girls alone, and others (Goodwin) seeing it only in mixed groups. In a slightly different context, Grant looked at classroom behaviors of students by race (white/black) and sex and found that whereas boys of both races tended to be more involved in aggressive episodes, black girls were much more likely to fight back verbally or physically than were white girls, though less likely to do so than were boys (Grant, 1984).

13. The maintenance of a "macho image" appears to be an important part of many traditionally male jobs: women working in such settings often hear direct expressions of this sentiment. Gigi Marino's description of being a merchant sailor notes that her problems came not from the work so much as from the men who told her she didn't belong there; she quotes one coworker: " 'How do you think it makes us feel,' he asked, 'to have you go out and do the same job as us?' " (Martin, 1988:183). In the same anthology, Marian Swerdlow, a subway conductor, comments that her coworkers found women more of a threat to their egos than to their jobs: "They saw themselves as doing a man's job. They had a big stake in believing they were doing a job only the superior sex could handle emotionally as well as physically" (Martin, 1988:195). Cockburn, finding the same sentiment tied to socioeconomic concerns, quoted one young man at length on the subject of how "some of the shine would go out of the job" for him with the entry of women and commented, "He is saying that the presence of woman, one woman, any woman, is enough to destroy the mystique that women could not do the work and its corollary, that men must be superior because they can" (Cockburn, 1983:180).

Consistent with this picture, the culture of the fire service is quite homophobic, with many jokes and insults directed at male homosexuality in particular. Not surprisingly, as of this writing there are no openly gay men in the Oakland Fire Department, and very few throughout the fire service. Segal points out that homophobia is a way of maintaining gender boundaries: "Although the persecution of homosexuals is most commonly the act of men against a minority of other men, it is also the forced repression of the 'feminine' in all men. It is a way of keeping men separated off from women, and keeping women subordinate to men" (Segal, 1990:16).

14. The implication always was that the old way was better. There was little or no recognition that modification of equipment or procedures could benefit everyone in the long run by taking a lesser physical toll.

15. There is some research that suggests that men tend to ascribe sexual connotations to behavior much more readily than do women (Abbey, 1982). Henley (1977) notes that when women engage in the nonverbal behaviors which in men are associated with dominance, they are interpreted sexually. In Gutek's survey on sexual behavior at work, men reported far more incidents of sexual touching than did women; on the basis of other responses as well as other research, Gutek concludes that "this reflects the finding that men are more likely than women to call a touch sexual if the person doing the touching is of the opposite sex" (Gutek, 1985:47).

16. One woman veteran felt she could only be accepted by looking like a boy; she described having been screamed at by a male coworker when she unbraided her hair temporarily one afternoon so she could massage her scalp (on the job, long

hair had to be worn up). Similarly, veterans were highly critical of a woman newcomer who at the end of her shift would let her hair down and put on a dress and
makeup.
17. The asymmetry applies to racial harassment as well. Traditional white firefighters
sometimes argue that coworkers often tease each other about their race or ethnicity
and that no one takes it seriously. However, when one group has historically been
dominant and the other oppressed, the "joke" can take on a more sinister meaning. An additional layer of meaning separates sexual from racial harassment, however, in that sexist joking can serve a special purpose for men—that of separating
intimacy from sexuality (see Lyman, 1987, on this).
18. Other studies of women entering male-dominated fields suggest that sexual banter is a way of reminding women that they are not members of the group
(Remmington, 1983). See also Enarson (1984) on the sexualization of women's
work and bodies in the forest service.
19. I never witnessed a firehouse fight, and none of my group of newcomers described
involvement in one, but several men alluded to occasions when they thought they
might have to physically engage someone and were prepared to do so. Women
occasionally spoke of being angry enough to "take someone out," but according
to their accounts of these occasions, they weren't trying to convey a willingness
to fight, as the men seemed to be. Reports of women physically responding to con-
frontations in the fire service or other male-dominated settings are rare and can
have positive or negative effects. One woman veteran in Oakland recalled being
tormented by a coworker to the point where she got into a physical fight, in the
course of which she picked up a hammer; at this point another coworker realized
how serious the situation was and stopped the fight. In her case, the physical confrontation was probably beneficial, but the outcome could be different. Enarson
describes a forest service woman whose verbal battles with her crew boss "erupted
in violence" with the result that he threw her to the ground and kicked her repeatedly, screaming in rage while the rest of the crew looked on (Enarson,
1984:113).

Chapter 5   *Proving Grounds*

1. Marianne's experience is similar to that of the first women police patrol officers
in Atlanta. Remmington (1983) found that the men's lack of confidence in the
women's ability was so great that the women were rarely allowed to assume or maintain responsibility for serious incidents. The effect was a self-fulfilling prophecy in
which the women were unable to learn, to prove themselves, and to develop self-
confidence.
2. Research has found a somewhat greater tendency toward spontaneous display of
aggression among males than females, though the difference is often slight and
appears likely to be heavily influenced by social conditioning (see Lips, 1989, for
a summary). Bandura's (1973) work, for example, shows the gender difference all
but disappearing when girls and boys have an equal incentive to display aggressive behavior.
3. When a female veteran objected to my characterization of the women as less willing
to free-lance than the men, she claimed that a number of the women in her academy class had been quite aggressive from the outset; however, when she named
them, they turned out to be women with previous firefighting experience. For example, Lillie Carlton, the young veteran mentioned in chapter 2 who took the
nozzle at her first structure fire, had spent a season or more in wild land firefighting
before coming to OFD.
4. Walshok (1981), in her study of blue-collar women, concludes that women whose

childhood experiences encouraged them to become risk-takers (in contrast to the norm for female socialization) were among those most likely to succeed in male-dominated blue-collar environments. Literature on gender differences in the experience of education notes the tendency to notice and reward assertive and risk-taking behaviors in boys more than in girls as well as other patterns of differences in reinforcement that produce similar results. See, for example, Gold, Crombie, and Noble (1987); Dweck et al. (1978); and Sadker and Sadker (1994).

5. Sadker and Sadker (1994).
6. For example, in Irvine's (1985, 1986) analyses of teacher-student interactions by race, sex, and grade level, she found that although in earlier grades white girls were the invisible members of the classroom—receiving significantly less frequent teacher communication than those in any other sex/race group—by the later elementary school years, black girls were also receiving significantly less feedback than either white or black boys or younger black girls. She notes that her findings seem to support the hypothesis of dissimilar early sex-role socialization in black and white girls, but their increasing similarity as a result of public school education. "The data from this research support the early salience of lower elementary black female students but suggest that teachers and schools have a significant influence on the socialization of black girls to traditional female behaviors. It appears that by the time black girls enter the upper elementary grades they have joined their white female counterparts in invisibility, thereby resulting in fewer interactions with teachers" (Irvine, 1986:18–19).
7. In her study of police officers, Martin (1980) found differences in the assertiveness of men and women faced with the uncertainty and unfamiliarity of the streets. In this case, women were not divided by race, but to some extent by neighborhood background: those who had grown up in poverty were most likely to feel confident on the streets, as opposed to either working-class or middle-class women. Of the gender difference, Martin notes that "when confronted with self-doubts, the normative patterns for men's and women's behavior are different: men are more inclined to act, women to avoid. . . . New policewomen must therefore learn new patterns of behavior" (Martin, 1980:123).
8. See Kanter (1977); Remmington (1983); Enarson (1984).
9. This extra effort was mentioned in one of Elena's written evaluations, but it is the informal comments among firefighters rather than formal performance reviews that form the basis for reputations and acceptance.
10. I did at "phase checks" occasionally see a man have difficulty starting a power saw, but no men ever related stories like these about drill experiences. It is impossible to tell if that is because men weren't drilled in a harassing way or if they chose not to discuss this in interviews.
11. Enarson describes the particular resistance to women in firefighting among forest service workers, some of which related to the question of physical ability. The formal physical test was widely criticized as irrelevant to firefighting duties, and the ability of women to pass the test was seen by some as an indication of its inadequacy. Enarson comments that in this context, "the real test is on the job and is virtually unpassable in the eyes of people convinced of male dominance" (Enarson, 1984:63). She also notes that one-on-one challenges could not be won by women because they were issued by the strongest men.
12. In fact, no one—male or female—was dismissed as a result of failing an academy or probationary examination, though there were occasionally poor performances in aspects of the testing. Some veterans put this result down to the department's reluctance to dismiss anyone in a "protected category," but the result remains that, under these circumstances, "Joe" probably couldn't fail either.
13. "Stereotypes," forms of social categorization, are useful in cognitive processing but

also can have biasing effects in terms of perceptions (Hamilton and Trolier, 1986). For example, Linville et al. (1986) report a variety of findings relating to perceived distributions of attributes among in-group versus out-group members. Most important, their experiments demonstrate that differentiation of individuals along a particular attribute scale (e.g., intellectual ability) is greater for in-group than out-group members, as commonly hypothesized (and supported by some other research). Variability, defined as breadth of distribution from the mean, is not always different for in-group versus out-group members, and in-group favoritism is also inconsistently demonstrated. Other studies have found that even small, arbitrary classifications of people can produce discriminatory behavior; in a summary of the literature on this point, Ross and Nisbett note that although the artificiality of some studies can be criticized, they "do suggest that the tendency to view the world in terms of 'we' and 'they,' with at least a working hypothesis that 'we' are somehow better and more deserving, is a rather basic aspect of social perception" (Ross and Nisbett, 1991:40).

Hamilton and Trolier (1986) provide an excellent review of the literature on stereotyping and the effects of such categorization on perception and interpretation. Briefly, the research indicates that group membership and social categorization have profound effects on perception and interpretation of behaviors that tend to favor in-group members and promote the continuation of stereotypes, but there are important exceptions and limiting conditions. Pettigrew and Martin in their analysis of ongoing racial discrimination cite a number of social psychological studies that "show the many ways we maintain our beliefs about people in the face of contrary evidence" (Pettigrew and Martin, 1987).

14. Linville et al. (1986); Hamilton and Trolier (1986).
15. In the classic Robbers Cave experiment of Sherif and his associates, boys attending the summer camp demonstrated a significant tendency to overrate the performance of in-group members and to underrate the performance of out-group members when intergroup hostility and distance were particularly great (Sherif et al., 1961). These effects were also most pronounced when the standard of judgment was ambiguous, consistent with other research.
16. Hamilton and Trolier (1986).
17. For an explanation of tokenism and its effects, see Kanter (1977); Spanger et al. (1978); Alexander and Thoits (1985), and Crocker and McGraw (1984). Most of these studies confirm the expectation of generally negative consequences for tokens, but Crocker and McGraw found that high-status tokens (men) did not suffer the negative consequences of low-status tokens (women) in solo situations. Yoder (1991) and Zimmer (1988) also offer critiques of the notion that disproportionate numbers alone are to blame, emphasizing the role of sexism. In addition, Yoder notes that the effects of tokenism seem to be worst in gender-inappropriate occupations, and she reminds us of the problem of "intrusiveness": increasing numbers of a subordinate group can lead to a more vehemently negative response by the majority.
18. This kind of attribution has been shown to increase a sense of helplessness and poor performance in the face of failure, an orientation to which girls may already be socialized (Dweck et al., 1978). Children who persist and succeed following failures are no more capable than those whose performance declines after failures, but they are different in their attribution: the former attribute failure to something other than ability—generally lack of effort or motivation—whereas the latter attribute failure to their own lack of ability (Dweck, 1975).

It should also be noted that sex stereotyping affects interpretations of performance in "sex-typed" jobs (i.e., those strongly associated with one sex or the other), so that women are likely to be given less personal credit for good performance in a male-dominated job. "According to attribution theory, it is only when an individual performs in accordance with expectations that the outcome is attributed to skill. When he/she performs inconsistently with expectations, the outcome is attributed to factors that enable interpretation of this event as an exception, unlikely to occur repeatedly. . . . Women's success at masculinely sex-typed jobs constitutes an inconsistency with expectations. Thus, female success might well be expected to be explained by factors other than skill more often than male success. . . . There is, in fact, research evidence attesting to this point" (Heilman, 1983:285). Note that Pettigrew and Martin make an analogous point with respect to assessments of black performance in white-dominated settings (Pettigrew and Martin, 1987).

Chapter 6   Learning in Relationship

1. See Coy (1989) and Lave and Wenger (1991). Note also that in OFD itself, lengthy academies are a recent development. In the 1970s, the academy training was only four weeks, and that was a significant increase over previous training. According to one veteran, the first wave of new hires after World War II received no academy training at all: recruits were simply assigned to a senior firefighter and told to "follow him and do what he tells you to do."
2. See Lave and Wenger (1991).
3. Walshok (1981) makes a strong point about the importance of these qualities in her analysis of women who succeeded or failed to do so in male-dominated blue-collar work. Similarly, Enarson (1984) notes that on-the-job training and informal instruction among foresters required that women be assertive and knowledgeable about the organization, and she emphasizes that even if a trainer is willing to share information—as not all are—the novice must know enough to ask the right questions. Martin (1980:121) found that rookie police officers who didn't inspire confidence in the veterans, were overly shy or self-conscious, didn't follow norms, or complained were "not likely to get adequate instructions." She also noted that those who avoided making mistakes through passivity received little assistance from veterans: "For a rookie the road to success is to ask a question rather than remain silent, and to do something, even if it is wrong, rather than do nothing" (1980:121). Haas (1989) emphasizes the importance of the newcomer's initiative and active impression management in the apprenticeships of both high-steel ironworkers and medical interns. Of the former he says, "sometimes it is necessary to take on new responsibilities without explicit direction. The point is that by taking on such new tasks and successfully performing them, he will be accepted by others as being competent" (1989:100).
4. The importance of such factors as self-esteem and assertiveness was highlighted in a survey of firefighters that found correlations between high levels of self-esteem/assertiveness and low levels of stress (Petrie and Rotheram, 1982).
5. This is often the case in apprenticeships. See, for example, the descriptions and discussions of apprenticeship in Cooper (1989), Goody (1989), Haas (1989), and Lave and Wenger (1991).
6. It might be argued that these characteristics describe *any* apprenticeship process, but there are differences in degree that amount to differences in kind, particularly in the importance of assertiveness or aggressiveness in the newcomer. Not all apprenticeships—indeed, not all episodes of fire service training—require the level of self-confidence generally required here and in similar occupational environments.
7. Women in many settings cannot count on receiving the same education as their male counterparts. Safilios-Rothschild observed that solo women in groups of Coast Guard cadets "tended to become marginal and to experience difficulties with regard

to even receiving basic training" (Safilios-Rothschild, 1978:194). Even in more integrated units, there were distinctions such as the tendency of instructors to allow male cadets repeated efforts at a task but to take over from a woman after a single failure. Safilios-Rothschild points out that this pattern is in accord with early female educational experiences. On this last point, see also Sadker and Sadker (1994).

8. See Dweck et al. (1978); Sadker and Sadker (1994).

9. The somewhat differing sentiments of white and black firefighters are similar to those reported in McCarl (1985). He noted that "the predominantly white fire fighting cultural value system is based on ability and performance during a fire" (McCarl, 1985:97). "To the whites, fighting fire is a culture—a way of thinking and doing that has a cultural value system all of its own. Blacks view the fire fighting culture as a white tradition and, although they do the same work, they only occasionally tap it for inside knowledge because they identify more strongly with an ethnic rather than an occupational way of life" (McCarl, 1985:99). McCarl also noted that black firefighters had closer ties to the urban community in which they worked than did the whites, many of whom had moved to the suburbs. As a result, the black firefighters felt more ambivalence at times about their role in the community—for example, putting out the fires set during the race riots of the late 1960s.

10. It should be noted here that while it might be expected that group differences could reflect different weights attached to the two major occupational roles of firefighting and emergency medical service (EMS) work, there was no evidence that this was the case. Although EMS calls now constitute the vast majority of firefighter responses in Oakland, the nature of the work is such that almost no one in this group sees these skills as paramount. When asked in their final interview if they were presented with a choice between a great firefighter–weak EMT and a great EMT–weak firefighter, all but one person, a white man, ultimately chose the strong firefighter.

Chapter 7   *Becoming an Insider*

1. Kanter offers a particularly good illustration of this relationship in her discussion of corporate alliances. Powerful sponsors, for example, can promote or inhibit another's career through teaching or coaching, advocacy, providing access to resources or information outside the regular channels, and extension of "reflected power"; ties with peers and subordinates can also be valuable (Kanter, 1977). Kanter points out that sponsorship is particularly important—but also harder to receive—for women whose own power in an organization is often so limited. As I illustrate in this chapter, Kanter's sponsorship functions operate in the fire service as well as in corporations, though they may be more muted or hidden in the former because of the paramilitary structure of fire departments that constrains discretion.

2. A report on gender integration in the New York City Fire Department noted the importance of the informal system in which "personnel were observed to 'cover' for each other" so that tasks would be performed, but individual failures would not be noticed. Women, however, were "not included in this informal system. As a result, we believe that sometimes minor infractions, which never appear on men's records because of informal 'solutions,' become significant incidents in the management of female firefighters. Reports from other cities on their experiences confirm this interpretation of reality" (Center for Social Policy and Practice in the Workplace, 1988:61).

3. An excellent illustration may be found in Norris and Reardon's description of the New York City Fire Department and its problematic efforts to develop a valid en-

trance examination (Norris and Reardon, 1989). The NYFD began by in 1973 hiring a consultant to analyze the work and develop a set of entrance examinations. The first round of these tests, given in 1977–1978, was subject to successful legal challenge on the basis of disparate impact and lack of job-relatedness. Women were hired pursuant to a special physical test, which then became the basis for a modified physical examination offered in 1983–1984. At this point, however, the written examination was so easy that it virtually failed to distinguish between applicants, and the physical results effectively determined an applicant's final score. This set of tests was also challenged, and a revision was ordered by the trial judge but reversed on appeal.

4. There is an important counterargument. Ignoring insulting sexually or racially biased behavior can imply that it is condoned, and failure to object can reinforce the hostility of the environment for nontraditional groups. This is a particularly powerful argument if one believes that an honest acceptance will never be achieved, or at least not achieved in the foreseeable future. But the experiences of many of these probationary firefighters suggest that a suspicious approach to others can be self-defeating.

5. The position of women in particular in the fire service is not unlike that of stigmatized individuals in the company of normals, and Goffman's (1963) analysis of their strategy is relevant. "The nature of a 'good adjustment' is . . . apparent. It requires that the stigmatized individual cheerfully and self-consciously accept himself as essentially the same as normals, while at the same time he voluntarily withholds himself from those situations in which normals would find it difficult to give lip service to their similar acceptance of him" (Goffman, 1963:121). He goes on to say that the real irony in the situation "is not that the stigmatized individual is asked to be patiently for others what they decline to let him be for them, but that this expropriation of his response may well be the best return he can get on his money" (Goffman, 1963:122).

6. The case of the one black woman in this class offers an unhappy example of the possibility of inordinate trust. She was disciplined for an infraction that by many accounts was no worse than behaviors commonly engaged in by others. Reflecting on her situation, another woman firefighter said that she had warned this woman to be more careful because as a black woman she couldn't rely on the same level of informal protection that others were given. Women interviewed for a study of the New York Fire Department "saw danger in being lulled into thinking they were ever accepted" (The Center for Social Policy and Practice in the Workplace, 1988:30).

7. The acceptance of some women was undoubtedly owing to a combination of factors, but it is worth noting here that the veterans could and occasionally did point to their fondness for a particular woman as "proof" of their nonsexist attitudes—in the manner of those who claim not to be prejudiced, "because some of my best friends are . . . "

8. This circumstance is analogous in some ways to the "reflected power" bestowed by sponsors in the corporate hierarchy (Kanter, 1977).

9. The importance of such interactions is reflected in a comment from the aforementioned report on gender integration in the New York City Fire Department, in which firefighters were asked to rate regulars, new recruits, men, and women separately on a variety of dimensions. Women were rated substantially below other categories on their ability to take hazing and pranks well. The report authors suggest that this judgment reflects a negative assessment of the women's interpersonal competence (Center for Social Policy and Practice in the Workplace, 1988).

10. Walshok found in her study of blue-collar women that successful women often had the advantage of some kind of familiarity with the work or the company that would

make them seem less strange: these experiences allowed the women to be "an-chored" in some context other than gender, which was the default anchor (Walshok, 1981).

11. To a female reader, Larry Brown's account of his life as a firefighter in Oxford, Mississippi, contains a striking number of sexual references; in particular, it seems that every time he refers to a body part, it is an ass or a breast (Brown, 1994). On reading the book, I was reminded of newcomer Valerie's comment that she couldn't believe how much the men in her station talked about sex and how boring it was to her.

12. In their summary of gender differences in conversational socialization and behav-ior, Maltz and Borker (1983) note that men are trained to be verbal entertainers in a way that women are not.

13. It is also possible that there was a self-fulfilling prophecy in action here, similar to that observed by Word et al. (1974) in their experiments on racial interaction. They found that whites unconsciously conveyed nonverbal distancing cues to blacks, who in turn unconsciously distanced themselves or otherwise performed poorly in an interpersonal interaction. In the case of women at the firehouse din-ner table, they may well be receiving cues that their contributions are unwanted and in turn react by withdrawing even more.

14. A possible exception would be lesbian firefighters who might appeal to lesbian civilians, but homosexuality is not something with which traditional veterans readily identify.

15. A number of women firefighters talked about putting up with the flirtatious com-ments and behaviors of their coworkers toward women on the street. They would tolerate this kind of behavior with fond teasing or mild expressions of disapproval but never with any kind of serious comment—as long as they themselves were treated as people rather than as sexual objects.

16. Thorne describes the brother-sister relationship as "one of the few powerful im-ages of relatively equal relationships between boys and girls, and between adult men and women" (Thorne, 1993:172, footnote omitted). But Enarson character-izes the "little sister" model used by some women foresters as "misleadingly be-nign"; it appears egalitarian but in fact involves unequal power and options (Enarson, 1984:77).

17. I am not unaware that there is tension and rivalry in the father-son model, but as a power struggle it does reflect the seriousness with which the son is taken as a rival. The daughter, by contrast, may be an object of greater fondness, but one who rarely inherits the father's position.

18. Thorne (1993), for example, describes the prominence of team sports in boys' as opposed to girls' play, with the latter more often consisting of small-group or one-on-one interactions. Sadker and Sadker (1994) point out the tremendous gender disparities in funding of and participation in organized sports in school. Rubin (1983:129–130) learned through interviews of over two hundred men and women that "women have more friendships (as distinct from collegial relationships or workmates) than men, and the difference in the content and quality of their friend-ships is marked and unmistakable. . . . Generally, women's friendships with each other rest on shared intimacies, self-revelation, nurturance, and emotional sup-port. In contrast, men's relationships are marked by shared activities." For a dif-ferent perspective, however, see Walker (1974), who found that although men and women described friendships in stereotypical gendered terms, their reports of spe-cific relationships often included "nongendered" behavior.

19. Brown and Gilligan, in their study of girls' psychological development, note that they, along with other researchers, have "found that an inner sense of connection with others is a central organizing feature in women's development and that psy-

chological crises in women's lives stem from disconnection" (Brown and Gilligan, 1992:3, footnote omitted). Psychiatrist Jean Baker Miller's comments could apply to some women firefighters: "Men are encouraged from early life to be active and rational; women are trained to be involved with emotions and with the feelings occurring in the course of all activity. Out of this, women have gained the insight that events are important and satisfying only if they occur within the context of emotional relatedness. They are more likely than men to believe that, ideally, all activity should lead to an increased emotional connection with others" (Miller, 1986:39).

20. A "route" is a repeating assignment to a series of several stations—for example, one east end route includes five shifts at Station 20, five shifts at Station 18, a shift at Station 27, and a shift at Station 29.

21. One black man, not among those described here, did resign, reportedly under pressure to do so. I do not have enough information on the case to judge how much his departure was influenced by his racial or outsider status.

Chapter 8   *Gender and Race in the Urban Fire Service: Policy Implications*

1. A consultant's report on gender integration in the New York City Fire Department found "widespread and deepseated antagonism toward women firefighters among a significant majority of departmental personnel" (Center for Social Policy and Practice in the Workplace, 1988:1). The authors add that contacts with people in other fire departments "suggest that the path to gender integration has been a difficult road to travel" (Center, 1988:66). This report did not assess problems of minority firefighters or compare the experience of women to the racial minorities; however, the report's literature review did note that "much more attention in the literature is paid to the problem of integrating women firefighters than to that of integrating minority men" (Center, 1988:62). The report questions whether this fact reflects the "larger threat" that women pose "to old ways" or if it reflects a greater comfort in looking at gender differences as opposed to race and ethnicity. The findings of my study in Oakland suggest that both factors are operating: racial integration is easier, *and* racism is less acceptable than sexism. On the last point see Reid and Clayton's (1992) discussion of differences between racism and sexism. These findings reflect the importance of situational variables in shaping interracial behavior. See Pettigrew (1961) for a discussion of the need to emphasize research on social context rather than attitudinal variables in racial tolerance.

2. As previously noted, there are conflicting effects of race for women in firefighter society. Whites have the advantage of easier familial alliance with veterans and of meeting prevailing standards of physical attractiveness. But black women may have been socialized to greater assertiveness and self-confidence. See Epstein (1973) on the success of professional black women and Reid and Clayton (1992) on the ambiguous effects of race within gender; see also Glenn (1985), Goodwin (1990), Grant (1984), and Sadker and Sadker (1994) on black women's self-esteem and assertiveness. Glenn observes that as a result of their difficult history, "black women were from the start exempted from the myth of female disability" (Glenn, 1985:95), and she goes on to argue that for black women, the family is a place where self-esteem and identity are built, not a source of oppression. I saw evidence of both positive and negative effects in the experiences of black and white women firefighters in Oakland.

3. McConahay et al. (1981) argue that prejudice against blacks remains but that modern racism is expressed in more subtle terms, consisting of political judgments rather than clearly discredited stereotypes of black ability. Gaertner and Dovidio (1986)

also maintain that although overt bigotry has diminished, a more subtle form of racism continues. "Aversive" racism tends to reflect more fear, discomfort, or disgust than hostility, motivating avoidance rather than overt destruction. This discriminatory behavior may derive more from in-group favoritism than anti-out-group bias. See also Pettigrew and Martin (1987) for a discussion of modern racism and its indirect manifestations: in effect, though prejudice remains, it is often subtle enough that it is denied by whites, who then attribute racial disparities to lack of motivation or ability and refuse to support political and social remedies such as affirmative action.

4. An example is in the east end–downtown division noted at the end of chapter 7. Some black activists are concerned that the relative absence of black officers from downtown stations means lower opportunities for advancement, and black firefighters sometimes also complain about the uneven division of work, particularly between the extremely busy east end stations and the "retirement homes" (hill stations) dominated by older white firefighters. At the same time, according to at least one black newcomer, many black firefighters prefer the east end because they believe there is greater acceptance by other firefighters.

5. Coleman (1993).

6. Ibid., 51.

7. One reason for making this claim is that the findings here resemble those of several related studies. An excellent example is Walshok's (1981) study of pioneering women in blue-collar fields. Her summary of the individual and situation characteristics that promoted success are strikingly similar to what I found in the Oakland Fire Department. Martin's (1980) characterization of the sexual integration of the District of Columbia police force also resembles my analysis in many ways. In fact, the similarity between the findings of these earlier works and my own is alarming to those of us looking for social change.

8. It goes without saying, for example, that firefighters must be in good physical health and of reasonable intelligence. Though there is still some debate about measurement of such qualities, particularly intelligence, they tend to be taken for granted and are therefore not elaborated here.

9. For example, the importance of self-confidence can be emphasized in the way the job is described to prospective applicants.

10. See Petrie and Rotheram (1982) on the association between self-esteem and assertiveness and lower levels of stress among firefighters. Also note that Louis (1990) mentions self-confidence as a newcomer quality that can ease the acculturation process by increasing necessary risk-taking.

11. This is a nationwide issue, not just a problem in Oakland and similar departments. The National Fire Protection Association has been engaged in an effort to develop acceptable national standards for physical fitness and performance since 1993 (the NFPA's previous standards, known as NFPA 1001, had been invalidated and were no longer in use). Lacking adequate funding for relevant research, the Physical Performance Task Group concluded that it could not develop a national physical performance standard for firefighters and instead has pursued the development of a "recommended practice" (RP). Published in 1994 for public comment, the draft of this RP (known as NFPA 1553) was widely and severely criticized, and as of January 1996 it had yet to be issued in final form ("Standards Council Sends 1583 Back to Committee," 1996).

12. Courts have invalidated entry-level tests in many cities on the basis of their disparate impact and lack of demonstrable job-relatedness. Critics have pointed out that tests include components that are unrelated to actual job requirements or sometimes even contrary to effective fireground practices. For example, a state Fair Employment Practices Agency (cited in Women in the Fire Service, 1993:87–88)

found that one city's test emphasized tasks and scoring "that were often testing for and rewarding behavior that is detrimental to effective firefighting. There were strong rewards for upper body strength and sprinting even when responsible firefighting prohibits sprinting. In a smoke filled environment it can lead to fatigue or smoke inhalation. Although upper body strength is a characteristic that can be tested for, it is not the sole characteristic that leads to effective firefighting skills." Common complaints against firefighter tests are the rank-ordering of candidates on the basis of physical test scores when there has been no demonstration that this order corresponds to actual performance, the use of current firefighters to establish passing scores when their abilities are in part the result of on-the-job training and experience, and the overemphasis of anaerobic capacity (speed) as opposed to aerobic capacity (stamina), which is equally if not more important. "Heart attacks consistently cause nearly 50 percent of firefighter line-of-duty deaths, yet many fire departments have no endurance component to their entry-level tests" (Women in the Fire Service, 1993:32, footnote omitted; similar criticisms may be found in Bahr, 1992, and Pranka, 1993). For a counterargument, see Davis (1993). See also L. Bell (1987) on testing for physical jobs and Norris and Reardon (1989) for a description of the New York Fire Department case.

13. A sense of the procedural fairness of decision-making processes is vitally important to people; it affects their reactions and compliance to decisions, independent of the favorability of outcomes. Judgments about fairness appear to be influenced by such factors as an opportunity to be heard, even if it does not directly affect the outcome; a sense of neutrality or a "level playing field"; trust that the decision maker is motivated by a desire to be fair; and a feeling of being treated with dignity and respect for one's rights. See Tyler (1989) and Tyler and Lind (1992) for a fuller explanation. It should be noted here that the current Oakland chief's practice of making promotions in rank order from the list of certified candidates is widely appreciated for its fairness.

14. Many veterans insist that firefighters who do not meet the old height requirements are unable to comfortably reach ladders, hoses, and other pieces of equipment on a fire rig, and this is certainly true *given the current inventory of vehicles.* But because departments regularly replace old equipment, they can make choices in their specifications for replacement rigs. If the department already employs people of smaller stature, then it orders rigs with more accessible equipment—often to the benefit of all firefighters because of the reduced need to lift heavy objects overhead. See LeCuyer (1994).

15. Oakland's experience with a proposed 1991 consent decree suggests that this would be possible. The proposed decree established some agility test components and named a particular outside expert to decide other issues; this proposal was agreed to by representatives of the various parties to the *Nero* and *Petersen* discrimination and reverse discrimination lawsuits, but it ultimately failed to win the approval of the union membership, who evidently opposed the proportion of women and the mandate for annual physical testing of veterans.

16. High school physical training programs have become a primary source of women candidates for the Seattle Fire Department (Center for Social Policy and Practice in the Workplace, 1988).

17. The Columbia University report on gender integration in the New York Fire Department gave two broad categories of recommendations: to support the women currently in the department and to ensure a "steady stream of women" into the department in the future (Center for Social Policy and Practice in the Workplace, 1988).

18. For example, in 1989 the department worked with representatives from different ethnic groups and women's organizations, linking them with other community

organizations that could sponsor recruitment and preparation efforts. The Oakland Black Fire Fighters Association held classes, the Asian/Filipino Firefighters worked with the Chinese Community Center, the Hispanic Firefighters with the Spanish-Speaking Unity Council, and the women's groups with the Private Industry Council (and of course, women could attend classes sponsored by other groups as well). Recruitment was also conducted through billboards, public service announcements, advertisements in minority publications, and other nontraditional venues.

19. Broader recruitment efforts have had more dramatic results in terms of minority male representation than female representation. Some members of the department feel that in time women's awareness of and interest in the job will grow and that the process will work for them as it has for minority men. In this context, community-based recruitment strategies represent long-term educational efforts.

20. The Menlo Park Fire Protection District in California made a point of involving its incumbent work force in the recruiting effort when the first serious push for integration occurred in the late 1980s; the department reports high satisfaction with the quality of the candidates and the increase in minority and female representation they were able to achieve in one recruitment campaign (Lee, 1988).

21. Kanter (1977) provides a particularly persuasive description of how such internal organizational characteristics can shape workers' behavior.

22. See Schultz (1990) and Walshok (1981) on the way women's work opportunities shape their expectations, behavior, and norms relating to work.

23. Though separations in earlier academies were not common, the classes were also considerably smaller, so that when terminations did occur they represented a larger proportion of the group.

24. This discussion does not address promotion practices, but a note about these is relevant here. Arguments about promotion procedures have gone back and forth in much the same way as the debate over hiring practices, and they are no more settled. Without recommending specific approaches, it can be noted that enhancing the members' trust in these practices is an important goal. Many Oakland firefighters expressed dissatisfaction with the emphasis on test performance as opposed to job performance, and there was also some concern about the tests and their administration.

25. Many probationary firefighters commented on the ways in which they felt the department failed to take EMS work seriously. Their concerns included questions about the adequacy of EMS training, the arrangement for ambulance and hospital tours to be conducted in much quieter Alameda rather than in Oakland, the delay in providing Hepatitis B immunizations to probationary firefighters, and the apparently ineffective screening of medical calls resulting in frequent dispatches to nonemergencies.

26. Somewhat similar recommendations were made in the Columbia report to the New York Fire Department. The report suggested that training of new women firefighters include information on department traditions and culture, hazing and harassment, and management of body privacy issues. It recommended that all women firefighters be trained in assertiveness, problem-solving techniques, and "effective communication within the cultural parameters of the fire department," among other things (Center for Social Policy and Practice in the Workplace, 1988:9). In addition, the Center advised that all probationary firefighters be prepared for work in a gender-integrated environment.

27. It is assumed here that the department will not again train a class as large as 1-91; those involved with that training seemed convinced that the class was far too large for the most effective training. Going back to a much smaller class size would re-

duce one major obstacle to the maximization of field training opportunities through appropriate station assignments.

28. In McCarl's study of District of Columbia firefighters, he concluded that a "rookie's entire fire fighting career can be shaped by his/her first assignment. If sent to a slow house or excluded from participation in the aggressiveness and spirit associated with a running company, it may take a fire fighter years to make up that missing experience" (McCarl, 1985:38, notes omitted). He also notes how overwhelming are a rookie's early days in the field, and the crucial importance of guidance given by veterans.

29. Implementation of this suggestion would obviously not be simple, but the effort could have a significant payoff. It is worth noting here that an alternative hiring program used in Kern County to facilitate the hiring of women and minority men places program trainees in one of four training stations, which are characterized by their types of apparatus, high level of activity, and officer's or engineer's interest in training (Women in the Fire Service, 1993).

30. See, for example, Tannen (1990) on differences in men's and women's communication styles, Blauner (1989) on some of the effects of race on personal and social experience, and Andersen and Collins (1992) for some unsettling first-person essays providing different perspectives on race, gender, and class.

31. See, for example, Hamilton and Trolier (1986), Sherif et al. (1961), and the summary in RAND (1993, chapter 10).

32. Ross and Nisbett (1991).

33. See, for example, Egan (1993); RAND (1993:140, 152, 389).

34. One firefighter insisted that the joke was really a put-down of *men*; when I suggested that it seemed a put-down of both men and women, he disagreed. My sense was that the joke could be offensive to women because of its crude reference to female body parts; the sensitivity of many women to this kind of language has not to do so much with delicacy or squeamishness as with vulnerability to sexual violence and domination. For women, having our sex referred to by sexual organs is dehumanizing. Because of the power asymmetry, the effect is not quite the same for men.

35. See Gutek (1985) for an extensive discussion of nonreporting along with other aspects of the sexual harassment problem.

36. See Women in the Fire Service (1993).

37. This view is based in part on observations by Enarson (1984:109), who offers the following analysis. "The term 'sexual harassment' seems to mean too little and too much. When it refers to dirty jokes or pin-ups, for instance, it is better seen as part of the sexualizing of the workplace and work relations. On the other hand, it does not fully convey the reality of sexual violence against women workers or economic retaliation against those who reject powerful men and resist demands for sexual services. Sexual aggression and extortion can and should be singled out, and the term 'sexual harassment' should be reserved for what it suggests—harassment, here called manhandling. It is interaction in and around the workplace which is sexually suggestive, objectionable, and nonreciprocal. Together, these different problems constitute a continuum of abuse, founded on women's fundamental economic and sexual vulnerability and reflecting a cultural tradition which sexualizes, objectifies, and diminishes women."

38. The episode mentioned earlier, concerning a woman's complaint about the telling of a dirty joke, was somewhat exceptional. First, the joke was told in a setting in which more serious harassment had been occurring, and second, the woman was herself more outspoken and perhaps more sensitive than most.

39. See RAND (1993), chapters 5 and 12.

40. For a description of this problem in an entirely different context, see Talbot's (1994) analysis of the implications of an overly rigid approach to sexual harassment concerns within a university setting. In her conclusion, she writes that "there is something lost when we get too punctilious about defining teaching as a business relationship. And what's lost isn't trivial" (Talbot, 1994:40). Enarson (1984:88) summarizes the mixed feelings of women in the forest service by noting that for some, "sexualization is all too apparent and asks too much; for others, it is precisely what makes their work lives meaningful and friendships at work so special."

41. Several writers have discussed the relationship between stereotyping and sexual harassment (as well as other forms of discrimination). Deaux (1995) and Burns (1995) both point out that an obvious implication of this relationship is the need to disrupt processes of stereotyping or group categorization in order to eliminate harassment—part of my argument here. In contrast to the views expressed here, however, they suggest that the elimination of pornography in the workplace is important because it "primes" men to see women in sexual terms. Pornography has been demonstrated to have such effects and clearly does contribute to stereotyping, but, as explained above, efforts to eradicate sexual materials from male workplaces are impractical and often counterproductive.

42. There is no doubt that mistrust of the selection and promotion procedures by traditional veterans fuels animosity toward women coworkers in particular. Some attention to procedural fairness concerns is needed to alleviate this kind of hostility and to address whatever legitimate concerns there may be about qualifications. On the importance of procedural fairness, see Tyler (1989) and Tyler and Lind (1992).

43. While lower-level-leadership commitment is important, there is no magic formula for achieving it. It is sometimes suggested that managers be evaluated and rewarded in part based on how they deal with diversity, but organizations should be wary of possible negative consequences when such a plan is implemented without careful design. For example, there was an occasion during this study when firefighters were surveyed by the city's human resource office as to their officers' support for diversity. One officer who had been described repeatedly by my interview subjects as both capable and supportive was upset when a crew member showed him the questionnaire, which the officer saw as a thoroughly unreliable and inappropriate form of evaluation. This example suggests that managerial support of diversity should be developed and assessed within a broader context of human resource management performance and that supervisors should be involved in training and evaluation procedures.

44. Note that some of this can happen through informal networks which the department may or may not be able to facilitate. One woman explained that in preparing for a promotional exam she participated in both a mixed and a woman-only study group; the latter was particularly helpful because of the comfort people felt in asking seemingly dumb questions.

45. See Women in the Fire Service (1993) and Center for Social Policy and Practice in the Workplace (1988) for discussions of the minimal accommodations made in many departments with respect to such issues as physical plants and maternity policies.

46. These points are also made in Women in the Fire Service (1993).

47. Martin (1980) reports that the first women to enter the District of Columbia Police Department were expected to conform to male norms and that the men actually resented the women's desire for better-fitting uniforms as a request for special treatment.

48. The lack of space for women can be attributed to the history of most urban de-

partments as single-sex environments. However, it should also be noted that there is evidence of a more general male domination of space in "integrated" environments such as offices and playgrounds (Henley, 1977; Thorne, 1993). One woman firefighter from another department explained to me that even in a station designed with women's quarters, the space was arranged in such a way that the women had to go through the men's locker room to get to "their" space.

49. A comparison of Women in the Fire Service surveys conducted in 1990 and 1995 concluded that problems with inappropriate gear and clothing are getting worse over time, as increasing proportions of women firefighters report difficulties (Floren, 1996).

Chapter 9   *Questions of Identity, Community, and Social Justice*

1. Alvarez (1979) makes this distinction and provides a conceptual approach to the analysis of allocations within organizations.

2. Kanter explains that the entry of tokens provokes a heightened awareness of the bond shared by members of the dominant group and an exaggeration of the elements of that bond against the threat to community represented by the tokens (Kanter, 1977).

3. See Rothman (1987) as well as the introduction and chapter 2 of this book.

4. For example, the culture that Everhart (1983) found in a group of rowdy junior high school boys bears a striking resemblance to the culture of firefighters; other observational studies of children report similar findings (Thorne, 1993). Similar patterns of behavior and values are reported in a wide variety of male-dominated work environments and social settings (see Schroedel, 1985; Martin, 1988; Walshok, 1981; Fine, 1987; Lyman, 1987).

5. Leserman (1981) found that medical school increased conservatism in both male and female students but that some gender differences in attitude remained. Remmington (1983) found early women police patrol officers taking on the cynicism, conservatism, and separation from the public common to male police officers despite their inability to be fully accepted by coworkers.

6. See Leserman (1981) as an example.

7. Foster's is one of the stories of nontraditional women workers included in Martin (1988).

8. Ibid., 229.

9. Ibid.

10. The argument might be made that firefighting mistakes are more dangerous and therefore justify a blunter response. I would submit that driving a big rig on a highway is probably as potentially hazardous to self and others as is firefighting, and that the distinction in approaches has more to do with gender socialization. Which one is most appropriate or effective is arguable.

11. A number of writers point out that the gendering of human relations (the creation and elaboration of gender categories in all aspects of life) includes not only distinctions between masculinity and femininity, but between different forms of each (see Carrigan et al., 1985; Connell, 1987; and Segal, 1990). Thus Connell speaks of a "hegemonic" form of masculinity that, while not the only way of being male, does dominate our general notion of male sexual character (Connell, 1987).

12. This is not to say that women always react more emotionally than do men under stress, but rather that they have cultural permission to express their feelings more readily. Within the context of the fire station and similar male-dominated environments women may learn to repress their feelings, but given an opportunity to

structure the environment differently, they might pay greater attention to the management of emotional stress. The comments of women interviewed for this study and the stories appearing in the newsletters of women firefighters' organizations attest to this difference (see, for example, Floren, 1993; Selk, 1993).

13. One benefit not mentioned here, but described by some male firefighters, is the potentially greater ease of social relations in women's culture. Gray (1992) offers some amusing comments on his own experience as a blue-collar union representative moving between male and female shop cultures. He found the latter something of a relief, noting that "when you ate at the women's table, you sat down to rest and relax. When you ate at the men's table, you sat down to fight" (Gray, 1992:475).

14. See Cox and Blake (1991) for a discussion of the benefits of diversity and brief references to literature suggesting that under proper circumstances, heterogeneity of work groups improves productivity, creativity, and problem-solving.

15. Numerous books and articles critique the liberal legal approach to social problems. For a particularly relevant discussion of the limits of this approach in conditions requiring discretion, see, for example, Handler (1986).

16. The basic argument is analogous to the critical legal analysis that legal rights operate within a context of oppression, not equality, and tend to favor those in power. Without a recognition of structural inequalities and an attempt to address these, the invocation of the law is likely to reproduce the status quo. As Taub and Williams (1985:830) summarize the argument, "We have accomplished relatively little, it seems to us, if all we can claim is that we have guaranteed for women born tall as the average man or willing and able to adopt traditional male life patterns and habits the right to move into the male world." They go on to assert, however, that a "dual system of sex-based rights and responsibilities" is equally pernicious, and that the answer lies in the elimination of practices with disparate impact. For an antiassimilationist feminist perspective that expounds a theory of difference, see Fineman (1990).

17. See, for example, Gilligan (1982) on the morality of care as an important alternative to the morality of justice; Miller (1986) on the value of a feminist ethic of connectedness; and Handler's (1990) discussion of some of the principles of feminist jurisprudence.

18. See Young (1994) for an editorial description of the case.

19. See Lacey (1993); Tamaki (1994); and Floren (1994a and 1994b).

20. Young (1994:3).

21. These are qualities that seem necessary for what Handler calls a "dialogic" community—i.e., one in which members are able to participate in ongoing, meaningful, and uncoerced dialogue, similar to the "ideal speech situation" of Habermas (Handler, 1990; see also Geuss, 1981, on Habermas and critical theory).

22. Most discussions of the problem of discrimination or the issue of diversity treat racism and sexism as essentially analogous. Each involves a disadvantage associated with group membership, but the different meanings of these disadvantages are not explored—even though it is sometimes noted that minority race and female sex carry different penalties. See, for example, Alvarez (1979); Burstein (1985); and Coil and Rice (1993). The literature on in-group–out-group perception and categorization also tends to treat racism and sexism as manifestations of the same underlying phenomenon; see Hamilton and Trolier (1986); Miller and Brewer (1986); and Linville et al. (1986).

23. Malveaux and Wallace (1987), for example, argue that black women are probably triply disadvantaged by the low economic status of their family members as well as their own membership in subordinate groups.

24. Discussions of racism generally focus on the effect of cumulative economic, po-

litical, and social disadvantage of minority, particularly black, status, with an emphasis on economic inequality (see D. Bell, 1987, among others). Sexism is also
analyzed in terms of reinforcing spheres of oppression, including the family and
the workplace, but it relies more heavily on the continued social construction of differences between people of different biological sexes (see, for example, Connell, 1987).
25. See, for example, Reid and Clayton (1992) and Wasserstrom (1977); also see Glenn
(1985) on the intersection of race, gender, and class.
26. The possibility of greater self-assertiveness and self-esteem in African American
women has already been noted here. In commenting on racial differences among
women, Reid and Clayton (1992) observe that "the family may be a source of resistance to oppression for women of color, rather than the source of oppression
that it has often been for white women" (Reid and Clayton, 1992:260, references
omitted). See also Glenn's (1985) argument on this subject. Epstein (1973) finds
this self-confidence among black women and also suggests that the effect of the
"double negative" of race and sex can be positive in some circumstances. For example, if black women are not seen as "women" in the way that white women
are, then they may also be more acceptable in nontraditional settings (in an effect similar to the possibly greater acceptance of lesbians in male work settings).
27. Black men have been employed as professional firefighters since at least the 1910s
(according to the International Association of Black Professional Fire Fighters'
Summer 1989 newsletter, the first black officer in New York was appointed in 1927
and had served on the force since early 1919). The first woman professional
firefighter was hired in Arlington, Virginia, in 1974 (Walker, 1974). Note that
some fire departments hired their first black employees much later, but still ahead
of the first women. Women have, however, been volunteer firefighters for more
than a century.
28. Women in the Fire Service (1993), citing the Affirmative Action Committee,
California Fire Chiefs Association, "CFCA Survey of Women Fire Fighters," 1976.
29. Many writers have commented on the kind of characterizations of women or implications of gender relations that would be unacceptable if the issue were race.
For example, Sadker and Sadker (1994) relate the open contempt expressed by
boys for girlhood and ask if we would expect equally strong and negative feelings
to be expressed regarding racial or ethnic differences. Goodenough (1987:440) reports on the devastating effect that sexist behavior has on young girls and notes
that "we would predict reactions like these if the target of the negative behavior
were children of another race. The curious thing is that we shield ourselves from
knowledge of such consequences when sexism rather than racism is involved." In
the present study, I often heard the expression "women don't belong in the fire
service," but I never heard someone say "blacks don't belong in the fire service."
30. Reid and Clayton (1992:250) point out that "although racial categorizations can
be enhanced or diminished by societal distinctions, sex is viewed as practically
immutable" and that "when race or gender-based distinctions are viewed as clearly
grounded in biological differences, they are seen as more legitimate because the
biological differences provide an explanation for the societal distinctions."
Wasserstrom (1977:589, 590) notes that "the ideology of sex, as opposed to the
ideology of race, is a good deal more complex and confusing" and as a result "does
not unambiguously proclaim the lesser value attached to being female rather than
being male, nor does it unambiguously correspond to the existing social realities.
For these, among other reasons, sexism could plausibly be regarded as a deeper phenomenon than racism. It is more deeply embedded in the culture, and thus less
visible. Being harder to detect, it is harder to eradicate. Moreover, it is less un-
equivocally regarded as unjust and unjustifiable."
31. Reporting on the experiences of "Agnes," a transsexual person who was raised as

a boy and eventually adopted a female identity, Garfinkel (1967:118) explains that for people like Agnes, "the work and the socially structured occasions of sexual passing were obstinately unyielding to attempts to routinize the rounds of daily activities. This obstinacy points to the omnirelevance of sexual statuses to affairs of daily life as an invariant but unnoticed background in the texture of relevances that comprise the changing actual scenes of everyday life." Bem (1981) theorizes that this socially constructed dichotomy actually structures cognitive processing as a result of the adoption of gender schema through socialization. For an extended exploration of how the gender dichotomy is constructed and maintained, along with some of its effects, see Kessler and McKenna (1978). See also West and Zimmerman (1987:126) on "gender as an accomplishment."

32. Thorne (1993) offers many such examples of the construction and maintenance of gender by teachers and students alike in the school setting.

33. Blau and Winkler (1989) report figures for 1987 that indicate a substantial degree of sex segregation in the workplace, particularly with respect to higher-status blue-collar jobs. Beller (1984:19) found some movement of women into nontraditional occupations during the 1970s but the changes were primarily at the white-collar level; "little such change appeared for the blue-collar occupations." She also found that declines in occupational segregation by sex were greater among nonwhites than whites during this period.

34. Gutek (1985) offers "sex role spillover" as an explanation for the problem of sexual harassment in the workplace.

35. Ibid.

36. See, for example, Williams's (1989) discussion of men in the field of nursing.

37. Many feminist writers have pointed out that the pervasive threat of sexual violence is a feature of patriarchal control that can imbue minor heterosexual actions with destructive meaning. See Sheffield (1989) and Martin (1989).

38. Women are much less likely than men to be appreciative of a sexual overture from a coworker; Gutek's (1985) survey found that 67 percent of male respondents but only 17 percent of female respondents indicated they would be flattered by a proposition from a coworker of the opposite sex.

39. Gutek (1985) observes that men's work environments tend to be much more sexualized than are women's. See also the observations of women in nontraditional work reported in Martin (1988) and Schroedel (1985) and Fine's (1987) observations about sexual language and humor in male-dominated restaurant kitchens.

40. Fine (1987:143) makes this argument and insists that there is "no unfriendly intent" in male behavior. He suggests that women in male work settings are, in Garfinkel's terms, "cultural dopes" who need to learn how to play along. His interpretation would be more persuasive if it were not for certain untenable assertions. For example, within the category of harmless "sexual teasing" he includes touching "of a playful nature," though he goes on to say that "it is touching that would be inappropriate if done by a female to a male or by a male to another male, such as when Ken, a cook at the Owl's Nest, playfully slapped a waitress's buttocks" (Fine, 1987:141). If this is simply playfulness, then why is it inappropriate behavior coming from a woman to a man?

41. See Lyman (1987) for a detailed analysis of the social functions served by a sexually colored fraternity prank. Among other things, he points out that by separating sex from intimacy, the joke allowed the men to avoid the "loss of control" inherent in male-female relationships. Segal (1990:211) observes that the sexuality common in masculine work cultures, particularly those involving manual labor, bonds men. "Collectively, it is clear, calling up images of male sexual performance serves to consolidate and confirm masculinity, and to exclude and belittle women."

42. The Columbia report refers to the "fear and rage evoked by the presence of women in some fire departments as reported in *Fire and Police Personnel Report*" and notes that these are more "concrete and blatantly expressed" than would be expected (Center for Social Policy and Practice in the Workplace, 1988:61). Expressions that I witnessed in Oakland were more muted but ubiquitous. Occasionally I would hear of a more extreme reaction, such as a male firefighter placing a plate of feces before a woman coworker at the dinner table, or a group of veterans throwing a publication about women in the fire service to the floor and stomping on it. Recall also the words of one of the Oakland women in chapter 4, on her sense of her male coworkers' "hatred" of women.

43. Stoller (1985):183.

44. See Stoller (1968; 1985), Chodorow (1978), and Dinnerstein (1976).

45. The point is made by Segal (1990), Carrigan, Connell, and Lee (1985), and Connell (1987). Carrigan et al. (1985:588) argue that gay liberation represents a "contestation of the subordination of women to men" because it challenges the fundamental definition of hegemonic masculinity (its heterosexuality).

46. Williams (1989) explains that an effort is made to maintain the gender difference in the marines by segregating women's roles and emphasizing their femininity (women marines are required to wear makeup and female uniforms, are instructed in makeup, poise, and etiquette, etc.).

47. Martin (1980:207).

48. Carrigan, Connell, and Lee (1985:592) argue that male dominance is sustained not only by the oppression of women, but by a hierarchy of masculinities: "the culturally exalted form of masculinity, the hegemonic model so to speak, may only correspond to the actual characters of a small number of men. . . . Yet very large numbers of men are complicit in sustaining the hegemonic model. There are various reasons. . . . But the overwhelmingly important reason is that most men benefit from the subordination of women, and hegemonic masculinity is centrally connected with the institutionalization of men's dominance over women." See also Connell (1987).

49. Caplow (1954:242) notes that in "underprivileged occupations, pride in the virile character of the work and involvement in its antifeminine culture usually compensate in some measure for the absence of more tangible rewards."

50. Connell (1987:180) cites several studies revealing the aggressively masculine cultures of blue-collar settings and argues that these are expressions of solidarity and "a rejection of the masculinity of the dominant group" (managers). Of these cultures, he notes that "the common elements are a cult of masculinity centering on physical prowess, and sexual contempt directed at managers, and men in office work generally, as being effete." Gray (1992) also argues that doing difficult physical labor allows working-class men to feel superior to both women and middle- and upper-class men.

51. James Baldwin (1962, 1988) gives a moving account of the relationship between white identity and black subordination. "In this case, the danger, in the minds of most white Americans, is the loss of their identity. Try to imagine how you would feel if you woke up one morning to find the sun shining and all the stars aflame. You would be frightened because it is out of the order of nature. Any upheaval in the universe is terrifying because it so profoundly attacks one's sense of one's own reality. Well, the black man has functioned in the white man's world as a fixed star, as an immovable pillar: and as he moves out of his place, heaven and earth are shaken to their foundations" (Baldwin, 1988:20). Both racism and sexism entail the construction of identity based in part on opposition and domination. In both cases, the definition of the other helps to define the self, certain dangerous qualities are denied in the self and projected onto the other, and the social posi-

tion of the other establishes a "floor" below which one's own position cannot fall. There are of course differences between the two processes, however, deriving from differences in the nature of race and sex. For example, in the case of sexual identity, the simple fact of not being a woman defines one (in the vast majority of cases) as a man; however, not to be a black person does not make one white. Similarly, the fact of being interracial is quite different from the fact of being intersexed.

52. Sadker and Sadker (1994:83). They report quotations from essays written in response to this question by upper elementary and middle school boys and girls in twenty-four classrooms in Maryland, Virginia, and Washington, D.C.

53. Ibid., 83.

54. Office for Sex Equity in Education, Michigan Department of Education. "The Influence of Gender-Role Socialization on Student Perceptions: A Report Based on Data Collected from Michigan Public School Students" (revised June 1990), cited in Sadker and Sadker (1994:84, 289).

55. Ibid., 84.

56. Ibid., 85.

57. Mee (1993).

58. See Goodenough (1987) for a particularly disturbing example in one of the four classes she studied.

59. For example, Goodenough (1987) describes the cross-sex behavioral patterns of four different kindergarten classes. Two of these classes displayed supportive, egalitarian environments, but the other two were quite sexist, one horrifically so. Goodenough analyzes the difference in terms of dominant group structures and influences in the different classrooms. Thorne (1993) in her study of children's play found some crossing of gender boundaries but also considerable inequality and division, as in boys' dominance of playground space, their invasion of girls' territory and activities, and the association of "pollution" or "contamination" with gender and sometimes race or class inequality.

60. Both Thorne (1993) and Sadker and Sadker (1994) discuss the asymmetrical social construction of adolescent development, and its relationship to gender differentiation and inequality.

61. See Sadker and Sadker (1994:125–26 especially) on the unequal athletic opportunities of boys and girls.

62. Chodorow (1978), Dinnerstein (1976), Williams (1989).

63. On the general point, see West and Zimmerman (1987), Thorne (1993), and Kessler and McKenna (1978); on the question of interacting spheres of dominance, see Connell (1987) and Segal (1990).

64. Kessler and McKenna (1978) argue persuasively that our dichotomization of gender is by no means the only feasible way of seeing the world and that it has unfortunate implications for social justice. In their conclusion they note that "where there are dichotomies it is difficult to avoid evaluating one in relation to the other, a firm foundation for discrimination and oppression" (Kessler and McKenna, 1978:164). Bem (1981:363) challenges our emphasis on gender in situations where it has no relevance and argues that "the concept of androgyny is insufficiently radical from a feminist perspective because it continues to presuppose that there is a masculine and a feminine within us all, that is, that the concepts of masculinity and femininity have an independent and palpable reality rather than being themselves cognitive constructs derived from gender-based schematic processing."

Wasserstrom (1977) is not entirely committed to an "assimilationist" ideal, but he does effectively counter many of the arguments used against it. He notes, for example, that "it is the socially created sexual differences which tend in fact to matter the most. It is sex-role differentiation, not gender per se, that makes men and women as different as they are from each other, and it is sex-role differences which are invoked to justify most sexual differentiation at any of the levels of society" (Wasserstrom, 1977:610, notes omitted). And he recognizes that the strongest moral argument for the assimilationist ideal is its improved potential for individual autonomy. For even if we could eliminate inequality from the "psychological, role, and status differences" between the sexes, these differences would remain "objectionable on the ground that they necessarily impaired an individual's ability to develop his or her own characteristics, talents, and capacities to the fullest extent to which he or she might desire" (Wasserstrom, 1977:614).

References

Abbey, Antonia. 1982. "Sex Differences in Attributions for Friendly Behavior: Do Males Misperceive Females' Friendliness?" *Journal of Personality and Social Psychology* 42 (5): 830–838.

Alexander, Victoria D., and Peggy A. Thoits. 1985. "Token Achievement: An Examination of Proportional Representation and Performance Outcomes." *Social Forces* 64 (2): 332–340.

Alvarez, Rodolfo. 1979. "Institutional Discrimination in Organizations and Their Environments." In *Discrimination in Organizations*, eds. R. Alvarez, K. G. Lutterman and Associates. San Francisco: Jossey-Bass Publishers.

Andersen, Margaret L., and Patricia Hill Collins, eds. 1992. *Race, Class, and Gender: An Anthology*. Belmont, Calif.: Wadsworth Publishing Company.

Bahr, Chris. 1992. "Using Women Firefighters to Validate Physical Agility Tests." *On the Scene. Newsletter of California Women in the Fire Service.* 4 (4): 1, 4–5.

Baldwin, James. 1988. *The Fire Next Time*. New York: Bantam Doubleday Dell Publishing Group.

————. 1962. *Nobody Knows My Name: More Notes of a Native Son.* New York: Dell Publishing Co.

Bandura, Albert. 1973. *Aggression: A Social Learning Analysis*. Englewood Cliffs, N.J.: Prentice-Hall.

Bell, Derrick. 1987. *And We Are Not Saved: The Elusive Quest for Racial Justice.* New York: Basic Books.

Bell, Laura. 1987. "Where Does Physical Testing Leave Women?" *Management Review* (December): 47–50.

Beller, Andrea H. 1984. "Trends in Occupational Segregation by Sex and Race, 1960–1981." In *Sex Segregation in the Workplace: Trends, Explanations, Remedies*, ed. B. F. Reskin. Washington, D.C.: National Academy Press.

Bem, Sandra Lipsitz. 1981. "Gender Schema Theory: A Cognitive Account of Sex Typing." *Psychological Review* 88 (4): 354–364.

Blau, Francine D., and Anne E. Winkler. 1989. "Women in the Labor Force: An Overview." In *Women: A Feminist Perspective*, 4th ed., ed. J. Freeman. Mountain View, Calif.: Mayfield Publishing Company.

Blauner, Bob. 1989. *Black Lives, White Lives: Three Decades of Race Relations in America.* Berkeley: University of California Press.

Boothe, Clare. 1937. *The Women*. New York: Random House.

Brown, Larry. 1994. *On Fire*. Chapel Hill, N.C.: Algonquin Books of Chapel Hill.

Brown, Lyn Mikel, and Carol Gilligan. 1992. *Meeting at the Crossroads: Women's Psychology and Girls' Development*. Cambridge, Mass.: Harvard University Press.

Burns, Sarah E. 1995. "Issues in Workplace Sexual Harassment Law and Related Social Science Research." *Journal of Social Issues* 51 (1): 193–207.

Burstein, Paul. 1985. *Discrimination, Jobs, and Politics: The Struggle for Equal Employment Opportunity in the United States since the New Deal*. Chicago: University of Chicago Press.

Caplow, Theodore. 1954. *The Sociology of Work*. Minneapolis: University of Minnesota Press.

Carrigan, Tim, Bob Connell, and John Lee. 1985. "Toward a New Sociology of Masculinity." *Theory and Society* 14 (5): 551–604.

Center for Social Policy and Practice in the Workplace. 1988. "Gender Integration in the New York Fire Department: A Review and Recommendations." New York: Columbia University School of Social Work.

Chodorow, Nancy. 1978. *The Reproduction of Mothering: Psychoanalysis and the Sociology of Gender*. Berkeley: University of California Press.

Cockburn, Cynthia. 1983. *Brothers: Male Dominance and Technological Change*. London: Pluto Press.

Coil, James H., and Charles M. Rice. 1993. "Managing Work-Force Diversity in the Nineties: The Impact of the Civil Rights Act of 1991." *Employee Relations Law Journal* 18 (4): 547–565.

Coleman, Ronny J. 1993. "Sticks and Stones May Break My Bones." *Fire Chief* 37 (8): 50–52.

Connell, R. W. 1987. *Gender and Power: Society, the Person and Sexual Politics*. Stanford, Calif.: Stanford University Press.

Cooper, Eugene. 1989. "Apprenticeship as Field Method: Lessons from Hong Kong." In *Apprenticeship: From Theory to Method and Back Again*, ed. M. W. Coy. Albany: State University of New York Press.

Cox, Taylor H., and Stacy Blake. 1991. "Managing Cultural Diversity: Implications for Organizational Competitiveness." *Academy of Management Executive* 5 (3): 45–56.

Coy, Michael. 1989. "From Theory." In *Apprenticeship: From Theory to Method and Back Again*, ed. M. W. Coy. Albany, N.Y.: State University of New York Press.

Crocker, Jennifer, and Kathleen M. McGraw. 1984. "What's Good for the Goose Is Not Good for the Gander." *American Behavioral Scientist* 27 (3): 357–369.

Davis, Paul O. 1993. "Not 'Strength' vs. 'Endurance,' but Both." *Fire Chief* 37 (10): 26, 27.

Deaux, Kay. 1995. "How Basic Can You Be? The Evolution of Research on Gender Stereotypes." *Journal of Social Issues* 51 (1): 11–20.

Dinnerstein, Dorothy. 1976. *The Mermaid and the Minotaur: Sexual Arrangements and Human Malaise*. New York: Harper & Row.

Dweck, Carol S. 1975. "The Role of Expectations and Attributions in the Alleviation of Learned Helplessness." *Journal of Personality and Social Psychology* 31 (4): 674–685.

Dweck, Carol S., William Davidson, Sharon Nelson, and Bradley Enna. 1978. "Sex Differences in Learned Helplessness: II. The Contingencies of Evaluative Feedback in the Classroom and III. An Experimental Analysis." *Developmental Psychology* 14 (3): 268–276.

Eder, Donna. 1990. "Serious and Playful Disputes: Variation in Conflict Talk among Female Adolescents." In *Conflict Talk: Sociolinguistic Investigations of Arguments in Conversations*, ed. A. Grimshaw. Cambridge: Cambridge University Press.

Egan, Timothy. 1993. "Teaching Tolerance in Workplaces: A Seattle Program Illustrates Limits." *The New York Times*, October 8, p. A12.

Enarson, Elaine Pitt. 1984. *Woods-Working Women: Sexual Integration in the U.S. Forest Service*. University, Ala.: The University of Alabama Press.

Epstein, Cynthia Fuchs. 1990. "The Cultural Perspective and the Study of Work." In *The Nature of Work: Sociological Perspectives*, eds. K. Erikson and S. P. Vallas. New Haven: Yale University Press.

———. 1973. "Positive Effects of the Multiple Negative: Explaining the Success of Black Professional Women." *American Journal of Sociology* 78 (4): 912–935.

Everhart, Robert B. 1983. *Reading, Writing and Resistance: Adolescence and Labor in a Junior High School*. Boston: Routledge and Kegan Paul.

Ferdman, Bernardo M. 1992. "The Dynamics of Ethnic Diversity in Organizations: Toward Integrative Models." In *Issues, Theory, and Research in Industrial/Organizational Psychology*, ed. K. Kelley. Amsterdam: North-Holland.

Fine, Gary Alan. 1987. "One of the Boys: Women in Male-Dominated Settings." In *Changing Men: New Directions in Research on Men and Masculinity*, ed. M. S. Kimmel. Newbury Park, Calif.: Sage Publications.

Fineman, Martha L. 1990. "Challenging Law, Establishing Differences: The Future of Feminist Legal Scholarship." *Florida Law Review* 42 (1): 25–43.

Floren, Terese. 1996. "WFS Survey: Protective Gear Fit, Part I." *Firework*. Newsletter of Women in the Fire Service. 14 (8): 2.

———. 1994a. "Anti-Harassment Policy Loses." *Firework*. Newsletter of Women in the Fire Service. 12 (8): 3.

———. 1994b. "L.A. County's Harassment Policy Challenged." *Firework*. Newsletter of Women in the Fire Service. 12 (3): 5.

———. 1993. "Caring for the Caregivers: A Decade of Progress?" *Firework*. Newsletter of Women in the Fire Service. 11 (11): 5.

Foster, Herbert L. 1986. *Ribbin', Jivin', and Playin' the Dozens: The Persistent Dilemma in Our Schools*. Cambridge, Mass.: Ballinger Publishing Company.

Gaertner, Samuel L., and John F. Dovidio. 1986. "The Aversive Form of Racism." In *Prejudice, Discrimination, and Racism*, eds. J. F. Dovidio and S. L. Gaertner. New York: Academic Press.

Garfinkel, Harold. 1967. *Studies in Ethnomethodology*. Englewood Cliffs, N.J.: Prentice-Hall.

Geuss, Raymond. 1981. *The Idea of a Critical Theory: Habermas and the Frankfurt School*. Cambridge: Cambridge University Press.

Gilligan, Carol. 1982. *In a Different Voice: Psychological Theory and Women's Development*. Cambridge, Mass.: Harvard University Press.

Glenn, Evelyn Nakano. 1985. "Racial Ethnic Women's Labor: The Intersection of Race, Gender, and Class Oppression." *Review of Radical Political Economics* 17 (3): 86–108.

Goffman, Erving. 1963. *Stigma: Notes on the Management of Spoiled Identity*. New York: Simon and Schuster.

Gold, Dolores, Gail Crombie, and Sally Noble. 1987. "Relations Between Teachers' Judgments of Girls' and Boys' Compliance and Intellectual Competence." *Sex Roles* 16 (7/8): 351–358.

Goodenough, Ruth Gallagher. 1987. "Small Group Culture and the Emergence of Sexist Behavior: A Comparative Study of Four Children's Groups." In *Interpretive Ethnography of Education: At Home and Abroad*, eds. G. and L. Spindler. Hillsdale, N.J.: Lawrence Erlbaum and Associates.

Goodwin, Marjorie Harness. 1990. *He-Said-She-Said: Talk as Social Organization among Black Children*. Bloomington: Indiana University Press.

Goody, Esther N. 1989. "Learning, Apprenticeship and the Division of Labor." In *Ap-*

prenticeship: From Theory to Method and Back Again, ed. M. W. Coy. Albany, N.Y.: State University of New York Press.

Gouldner, Alvin. 1954. Patterns of Industrial Bureaucracy. Glencoe, Ill.: The Free Press.

Grant, Linda. 1984. "Black Females' 'Place' in Desegregated Classrooms." Sociology of Education 57: 98–110.

Gray, Stan. 1992. "Sharing the Shop Floor." In Race, Class, and Gender: An Anthology, eds. M. L. Andersen and P. H. Collins. Belmont, Calif.: Wadsworth Publishing Company.

Griggs v. Duke Power Co. 401 U.S. 424, 91 S.Ct. 849, 28 L.Ed.2d 158 (1971).

Gutek, Barbara A. 1985. Sex and the Workplace: The Impact of Sexual Behavior and Harassment on Women, Men, and Organizations. San Francisco: Jossey-Bass Publishers.

Haas, Jack. 1989. "The Process of Apprenticeship: Ritual Ordeal and the Adoption of a Cloak of Competence." In Apprenticeship: From Theory to Method and Back Again, ed. M. W. Coy. Albany: State University of New York Press.

———. 1977. "Learning Real Feelings: A Study of High Steel Ironworkers' Reactions to Fear and Danger." Sociology of Work and Occupations 4 (2): 147–170.

Hamilton, David L., and Tina K. Trolier. 1986. "Stereotypes and Stereotyping: An Overview of the Cognitive Approach." In Prejudice, Discrimination, and Racism, eds. J. F. Dovidio and S. L. Gaertner. New York: Academic Press.

Handler, Joel. 1990. Law and the Search for Community. Philadelphia: University of Pennsylvania Press.

———. 1986. The Conditions of Discretion: Autonomy, Community, Bureaucracy. New York: Russell Sage Foundation.

Heilman, Madeline E. 1983. "Sex Bias in Work Settings: The Lack of Fit Model." Research in Organizational Behavior 5: 269–298.

Henley, Nancy M. 1977. Body Politics: Power, Sex, and Nonverbal Communications. Englewood Cliffs, N.J.: Prentice-Hall.

Henley, Nancy M., and Cheris Kramarae. 1991. "Gender, Power, and Miscommunication." In "Miscommunication" and Problematic Talk, eds. N. Coupland, H. Giles, and J. M. Wiemann. Newbury Park, Calif.: Sage Publications.

Honeycutt, Neil. 1994. "Oakland Fire Department: 125 Years of Service." Fire News. Newsletter of the International Association of Fire Fighters, Local 55. Number 124 (March): 3.

Hull, et al. v. Cason, et al., 88 Cal.App.3d 768, 151 Cal. Rptr. 438 (1978).

———. Alameda Superior Court No. 451337-9 (1974).

Irvine, Jacqueline Jordan. 1986. "Teacher-Student Interactions: Effects of Student Race, Sex, and Grade Level." Journal of Educational Psychology 78 (1): 14–21.

———. 1985. "Teacher Communication Patterns as Related to the Race and Sex of the Student." Journal of Educational Research 78 (6): 338–345.

Jacobs, Jerry. 1989. Revolving Doors: Sex Segregation and Women's Careers. Stanford, Calif.: Stanford University Press.

Jones, James M. 1986. "Racism: A Cultural Analysis of the Problem." In Prejudice, Discrimination, and Racism, eds. J. F. Dovidio and S. L. Gaertner. New York: Academic Press.

Kanter, Rosabeth Moss. 1977. Men and Women of the Corporation. New York: Basic Books.

Kapalczynski, Ignatius. 1993. "The National Run Survey 1992." Firehouse (June): 50–79.

Kessler, Suzanne J., and Wendy McKenna. 1978. Gender: An Ethnomethodological Approach. Chicago: University of Chicago Press.

Lacey, Marc. 1993. "ACLU, Playboy Magazine Join Fireman to Fight Ban." Los Angeles Times, December 17, p. B1.

Lamphere, Louise. 1985. "Bringing the Family to Work: Women's Culture on the Shop Floor." *Feminist Studies* 11 (3): 519–540.

Lave, Jean, and Etienne Wenger. 1991. *Situated Learning: Legitimate Peripheral Participation.* Cambridge: Cambridge University Press.

LeCuyer, John. 1994. "Where Tools and People Meet." *Fire Chief* (February): 35–41.

Lee, Renee McEntire. 1988. "One Fire Department's Approach to Affirmative Action Hiring." *Western City* (October): 23–48.

Leserman, Jane. 1981. *Men and Women in Medical School: How They Change and How They Compare.* New York: Praeger.

Linville, Patricia, Peter Salovey, and Gregory Fischer. 1986. "Stereotyping and Perceived Distributions of Social Characteristics: An Application to Ingroup–Outgroup Perception." In *Prejudice, Discrimination, and Racism,* eds. J. F. Dovidio and S. L. Gaertner. New York: Academic Press.

Lips, Hilary M. 1989. "Gender-Role Socialization: Lessons in Femininity." In *Women: A Feminist Perspective,* 4th ed., ed. J. Freeman. Mountain View, Calif.: Mayfield Publishing Company.

Louis, Meryl Reis. 1990. "Acculturation in the Workplace: Newcomers as Lay Ethnographers." In *Organizational Climate and Culture,* ed. B. Schneider. San Francisco: Jossey-Bass Publishers.

———. 1980. "Surprise and Sense Making: What Newcomers Experience in Entering Unfamiliar Organizational Settings." *Administrative Science Quarterly* 25 (June): 226–251.

Lyman, Peter. 1987. "The Fraternal Bond as Joking Relationship: A Case Study of the Role of Sexist Jokes in Male Group Bonding." In *Changing Men: New Directions in Research on Men and Masculinity,* ed. M. S. Kimmel. Newbury Park, Calif.: Sage Publications.

McCarl, Robert. 1985. *The District of Columbia Fire Fighters' Project: A Case Study in Occupational Folklife.* Washington, D.C.: Smithsonian Institution Press.

Maclean, Norman. 1992. *Young Men and Fire.* Chicago: University of Chicago Press.

McConahay, John B., Betty B. Hardee, and Valerie Batts. 1981. "Has Racism Declined in America? It Depends On Who Is Asking and What Is Asked." *Journal of Conflict Resolution* 25 (4): 563–579.

McKinney, Joan, and Sue Soennichsen. 1979. "Oakland Getting Its First Woman Firefighter." *The Oakland Tribune,* December 11, p. B1.

Majors, Richard, and Janet Mancini Billson. 1992. *Cool Pose: The Dilemmas of Black Manhood in America.* New York: Lexington Books.

Maltz, Daniel N., and Ruth A. Borker. 1983. "A Cultural Approach to Male-Female Miscommunication." In *Language and Social Identity,* ed. J. J. Gumperz. Cambridge: Cambridge University Press.

Malveaux, Julianne, and Phyllis Wallace. 1987. "Minority Women in the Workplace." In *Working Women: Past, Present, Future,* eds. K. S. Koziara, M. H. Moskow, and L. D. Tanner. Washington, D.C.: The Bureau of National Affairs.

Martin, Molly. 1988. *Hard-Hatted Women: Stories of Struggle and Success in the Trades.* Seattle, Wash.: The Seal Press.

Martin, Susan Ehrlich. 1989. "Sexual Harassment: The Link Joining Gender Stratification, Sexuality, and Women's Economic Status." In *Women: A Feminist Perspective,* 4th ed., ed. J. Freeman. Mountain View, Calif.: Mayfield Publishing Company.

———. 1980. *Breaking and Entering: Policewomen on Patrol.* Berkeley: University of California Press.

Mee, Cynthia S. 1993. "Middle School Voices and Gender Identity." Proceedings of pre-convention symposium: Gender Issues in the Classroom and on the Campus: Focus on the 21st Century. Annual Convention of American Association of University Women. Minneapolis, Minn.

Miller, Jean Baker. 1986. *Toward a New Psychology of Women.* 2d ed. Boston: Beacon Press.

Miller, Norman, and Marilynn B. Brewer. 1986. "Categorization Effects on Ingroup and Outgroup Perception." In *Prejudice, Discrimination, and Racism,* eds. J. F. Dovidio and S. L. Gaertner. New York: Academic Press.

Myers, Steven Lee. 1992. "Racial Barriers Slow to Fall in Fire Department." *The New York Times,* April 17, p. A18.

Nero, et al. v. City of Oakland, et al., USDC ND Cal. No. C-85-8448 WHO (1985).

Newbergh, Carolyn. 1988. "911 False Alarms Overwhelm Firefighters." *The Oakland Tribune,* August 30, pp. A9, A12.

Norris, Wessie L., and Maryellen Reardon. 1989. "Employment Screening, Qualifications, and Gender Discrimination: A Case Study of the New York City Firefighters." In *Affirmative Action in Perspective,* eds. F. Blanchard and F. Crosby. New York: Springer-Verlag.

Patterson, James, and Peter Kim. 1991. *The Day America Told the Truth: What People Really Believe about Everything That Really Matters.* New York: Prentice-Hall Press.

Petersen, et al. v. City of Oakland, et al., USDC ND Cal. No. C-89-2784 WHO (1989).

Petrie, Keith, and Mary Jane Rotheram. 1982. "Insulators Against Stress: Self-Esteem and Assertiveness." *Psychological Reports* 50: 963–966.

Pettigrew, Thomas F. 1961. "Social Psychology and Desegregation Research." *American Psychology* 16: 105–112.

Pettigrew, Thomas F., and Joanne Martin. 1987. "Shaping the Organizational Context for Black American Inclusion." *Journal of Social Issues* 43 (1): 41–78.

Pranka, Carol. 1993. "Firefighter Physical Performance Standards." *Firework.* Newsletter of Women in the Fire Service. 11 (10): 1–3.

RAND National Defense Research Institute. 1993. *Sexual Orientation and U.S. Military Personnel Policy: Options and Assessment.* Report prepared for the Office of the Secretary of Defense. Santa Monica: RAND.

Raphael, Ray. 1988. *The Men from the Boys: Rites of Passage in Male America.* Lincoln: University of Nebraska Press.

Reid, Pamela Trotman, and Susan Clayton. 1992. "Racism and Sexism at Work." *Social Justice Research* 5 (3): 249–268.

Remmington, Patricia Weiser. 1983. "Women in the Police: Integration or Segregation?" *Qualitative Sociology* 6 (2): 118–135.

Reskin, Barbara, and Patricia Roos. 1990. *Job Queues, Gender Queues: Explaining Women's Inroads into Male Occupations.* Philadelphia: Temple University Press.

Riccucci, Norma M. 1990. *Women, Minorities, and Unions in the Public Sector.* New York: Greenwood Press.

Rockwell, Paul. 1989. "Fighting the Fires of Racism." *The Nation* (December 11): 714–718.

Ross, Lee, and Richard E. Nisbett. 1991. *The Person and the Situation: Perspectives of Social Psychology.* Philadelphia: Temple University Press.

Rothman, Robert A. 1987. *Working: Sociological Perspectives.* Englewood Cliffs, N.J.: Prentice-Hall.

Rubin, Lillian B. 1983. *Intimate Strangers: Men and Women Together.* New York: Harper & Row.

Sacks, Karen Brodkin. 1988. *Caring by the Hour: Women, Work, and Organizing at Duke Medical Center.* Chicago: University of Illinois Press.

Sadker, Myra, and David Sadker. 1994. *Failing at Fairness: How America's Schools Cheat Girls.* New York: Charles Scribner's Sons.

Safilios-Rothschild, Constantina. 1978. "Young Women and Men Aboard the U.S. Coast Guard Barque 'Eagle': An Observation and Interview Study." *Youth and Society* 10 (2): 191–204.

Schein, Edgar H. 1992. *Organizational Culture and Leadership*. San Francisco: Jossey-Bass Publishers.

Schroedel, Jean Reith. 1985. *Alone in a Crowd: Women in the Trades Tell Their Stories*. Philadelphia: Temple University Press.

Schultz, Vicki. 1990. "Telling Stories about Women and Work: Judicial Interpretations of Sex Segregation in the Workplace in Title VII Cases Raising the Lack of Interest Argument." *Harvard Law Review* 103 (8): 1749–1843.

Segal, Lynne. 1990. *Slow Motion: Changing Masculinities, Changing Men*. New Brunswick, N.J.: Rutgers University Press.

Selk, Laila. 1993. "A Tough Call." *On the Scene*. Newsletter of California Women in the Fire Service. 5 (1): 1, 6.

Sheffield, Carole J. 1989. "Sexual Terrorism." In *Women: A Feminist Perspective*, 4th ed., ed. J. Freeman. Mountain View, Calif.: Mayfield Publishing Company.

Sheldon, Amy. 1991. "Conflict Talk: Sociolinguistic Challenges to Self-Assertion and How Young Girls Meet Them." *Merrill-Palmer Quarterly* 38 (1): 95–117.

Sherif, Muzafer, et al. 1961. *Intergroup Conflict and Cooperation: The Robbers Cave Experiment*. Norman: The Institute of Group Relations, University of Oklahoma.

Smith, Dennis. 1972. *Report from Engine Company 82*. New York: Dutton.

Spanger, Eve, Marsha A. Gordon, and Ronald M. Pipkin. 1978. "Token Women: An Empirical Test of Kanter's Hypothesis." *American Journal of Sociology* 84 (10): 160–170.

Spiegelman, Paul J. 1985. "Court-Ordered Hiring Quotas after Stotts: A Narrative on the Role of the Moralities of the Web and the Ladder in Employment Discrimination Doctrine." *Harvard Law Review* 20: 339–424.

"Standards Council Sends 1583 Back to Committee." 1996. *Firework*. Newsletter of Women in the Fire Service. 14 (8): 3.

Stoller, Robert J. 1985. *Presentations of Gender*. New Haven: Yale University Press.

———. 1968. *Sex and Gender: On the Development of Masculinity and Femininity*. New York: Science House.

Stuhlmiller, Cynthia. 1990. "An Interpretive Study of Appraisal and Coping of Rescue Workers in an Earthquake Disaster: The Cypress Collapse." Ph.D. diss., University of California, San Francisco School of Nursing.

Sullivan, Cheryl. 1988. "Public-Safety Jobs in U.S. Still Mainly Held by Whites." *The Christian Science Monitor*, January 22, pp. 3, 4.

Swidler, Ann. 1986. "Culture in Action: Symbols and Strategies." *American Sociological Review* 51 (April): 273–286.

Talbot, Margaret. 1994. "A Most Dangerous Method." *Lingua Franca* (January/February): 1, 24–40.

Tamaki, Julie. 1994. "Judge Says County Cannot Bar Playboy Magazine in Firehouses." *Los Angeles Times*, June 10, p. B1.

Tannen, Deborah. 1990. *You Just Don't Understand: Women and Men in Conversation*. New York: Ballantine Books.

Taub, Nadine, and Wendy W. Williams. 1985. "Will Equality Require More Than Assimilation, Accommodation or Separation from the Existing Social Structure?" *Rutgers Law Review* 37 (4): 825–844.

Taylor, Charles. 1985. *Philosophy and the Human Sciences: Philosophical Papers 2*. Cambridge: Cambridge University Press.

Thorne, Barrie. 1993. *Gender Play: Girls and Boys in School*. New Brunswick, N.J.: Rutgers University Press.

Tyler, Tom R. 1989. "The Psychology of Procedural Justice: A Test of the Group-Value Model." *Journal of Personality and Social Psychology* 57 (5): 830–838.

Tyler, Tom R., and Alan E. Lind. 1992. "A Relational Model of Authority in Groups." *Advances in Experimental Social Psychology* 25: 115–191.

U.S. Bureau of the Census. 1990. *EEO File: United States, Detailed Occupation by Sex by Race.* CD ROM File.

———. 1980. *Characteristics of the Population: United States Summary.* Washington, D.C.: Government Printing Office.

———. 1980. *General Population Characteristics: California.* Washington, D.C.: Government Printing Office.

———. 1970. *Characteristics of the Population: United States Summary.* Washington, D.C.: Government Printing Office.

Van Maanen, John. 1973. "Observations on the Making of Policemen." *Human Organization* 32 (4): 407–418.

Van Maanen, John, and Stephen R. Barley. 1984. "Occupational Communities: Culture and Control in Organizations." *Research in Organizational Behavior* 6: 287–365.

Walker, Connecticut. 1974. "Judy Livers: America's First Firewoman." *The Oakland Tribune, Parade,* September 1, pp. 6–8.

Walshok, Mary Lindenstein. 1981. *Blue-Collar Women: Pioneers on the Male Frontier.* Garden City, N.Y.: Anchor Books.

Wasserstrom, Richard A. 1977. "Racism, Sexism, and Preferential Treatment: An Approach to the Topics." *UCLA Law Review* 24: 581–622.

West, Candace, and Don H. Zimmerman. 1987. "Doing Gender." *Gender & Society* 1 (2): 125–151.

Weston, Kath. 1990. "Production as Means, Production as Metaphor: Women's Struggle to Enter the Trades." In *Uncertain Terms: Negotiating Gender in American Culture,* eds. F. Ginsburg and A. L. Tsing. Boston: Beacon Press.

Westwood, Sallie. 1984. *All Day, Every Day: Factory and Family in the Making of Women's Lives.* Chicago: University of Illinois Press.

Williams, Christine L. 1989. *Gender Differences at Work.* Berkeley: University of California Press.

Wilson, William Julius. 1987. *The Truly Disadvantaged: The Inner City, the Underclass, and Public Policy.* Chicago: University of Chicago Press.

Women in the Fire Service. 1993. *The Changing Face of the Fire Service: A Handbook on Women in Firefighting.* Washington, D.C.: U.S. Fire Administration, Federal Emergency Management Agency.

Word, Carl O., Mark P. Zanna, and J. Cooper. 1974. "The Nonverbal Mediation of Self-Fulfilling Prophecies in Interracial Interaction." *Journal of Experimental Social Psychology* 10: 109–120.

Yoder, Janice D. 1991. "Rethinking Tokenism: Looking Beyond Numbers." *Gender & Society* 5 (2): 178–192.

Young, Anne. 1994. "Eternal Vigilance Is the Price of Freedom, Or, With Friends Like the ACLU . . . " *On the Scene.* Newsletter of California Women in the Fire Service. 6 (2): 1, 3.

Zimmer, Lynn. 1988. "Tokenism and Women in the Workplace: The Limits of Gender-Neutral Theory." *Social Problems* 35 (1): 64–77.

Index

acceptance: earning, 83, 87, 94, 152; expectations about, 132–133; importance of, 131–132; after initiation, 61–62, 67, 133; levels of, 134–135; signs of, 147; social vs. professional, 135; struggle for, 5, 58, 154, 157, 176; variations in, among women, 52, 55, 135–136, 138, 148–149, 152, 155

access, 110, 116, 120, 124, 169; in police work, 208n1

accommodation: need for, 156, 183; strategies: 133–134, 137–139. *See also* women: accommodation strategies of

acculturation: process of, 10; gender differences in, 181

affirmative action, 5, 8, 20–21, 51, 58, 66, 86, 165, 168, 206n5

African Americans: achievement of membership in OFD, 155, 215n21; concern for respect, 57, 67–68, 101, 127; differences among, by sex, 9; fire service connections of, 44–46, 117, 166, 195t (*see also* Oakland Black Fire Fighters Association); experience with verbal contests, 70–71; image of the good firefighter, 126–127; nontraditional attitudes of, 53, 149–150, 212n9; Oakland backgrounds of, 46, 48–49, 53, 129; as outsiders, 156;

political activism of, 19, 158, 185, 186; representation in the fire service, 8–9, 186; representation in OFD, 19, 20, 70; representation in police, 8–9; station preferences of, 120, 146, 147–148, 151

aggressiveness, 21, 30, 48, 90, 94, 109, 110, 111, 112, 116, 125, 182; and gender, 91–93, 128, 208n2

artifacts, 204n32

Asian Americans: fire service connections of, 46, 195t, 217n18; image of the good firefighter, 125–126; representation in OFD, 19, 20; station preferences of, 151, 152; use of term to include Filipinos, 205n2

assertiveness, 111, 161, 163–164; and gender, 121, 169

athletic experience, 46, 143, 163, 164, 191

attribution theory, 210n18

bathrooms. *See* privacy, physical

belonging, sense of, 4, 139, 146–149, 152–153, 185

blue-collar work: culture of, 181, 189, 222n13, 224n41; newcomer experience in, 44, 46, 140, 164; racial integration of, 9; sexual integration of, 9, 224n33

bond of masculinity, 76, 82, 139, 140–141, 148, 188
boundaries, 6, 35, 36–37, 140–141, 148, 153–154, 156, 180

class, socioeconomic, 7, 13, 36, 189, 222n23, 226n59. *See also* blue-collar work
coaching, 116, 117, 119, 121, 122, 123–124, 126, 129; absence of, 111, 112, 115, 123
confidence, 43, 84, 85, 86, 88, 113, 114–115, 121, 153; process of building, 89, 90–91, 103, 119, 122, 127, 144, 149, 161, 163–164, 169
crew. *See* firehouse environment; relationship between veterans and newcomers; station differences
culture, occupational, 28–37, 200n20; and diversity policies, 164, 170, 172, 189–190; and exclusion by gender, 10–11, 36, 80, 111, 112, 160, 180, 188–189, 204n34; and exclusion by race, 10–11, 36, 80, 111, 160, 180, 204n34; masculine quality of, 37, 57, 62, 70, 76, 111, 161, 180–181, 182; possibility of change, 164, 180, 182–183; and twenty-four-hour shift, 26–27, 182; and work, 17–18, 27, 28, 31, 34–35, 99–100, 180, 182

discrimination, institutional, 8, 19, 20, 179–180
disparate impact, 20, 132, 165, 179–180
diversity: in the fire service, 5, 8, 19–20; in OFD promoted ranks, 19, 157, 175; in OFD training staff, 55, 167; symbolic value of, 7; training, 1, 168–169, 170–172, 186. *See also* Oakland Fire Department
"dozens," the, 70–71

equipment, 17, 18, 97–100, 103, 105–106, 125, 165, 175–176. *See also* nozzle
ethnography: comment on, 193–198; dilemmas of, 196, 197; position of ethnographer, 13, 196, 197. *See also* fieldwork

exclusion, by race vs. sex: in blue-collar jobs, 9; in firefighter culture, 37, 107; in fire service history, 80; in newcomer experience, 53–54, 57–58, 59, 73–74, 82, 139, 155, 156–161; in OFD history, 20; and social identity, 185–189
exposure to action, 89–90, 98–99, 114–115, 116, 119, 120, 130, 133, 161, 169. *See also* access

fairness, concerns about, 20–21, 50–51, 80, 104–105, 120, 165, 168, 174–175, 190, 217n13
femininity as stigma, 65, 71, 75, 76, 188, 190, 213n5, 226n59
fieldwork: access, 11, 194–196; methodology, 10, 11, 193–198, 200n19; participant characteristics, 11, 12, 194, 195t; participant selection, 193, 194; personal experience of, 13, 196–197; sample limitations, 12. *See also* ethnography
Filipino Americans. *See* Asian Americans
firefighters: bonds among, 7, 22, 27, 28, 34, 139, 142–143, 183; necessary qualities of, 23, 25, 26, 27, 30, 37. *See also* fire service; Oakland Fire Department
firehouse environment: anticipation of, 56–59; preparation for, 29, 70–71, 100, 111, 113, 132, 140, 143–144, 164, 168–169; sexualization of, 76–82, 171–172, 183–184; social styles in, 140, 141, 142. *See also* privacy, physical
fire service: changing work of, 24, 183, 212n10; desirability of, as work, 7, 28, 40; integration of, 7–10, 186, 159, 175, 191; gender exclusion in, 8, 19, 20, 36–37, 50, 87, 129, 159, 186; racial exclusion in, 8, 19, 36–37, 67, 129, 159, 186; salaries, 7; working conditions, 21–27. *See also* firefighters; Oakland Fire Department

gender: "advantage" of women, 117;

construction of, in firefighter culture, 37, 96–97, 103, 106, 117, 161, 176–177, 182; disadvantage, 9, 71, 118, 156, 179, 185; and evaluation, 96, 103, 129; hostility based on, 4, 20, 54, 58, 73–74, 75, 82, 103–104, 136–139, 191, 214n13, 225n42; omnirelevance of, 187; oppositional construction of, 188–189, 190–191, 221n11; as social and analytic category, 13, 36, 37, 87, 223n30, 226n64; and traditionalism, 50; use of term, 199n4. *See also* exclusion, by race vs. sex; women

gossip, 33–35, 93, 104, 140, 145

harassment, general: interpretation of, 136–139, 171, 183; newcomer attitudes toward, 67–69, 136; responding to, 32, 62–65, 136, 183; as testing, 32, 62–64, 172. *See also* hazing; teasing

harassment, racial, 36, 65–67, 136–137, 138, 158–159, 186–187, 213n4; asymmetry of, 208n17; policies, 172

harassment, sexual, 36, 76–82, 139, 171; asymmetry of, 80, 187–188; clarification of, 169, 171, 174; and context, 80–81, 82, 174, 188; levels of, 173–174, 183–184; meaning of, in male work culture, 186–188; paranoia about, 3, 71–72, 73, 82, 153, 172, 174; and physical privacy, 176; policies, 77, 172, 174, 183–184; as resistance to women, 5, 20, 174; responding to, 77–82, 153, 172–173, 213n4; training about, 170–172, 203n14; and vulnerability, 77, 80, 187–188, 219n34, 219n37, 224n37. *See also* women: hostility to

hazing, 2–3, 31, 32, 61, 171, 181; being ignored as a form of, 2, 3, 75; of women, 71–75, 213n9

Hispanics: firefighter/EMS experience of, 43–44, 88, 98, 116, 118–119, 195t; fire service family connections of, 43–44, 48, 88, 116, 117, 118–119, 195t; image of the good firefighter, 124–

125; in lawsuit, 21; representation in fire service, 8; representation in OFD, 19, 20; station preferences of, 119, 146, 151, 152; use of term, 199n2

homosexuality, 79, 159–160, 188, 207n13, 214n14. *See also* women: lesbian

housework, 94–97

identity, occupational: achievement of, 155; development of, 10, 109, 110, 124; in images of the good firefighter, 124–130; and masculinity, 18, 37, 50, 59, 73, 106, 124, 146, 185, 188–189; newcomer feelings about, 57; and race or gender, 36, 59, 73, 124, 129–130, 160, 189–190; in relation to newcomer identity, 10, 49–56, 201n25; in relation to working conditions, 27; traditionalism in, 17–18, 50

impression management, 10, 31, 84, 102, 211n3

in-group–out-group perceptions, 106, 170, 222n22

isolation, sense of, 4, 5, 186

Latinos. *See* Hispanics

legalism, 174, 183–185

manhood, 67, 71, 188–189

membership, 6, 139, 146–149, 150–151, 152–153, 175, 176

men: differences among, by race, 9, 67–69, 95, 126, 129, 151, 152; and women as coworkers, 20, 58, 59, 71–72, 78–79, 82, 117–118, 135, 142, 164, 169, 174, 187, 220n41

minorities: beliefs about competence of, 66, 186, 215n3; and networking, 166; representation in OFD, 5, 20, 70. *See also specific groups*

Native Americans: in lawsuit, 21; representation in OFD, 19, 20

newcomer success: personal factors in, 64, 84, 97, 118, 130, 139, 155, 161–162, 163–165, 167; situational factors in, 155, 161–162

nozzle, 35–36, 42, 87, 92, 98, 109, 110, 111, 112, 115, 128, 130
numbers, importance of, 70, 93, 106, 157, 159–161, 165–166, 185, 190

Oakland Black Fire Fighters Association (OBFFA), 19, 20, 158, 161, 194, 217n18
Oakland Fire Department (OFD): activity level, 18–19, 24, 25; and consent decree, 5, 20; history, 18; integration efforts, 19–21, 186; participation in study, 11; racial conflict in, 137, 158–159; and study findings, 162; work of, 21–27; work force, by race and sex, 19; traditionalism of, 17–18, 21, 48, 49
occupational segregation, 6, 187, 188–189

people of color. See minorities
physical size and strength, 58; as defining manhood, 189; emphasis on, 103, 104, 156, 160–161, 164; gender differences in development of, 191; as intimidation factors, 65, 82, 136; in relation to equipment, 18, 176, 207n14; relative value placed on, 125, 127, 128, 129; standardized testing for, 156, 165, 212n3; training for, 167; usefulness of, 105, 160–161, 161–162, 165, 186
police, integration of, 7, 9
privacy, physical, 20, 175–176
proving oneself. See testing
public safety jobs. See firefighters; fire service; police, integration of

race: in dealings with civilian community, 126, 129, 152; disadvantage, 9, 118–119, 156, 179, 185; and evaluation, 85, 129, 158; and favoritism, 120, 137; hostility based on, 19, 65–67, 85, 120, 136–139, 158–159, 214n13, 226n59; identification of, in text, 13; oppositional construction of, 225n51; as social and analytic category, 13, 36–37, 87, 223n30; and traditionalism, 50. See

also specific groups; exclusion, by race vs. sex
racism. See under race: disadvantage; and evaluation; and favoritism; hostility based on
recruitment, 28, 162, 163, 165, 166, 217n18, 218n19
relationship between veterans and newcomers, 29, 30, 31, 62, 63, 95, 110, 116, 166; effect on professional development, 119, 131; and respect for experience, 56–57, 95; shaped by newcomer openness, 138–139
reputation, 30, 31, 36, 96, 144–145; veterans' control over, 2, 68. See also gossip
research methods. See fieldwork
respect: and gender, 57–58, 73, 76, 79, 81, 91, 114, 127, 129, 167–168, 174; and race, 57–58, 95, 105, 127, 129
risk-taking. See aggressiveness; assertiveness
rituals, 35–36, 100
role modeling, 7–8, 43, 48, 167
route, 215n20

sample. See under fieldwork: participant characteristics; participant selection
San Francisco Fire Department, 19, 206n6
selection procedures, 20–21, 28, 162, 218n24
self and community, 86, 183–185
self-esteem. See confidence
sex. See gender
sexism. See under gender: disadvantage; and evaluation; hostility based on; see also under women: beliefs about competence of; hostility to; judgments about; negative talk about; as outsiders
sexualization of the workplace, 76–82, 171–172, 173–174, 183, 186–188. See also firehouse environment: sexualization of
sponsorship, 44–45, 64, 116–117, 133, 162, 166, 212n1, 213n8
sports, familiarity with, 3, 53, 140

station differences: in activity, 89–90, 151; in harassment, 67–68; in racial diversity and attitudes, 120, 151, 158; in support of newcomers, 85, 119–124, 162, 181–182; in teaching, 119–124, 162, 169–170; in testing, 86; in treatment of women, 86, 121–122, 148, 150

storytelling. *See* gossip

subjugation of newcomers, 28–31, 57, 61, 68–69, 95

success, factors influencing. *See* newcomer success

teamwork, 22, 23, 25, 31, 34; in training, 53, 131, 167

teasing, 4, 63, 78, 81. *See also* harassment, general; hazing

testing, 83–84, 91, 94, 110, 111, 118, 140–141, 180, 182; as harassment, 103, 104, 105; newcomer attitudes toward, 84–85, 86, 99–102; psychological, 2, 31–32, 33, 62–64; quizzing, 99–101, 102; of self, 83, 88, 89, 91, 163; of women, 54, 74, 79, 80, 95, 96, 99, 102–106

tokens. *See* numbers, importance of

"Tower," the, 199n1

traditionalism, 45; vs. change-orientation, 49–56, 105, 164; in field training, 109, 124, 130; in initiation, 56; newcomer attitudes toward, 49, 52–53, 69, 94–95; in white and Hispanic men, 2, 48, 50–52, 85, 112, 124–125

transcript conventions, 203n19

white men: firefighter/EMS experience, 43–44, 97–98, 116, 118–119, 195t; fire service family connections of, 39, 43–44, 48, 64, 117, 118–119, 195t;

image of the good firefighter, 124–125; in lawsuit, 21; station preferences of, 119, 151

women: acceptance of, 52, 55; accommodation strategies of, 55–56, 77–78, 81, 134–136, 137–139, 142, 149, 153; apprehensions about work and coworkers, 41, 49, 57–59; attitudes toward physical labor, 41–43, 162–163, 164; beliefs about competence of, 20, 74, 86, 89, 95, 96, 103, 156, 164; as coworkers, 164, 169, 174, 176; differences among, by race, 9, 71, 93, 118, 156–157, 215n2, 223n26; fire service connections of, 39, 46–47, 195t; hostility to, 54, 72, 73–75, 82, 103, 104, 136, 138, 148, 156, 157, 184; image of the good firefighter, 127–128; invisibility of, 5, 75, 97, 140; judgments about, 55, 58, 93, 134–135, 145, 156; lesbian, 79, 153, 157, 214n14; negative talk about, 3, 41, 54, 58, 74, 86, 140–141; occupational culture of, 181, 182; as outsiders, 5, 54, 76, 82, 140, 142, 143, 153, 156, 175–176, 212n2; possible roles for, 142, 187; and protection, 117, 118, 139, 162; representation in OFD, 5, 19, 20, 70, 106; representation in fire service, 8, 20, 106; representation in police, 9; and sexuality, 79, 118, 188; socialization of, 71, 93, 122, 157; station preferences of, 151; support for, 100–101, 121–122, 127, 138, 150, 220n44

women of color: added disadvantage of, 118, 156–157, 185, 213n6; socialization of, 71, 93, 185; in study, 12. *See also* women: differences among, by race

work-family policies, 175–176

About the Author

Carol Chetkovich holds a Ph.D. in Public Policy from the University of California at Berkeley, and is an assistant professor of public policy at the John F. Kennedy School of Government, Harvard University. She has taught qualitative research methods, affirmative action, public policymaking, organization theory, and administrative behavior, at UC Berkeley and Mills College. She has conducted research in a variety of policy areas, including race/gender pay equity, employer-supported child care, low-income women's access to family planning, and social services to people with disabilities.